Stories of Desire and Narratives of Faith
―――――――――――――――――

Stories of Desire
and Narratives of Faith

From Neanderthals to the Postmodern Era

VICTOR HUNTER, MDIV, DMIN
LANNY HUNTER, MD

CASCADE *Books* • Eugene, Oregon

STORIES OF DESIRE AND NARRATIVES OF FAITH
From Neanderthals to the Postmodern Era

Copyright © 2019 Wipf and Stock. All rights reserved. Except for brief quotations in critical publications or reviews, no part of this book may be reproduced in any manner without prior written permission from the publisher. Write: Permissions, Wipf and Stock Publishers, 199 W. 8th Ave., Suite 3, Eugene, OR 97401.

Cascade Books
An Imprint of Wipf and Stock Publishers
199 W. 8th Ave., Suite 3
Eugene, OR 97401

www.wipfandstock.com

PAPERBACK ISBN: 978-1-5326-6227-0
HARDCOVER ISBN: 978-1-5326-6228-7
EBOOK ISBN: 978-1-5326-6229-4

Cataloguing-in-Publication data:

Names: Hunter, Victor, author. | Hunter, Lanny, author.
Title: Stories of desire and narratives of faith : from neanderthals to the postmodern era / Victor Hunter and Lanny Hunter.
Description: Eugene, OR: Cascade Books, 2019 | Includes bibliographical references.
Identifiers: ISBN 978-1-5326-6227-0 (paperback) | ISBN 978-1-5326-6228-7 (hardcover) | ISBN 978-1-5326-6229-4 (ebook)
Subjects: LCSH: Human evolution—Religious aspects. | Theological anthropology. | Religion.
Classification: BL 256 .S60 2019 (print) | BL 256 (ebook)

Manufactured in the U.S.A.   MARCH 18, 2019

For Our Children

Heather	Wendy
Charisa	Lisa
Lance	Courtney
	Scott

And Grandchildren

Iona	Alanna	Leotie	Bodø	Shane
Callum	Conor	Atticus	Jaeger	Kendra
	Carter			

"When your children ask you the meaning of the testimonies, you shall tell them the story of freedom."

—Paraphrase of Deuteronomy, Chapter 6

Table of Contents

Prologue 1

PART ONE
What? The Evolution of Practically Everything

Chapter 1: Mommy, Tell Me a Story 11

Chapter 2: Language 15

Chapter 3: Writing 19

Chapter 4: Stories, Songs, and Poems 26

Chapter 5: A Long And Longing Journey Through Colliding Narratives 30

Chapter 6: Certitude 41

Chapter 7: The Quest for Truth That Makes Us Free and Whole 42

Chapter 8: The Atomic Age and the Quantum Universe 49

Chapter 9: Space, Time, and Mass 56

Chapter 10: Molecules, Cells, and Creatures 63

Chapter 11: Narrative and Metanarrative 72

Chapter 12: The Human Tribe and Its Planet 81

Chapter 13: Societies and Stratification 86

Chapter 14: Civilization in Contention:
　　Tensions Between Civil Power and Religious Authority 92

Chapter 15: Pushing the Boundaries of Survivability 100

Chapter 16: Thinking About Thinking 110

Chapter 17: Ancient Text-Based Religions 117

Chapter 18: Religion: Seers, Sages, Saviors, and Renouncers 134

Chapter 19: Informed Critique and Rambling Notions 141

Chapter 20: Science and Religion: How Do We Know Things? 149

PART TWO
So What? Religion: A Christian Perspective on the Dynamic of Faith

Chapter 21: Beings of Desire: The Yearning Heart 161

Chapter 22: Narrative Theology 166

Chapter 23: Christian Identity: From Pentecost to the Present Moment 181

Chapter 24: Functions of Narrative for Christian Theology 190

Chapter 25: A Coherent Christian Faith 196

Chapter 26: Giving an Account 202

Chapter 27: A Coherent Christian Hope 212

Epilogue 217

Bibliography 221

"May I, composed like them
Of Eros and of Dust,
Beleaguered by the same
Negation and despair,
Show an affirming flame."
> —W. H. Auden
> Poet

"Mystery is the fundamental emotion that stands
At the cradle of all true art and science.
Anyone who can no longer wonder and stand rapt in awe,
Is as good as a snuffed out candle."
> —Albert Einstein
> Theoretical Physicist

Prologue

"Rationalistic accounts of mind and self do not suit their subject any better than a mechanistic physics suits a quantum universe."
—Marylynne Robinson
  Novelist and Essayist
  From *The Givenness of Things*

Humankind—creatures of planet Earth—evolved, transmuted and transformed, are shaped by molecular and biological phenomenon. Humankind is also shaped by numinous and transcendent experiences. From the beginning, humans faced a stark reality of their existence. Life was hard, often unsatisfactory, and then you died. Not yet possessing sophisticated language, they nevertheless asked an existential question: "What does it all mean?" The urge to know and discern—make meaning—is grounded in the desire to live mindfully, and springs from the depths of what it means to be human.

Meaning-making has the force of instinct, ranking just behind the hardwired, biological urges for physical survival: rooting and sucking; fight, flight, or freeze; and sexuality. Struck with wonder and dread about cosmos and creature, humankind was driven to find reliable answers. That effort spun off natural science and religion. These two disciplines became foundational for meaning-making and invested with authority over humankind's doings. In our Stone Age beginnings, the concepts and tools—and even the language—used in science and religion had little that distinguished them. Tens of thousands of years passed and methodologies were established that culminated in the Western Renaissance, the

Enlightenment, and were foundational for the industrialized Scientific Age. Knowledge, over these millennia, became subjected to a new standard of truth: evidence-based technique. Evidence-based knowledge begins with the premise that the pursuit of truth is unfinished business. Knowledge is always subject to modification and revision. Good science pays tribute to that concept by appending the words "Pending further study" to its pronouncements. Good religion should append the words "Pending further experience of the mystery" to its pronouncements.

Evidence-based, after everything, is grounded in one essential condition: it actually works when put to the test! Science requires more than *theory*; it must be functionalized in a gizmo that works. Whether on Main Street, Mesopotamia, or Main Street, the Moon. Religion requires more than *cerebral* knowledge: it must be functionalized in the gizmo of a lived life. The phrase "evidence-based science" falls trippingly off the tongue for postmoderns. Postmoderns may choke on the phrase, "Faith-based religion." In recent centuries, religion has gradually lost credibility in the struggle for authority in meaning-making. Yet religion, in spite of increasing secularization, has survived all attempts to suppress or destroy it. Faith-based understanding continues to compete with evidence-based knowledge for the soul of humankind because—to echo the words of Auden and Einstein, a poet and a scientist—an *affirming flame* of desire burns within the human heart for coherent narratives that sustain faith and prevent life from being *snuffed out* like a candle.

* * * * *

Three people walk into a supra-terrestrial bar: *Homo neanderthalensis sapiens*, Abigail Adams, and Alan Shepard. *Neanderthalensis* scratched his scabetic skin and gripped his spear defensively. The spearhead had been carefully knapped to a fine point and the base scored with a decorative pair of grooves. His fur vestment was encrusted with mud and blood. It had been a tough period of glaciation, hard traveling, lean living, and god-awful dying.

Abigail Adams endured the discomfort of her constricting bodice of whalebone and silk and allowed herself to be maneuvered to a barstool where she could be shared by the gentlemen. Her husband, John, arguing politics at the Continental Congress in Philadelphia, had just received a letter from her: "Remember the Ladies... Ladies will not hold ourselves bound by any Laws in which we have no Voice or Representation."

Alan Shepard rested the head of his Wilson six-iron against the polished, mahogany bar. The retired rear admiral and president of Seven Fourteen Enterprises (his business company named for space capsules Freedom 7 and Apollo 14) was dressed impeccably in a gray suit accented with a burgundy tie. A discreet red, white, and blue bar on the left lapel of his suit coat identified him as a recipient of the Distinguished Flying Cross. Shepard cupped the head of his golf club as his mind drifted to the moment on the moon when he hit a golf ball, as he once said dreamily, "miles and miles and miles."

The three eyed each other with a happy hour mix of skepticism and curiosity and tentatively clinked drinking vessels. *Neanderthalensis'* concave stone was filled with a fortuitously discovered raw ferment. Abagail's handblown stem-glass held a fine French Port. Alan's shot glass shimmered with an eighteen-year-old single malt Scotch. Abigail wasn't sure which was worse. The rank odor of the cave man seated to her left, or the cologne of the urbane gentleman seated on her right. She took the spear from *Neanderthalensis* and the golf club from Alan and let them clatter to the floor. "Men are useless without their stick in their hand."

Neanderthalensis leaned heavily past Abigail. "How was it up there?"

"How was it back there?" Shepard replied.

Neanderthalensis studied his companions a long moment. "I'm gonna tell you a story." He chugged his drink.

Abigail and Alan paused, glasses halfway to their lips, immediately hooked.

"I hunted the Neander Valley. My clan was starving. We did the ritual for the hunt, but I took nothing. We danced for rain. The sky burned clear. The earth was parched. We danced the war dance and raided a thriving neighboring clan, but were defeated. I had three girl children in as many years. My fourth child was a male, but my woman died birthing him. Prior to his manhood, he developed fever. I practiced the healing ceremony. He died. He was buried face-down with no implements to sustain him in his dawn so he would not carry forward the misfortunes." He raised his right hand and revealed a pattern of scars burned into the palm. "The clan marked me as the bearer of adversity and I was driven out to reverse our tribulations. I died alone and was eaten by scavengers."

"I lived in Boston," Abigail said. "A city of religion, politics, tea, and liberty. Not far from my home a half century before I was born, twenty people, fourteen of them women, were executed as witches. The trials in Salem will avert a theocracy for America, I think, thank God." Abigail took *Neanderthalensis*'s right hand and traced the scars in his mutilated palm. "All men would be tyrants, if they could. Since God created Adam, men think history is just his story. Her story is a cipher. Men regard a female birth regrettable and the girl child inferior. There is not one woman at the Continental Congress. At least half the brains and half the heart of the colonies are disenfranchised. In the Republic women will have their place, but I didn't live to see it. I died of typhoid and was buried in a crypt at the United First Parish Church in Quincy." Abigail released *Neanderthalensis*'s hand. "As sure as I died believing the Father alone is God, and no reasoning can convince me that three is one and one is three, I believe scapegoating will not solve your clan's troubles."

"My faith was Christian Science," Alan said. "My love was flying. My profession—career military. I was a Navy man. Straight from the Academy to a destroyer in 1944." He rapped the mahogany bar with his Academy ring. "We fought the people where you hail from," he said to *Neanderthalensis*. "The Germans, a brilliant nation of scientists, theologians, philosophers, and artists, followed a madman off a cliff. They began by burning books and ended up burning people. Millions . . ." His voice trailed off before he added quietly, "America incinerated 200,000 Japanese and irradiated thousands more with two nuclear bombs to end that war. I became a Naval aviator and logged over 8,000 hours in piston engines and jets. I ended my career as an astronaut. I was the first American in space and the fifth man to walk on the moon." He smiled wistfully. "The Earth was a luminous, blue orb suspended in the blackness of space." He glanced at his machine-tooled six-iron resting on the floor beside the handcrafted spear. "I think I could have driven a golf ball from the moon to Pebble Beach. I died of leukemia and my ashes were scattered in the cove off the eighteenth green." He lifted his Scotch. "*Neander*-buddy, between the time you stepped out of your cave spear in hand, through the time Abby took pen in hand to stand her ground for her gender, to the time I stepped off the lunar module six-iron in hand, civilization happened."

"What's civilization?" asked *Neanderthalensis*.
"The progress of all mankind," Shepard replied.
"Humankind," Abigail corrected.
"So what?" *Neanderthalensis* grunted.

* * * * *

Stories are what our disparate, happy hour souls had in common. The words, "I'm gonna tell you a story," possess power disproportionate to their brevity. We sense they are not uttered casually, but spoken after some deliberation. Our response is, at the very least, bemusement, if not a shiver of anticipation. The hairs may stand up on the back of our neck or our stomachs turn over. The words set us on pins and needles, not only from eagerness, but from apprehension, foreboding, even dread. The words imply intimacy. Something significant will be divulged. A secret, possibly. Or some critical bit of information or insight. Perhaps words of gravity, grief, dismay or alarm. A mystery will be made plain. "I'm-gonna-tell-you-a-story" is a singular proposition and one we rarely refuse, despite misgivings.

Stories are alive! They live in us and we live in them. Some stories are immortal, linking the present to the past and projecting an overarching theme toward a meaningful future. Such narratives create the scaffold on which we structure our lives. They contain the powerful bias that serve as our gauge for measuring reality. They provide rationales for justifying assumptions. They provide checks and balances for behavior. They serve as a guard against chaos. Coherent narratives are stories so perceptive that they hold within them insights for living and sometimes kindle convictions that enter the realm of faith, even foreshadowing a life beyond death.

Stories of both science and religion are powerfully captivating. They hold us in thrall because their themes drive to the heart of personal experience. Both sometimes seem improbable, as some of their claims beggar the imagination. Science observed that fire reduced some elements to liquids and hardened others, and fired clay to make a bowl. Religion placed the bowl in the grave beside the corpse for use in the life to come, and asked, "Where do the dead go?" Science challenges us "to know" through observation. Religion challenges us "to perceive" through paying attention. Bound by context, each thereby plumbed the essence and extremities of its discipline because each works with a different data base. Test tube and text are not the same things, nor accessible by the same methods. Yet for both, storytelling was the medium. Meaning-making was the message. Coherence was the goal. Our intention in this book is to "explore science," "do theology," and "engage faith" by the lights of civilization's accumulated narratives of "What is it?" and "What does it mean?"

This book is divided into two sections. Part I (*What?*) is composed of scientific stories of the cosmos and planet Earth. It traces the geological evolution of our solar system and the biological evolution of life on planet Earth. It charts the nature of the civilizations and cultures humankind has developed for itself. The stories of Part I inspire awe and establish a context of "givens" for the stories of Part II. Part II (*So What?*) recounts religious and philosophical stories bequeathed to the world and transcribed into permanent texts during the first millennium BCE and the first millennium CE. Our goal is to use precise, yet accessible language in the hope of making scientific jargon and god talk comprehensible to all, regardless of educational emphases. In describing complex scientific, societal, and religious issues, we have not teased out every nuanced thought. We believe this isn't oversimplification, but a "limited edition" that democratizes the subject matter. We don't dismiss the academy, but seek a broad audience including the academy. We hope to offer fresh air and breathing space for people like us who have been, and no doubt still are, to some degree, trapped in an inadequate and limiting conversation between science and religion.

The authors of this book are brothers from a small farming community in southwestern Kansas. Together, we share 150 years of life experience and over fifty years of formal education. A theologian and a scientist, we each have served more than a half century in our chosen professions of pastor and physician. We also write as confessing Christians, rooted in the rationalistic, conservative Protestantism that arose on the American frontier during the eighteenth and nineteenth centuries. We acknowledge the Bible, a narrative that begins with the Jewish Old Testament and was brought to fruition, we believe, in the New Testament. These two anthologies grew out of history and were written to preserve history. At each moment of writing, the history was theologized and the theology was historicized. This concept is vital for understanding the function of narrative theology in addressing meaning-making within the context of the Bible. We have chosen the lenses of desire, narrative, and faith to gather light and provide focus for exploring meaning-making in a world of science and religion. We will give an account—a time-honored Christian tradition—of the reasons we continue to live in the biblical story with faith, as well as the metamorphosis of this faith over our life-spans.

We believe the Bible is not the only text to arise out of history that addresses meaning-making. During our long—and longing—journey, we have become hospitable to stories other than our own. We attempt to address the plurality and complexity of diverse text-based religions that had their origins in antiquity. Our question is not, "Which is better, science or religion?" Or, "Which religion is the best or truest?" Rather, "Where, and in what manner, have we searched for a coherent narrative in this era of cultural pluralism where the stories of modern science and world religions intersect?" It is vital to pay attention to narrative. Otherwise, we will be overwhelmed with data, but miss the point.

PART ONE

WHAT?
The Evolution of Practically Everything

"The time has come, the Walrus said,
To talk of many things:
Of shoes—and ships—and sealing wax—
Of cabbages and kings—
And why the sea is boiling hot—
And whether pigs have wings."
　—Charles Lutwidge Dodgson (*aka* Lewis Carroll)
　　Author, Mathematician, and Anglican Cleric

1

Mommy, Tell Me a Story

"In my world, history comes down to language and art. No one cares much about what battles were fought, who won them and who lost them—unless there is a painting, a play, a song or a poem that speaks of the event."

—Theodore Bikel

The fountainhead of meaning-making and socialization is the mother's first story to her child. We meet that head-on every time we converse with a child who asks a question and responds to our every answer with a repetitive series of, "Why?" Their "Whys?" never stop. Erudition is stymied by the inquisitive mind of a child. The child's "Why?" is only satisfied by, "Mommy, tell me a story."

Stories address the abiding curiosity that is fundamental to being human. Stories express the facts, imaginings, hopes, fears, dreams, and beliefs of the human race. Stories pose a problem and set out to find a solution—or bear witness to its failure to do so. The tension created in the search for answers is what makes stories compelling. The story's solution, or resolution, advances understanding and provides insight and satisfaction. Stories have a beginning, a middle, and an ending. Stories may be short or long, and may be plain-spoken or grandiloquent, intimate or epochal. Stories are also infused with an elixir of unspoken or unwritten insights that evoke intensity and emotion.

Stories may express truth and beauty, be whole and sound, false and distorted, warped and twisted, healing or wounding, uplifting or dehumanizing. A story may be too small or too inflated. It may claim too little or too much. Sometimes stories are perverse and intended to deceive. We may judge—our prerogative—some stories to be flawed. The antidote to flawed stories is more stories, contingent, of course, upon accurate listening and thoughtful discernment.

Stories aren't spoken into a void, but into a world of stories where they intersect, embrace, repel, fuse, fade away or disintegrate, but in any case are altered forever. Avoiding insular stories is the best corrective to exclusive claims of truth. Sometimes we find our most cherished beliefs are ill-conceived, reinforced prejudice or refined ignorance. Telling stories in community, where stories are reassessed, challenged, broadened or abridged, is invaluable for appraisal and analysis. An unexamined life, Socrates said 2,500 years ago, isn't worth living. Unexamined living can only be remediated by paying attention to one's personal story within the world of stories. Reflective living is essential because the limits of our meaning-making story determines the limits of our world.

Ultimately, personal identity is a constructed narrative drawn from the many narratives in which we live—gender, racial, ethnic, personal, familial, economic, educational, scientific, religious, national, political, global . . . and more. We sift through events, places, persons, and things. We make judgements, we interpret, and we choose, consciously and unconsciously. Not every aspect of our narratives are necessarily true or truthful, nor healthy, congruent, edifying, or liberating. We must come to terms with the fact that self-deception lurks in the shadows to hoodwink us. Furthermore, life is a continual encounter of our narratives with *other* narratives and *others'* narratives, which are also constructed narratives, possibly flawed, and marked with the same potential for self-deception. The raw data of experience is filtered through selective memory, interpreted, reappraised, and charged with purpose according to a complex matrix of personal, emotional, and social needs. *All* data, even *raw* data, is *interpreted* data. There is no such thing as pure objectivity—there is only perception. Henry Ward Beecher reminds us: "We not only perceive things as *they* are, we perceive things as *we* are." Stories are necessarily an interpreted muddle of facts, distortions, self-deceptions, yearnings, illusions, visions, dreams, fabrications, fallacies, lies and damned lies. Pure objectivity is a fetish left over from the heady days of modern natural science.

Nearly all human conceptualizations—creeds, morality, ethics, dogma, and law, as well as evidenced-based realities—hold within them a smidgen of truth. All are also infused with subtlety, nuance, and a whiff of mystery. Absolute truth is no doubt abroad in the cosmos—and in our personal worlds—but most human understandings are true contextually. Many avowed claims have historical settings and aren't necessarily universally valid. Each person brings the formative and deformative influence of his or her own life history to everything they encounter. But abandoning the effort of rational discourse and evidentiary facts relinquishes the field of meaning-making to liars, cheats, and demagogues. Our plural, global, transnational world has taught us that humankind's fundamental efforts and institutions are naturally directed toward consolidating their own power. Goals may be accomplished through claims of closely held, personal truths, but absolutism and exclusivity fuels self-deception and leads to fanaticism. It necessarily follows that most activities and proceedings operate, to some degree, at the expense of other humans and institutions.

Paradigm shifts of what constitutes reality have been the by-product of all social and cultural change, from the Neanderthals to the twitter twits. Each shift might be considered a betrayal of the previous "givens," but should be construed as a time where understanding is broadened and refined. Still, we need not be left to a universal sectarianism in which each person has their own truth, and one truth is as good as any other. We can recognize that pure, ideological neutrality is rare to the point of nonexistence, and still strive for rational discussion of evidence-based realities as foundational to meaning-making. Distillation of knowledge from all credible persons, disciplines, philosophies and religions is required to approximate the whole of consequential subjects. Even so, we are left, in most cases, with the partial, the fragmentary, and the mysterious. That doesn't mean humankind is adrift in the cosmos with no compass. Our ever-enlarging data pool has been perceived and refined through language, the arts, signs, symbols, and rituals, and cast in meaning-making stories.

Stories are *composed* of what we have absorbed from personal experience, but also drawn from the tales we have been told. Education (book learning) adds to our storehouse of narratives. Stories can also be an invention of the mind—a feat of imagination—which raises the question, "Are they true?" Or, "In what way are they true?" Stories are *accessed* by memory, a mystifying feat of the brain. Memory is capricious. It ambushes us when we least expect it and deserts us when we most need it. Memory is subjective, selective, sanitizing, self-protective, and self-serving. Stories are *assessed* by rational thought and measured against knowledge, experience, imagination, and common sense. Stories are *imprinted* by feelings—one means of "knowing." We feel things in our bones and in our gut. Germans have a word for this—*gestalt*. This is disquieting because *gestalt* is not a magnetic compass, but a profound inkling. *Gestalt* is more than a hunch and less than a fact, but looms large in comprehension. And yet, we also know that feelings can mislead us.

Credible stories acquire an all-consuming wholeness that goes beyond a summation of individual details. Stories that are confused, compartmentalized, counterfeit, or incoherent impede meaning-making. We must each decide which of our stories, or parts thereof, are true. Which, or what parts, are flawed? And which, or what parts, are indispensable? We can remain stuck in a misconceived story and spend our lives trying to shoehorn the actual world into it. Reflective, intuitive people engage in the process of revision, recasting, and reconstruction of their stories. Reappraisal of story is not a one-time thing—although epiphanies may occur—but a lifelong process. From the beginning, humankind has searched among the fossils, funerals, fables, fairy tales, flannel graphs, files, foot lockers, fights, fornication, foolishness, facts, fiction, footnotes, foxholes, fantasies, and follies in hopes of garnering a few meaning-making stories. Humankind had no way to pass along their stories for thousands of years except language—a complex, intricate, incredible artifice that set our genus apart from all other creatures in our family tree. Language is the beast of burden for meaning-making narrative and must be addressed at our beginning.

2

Language

"What makes us human, I think, is an ability to ask questions, a consequence of our sophisticated spoken language."
—Jane Goodall
   Primatologist and Anthropologist

LANGUAGE IS A DEVICE of both mechanics and mentation. The mechanics of speech were initiated eons ago when a pair of pouches budded from the upper end of the primitive alimentary canal and developed into a respiratory tract. This allowed some aquatic creatures access to an existence on land and creatureliness took a whole 'nother track. In addition, the lungs worked as a bellows, forcing exhaled air between a paired band of throat muscles that vibrated and made noise. Ungoverned noises, however, are not language. Coincident with the evolution of the anatomy of vocalization, the human brain evolved distinct neural structures to govern speech. Different anatomical sites developed for speech and music and neuroanatomy included connections to create a continuum. These higher centers worked in concert with vocal anatomy and muscles to make distinctive sounds. Sounds stuttered along in a babel of noise, influenced by isolation, ethnicity, and culture. Over an incalculable period of time words were conceived. Words became culture bound and emotionally loaded. Vocabulary was expanded and grammar was refined. Metaphor, simile, allegory, analogy, idiom, dialect, slang, patois, and other constructs were devised. Rapid, versatile, verbal bursts of cognitive speech were strung together in evermore complex fragments. Communication settled into varied patterns and rhythms. Speech manifested itself as different languages.

Human speech, as we might recognize it, began about 200,000 years ago. Humankind gained a tremendous communication advantage over other noise-making creatures. There is no doubt that other creatures communicate with the sounds they make. Walt Disney's imagination may correctly portray the speech of Bambi and Thumper, but *Homo sapiens sapiens* (anatomical modern humans) outdistanced all other species in linguistic sophistication. Language satisfied humankind's gabby instincts, but more than that, empowered eloquence through labyrinthine, expressive vocalization enhanced by volume, pitch, tone, inflection, shading, precision, and emphasis. Concepts could be rhapsodized and infused with emotional intensity.

Incrementally, chatter became conversation, notions became ideas, and talk was surpassed by disquisition and oration. Information was expanded into tutorial. Rumination became elevated to theory. Enlightened discourse evolved into scholarly disciplines. The universes of discourse began to assemble around a common table for the cross-fertilization of thought and universities were established. Time passed . . . Oxford University Press published the first edition of the *Oxford English Dictionary*, the main historical dictionary of the English language, as recently as 1928. Speech soared to the heights of rhetoric on the wings of vocabulary, elocution, and imagination. Winston Churchill spun them into language that inspired a nation and held it together in a time of catastrophic crisis. Humankind, with brain, larynx, lungs, and air (breath) acquired a voice. Creativity and diligence forged an instrument. It seems both prophetic and poetic that humankind's crucial gift of producing audible sound was a medium wafted on the breath of life. Breath gave us both life and language. Humans came to ask not only, "What is the breath that gives words?" but, "What is the word that gives life?"

Humans, from the beginning, were both telling and listening to stories. We told stories about ourselves because of narcissism, stories about others because of connections, stories about events because of their import, stories of explanation for justification, stories of clarification to elucidate, beguiling stories for enchantment, and speculative stories about the wonder of the cosmos. Storytelling made meaning and was the foundation for the cooperative venture of socialization, culture, and civilization. Narration was loosed upon the earth. Yet, humankind did not abandon its earlier forms of communication—mimicry and ritual.

Narrative, mimicry, and ritual were forged into a powerful, persuasive trinity. Narrative provides content and context for storytelling. Mimicry enacts the story and the body language adds power to the words. Ritual (a prescribed order of performance) formalizes the story and makes it tangible, accessible, and repeatable. Ritual reigns supreme to reinforce fact as it summons memory, supplicates and provides protection. Ritual assisted primitive and archaic humans in the arduous task of survival. There were rituals for birth, coming of age, and death. There were rituals for fertility. They were rituals for the hunt and for harvest. Rituals to govern. Rituals to preserve from illness, predators, and natural disasters. Rituals to influence war and peace. Ritual held within it a hope for humankind's deepest longings—for the way things ought to be. And ritual, although of primitive origin, has never been abandoned by humankind because it is transcendent. It overcomes factionalism, binds souls together, and makes society possible. It inspires the parlor game of charades, informs social and business transactions, pervades religion, makes possible a presidential inauguration, and saturates a societal enterprise like war. The net result is a vast repertoire of narration, mimicry, and ritual that remains vital to our species for communication.

This communicational advantage was propelled by the fundamental social unit of our species—the family. Mating and procreation established a family, but family members must pay attention and share attention—keen listening and incisive processing—or there is no family. Without another being, there is no one to mimic. The family both observes and participates in ritual. The family is a theater in the round. It was (and is) the fast track for learning and the foundation for language, integrated thought, communication, socialization, and culture. To be human is to have a his-story and a her-story. At birth, each person enters into history: at death each person departs history. These pilgrimage bookends encompass a life lived in narrative form, in which the entire world is discovered through one's own personal experience and which can only be expressed in stories that impart something to humankind's story.

Personal stories differ, of course, as they arise out of different geographies, time frames, societies, and cultures. Despite these differences, there are common themes in every story. Each narrative has personal, familial, communal, national, political, and cosmic elements. Every individual selectively chooses and imprecisely remembers—in ways complex beyond understanding—the anecdotal components of their stories. Psychology tells us that the anecdotal components that are "forgotten" or "repressed" are not totally lost to conscious behavior. To paraphrase American author William Faulkner, "Not only is the past not forgotten; the past is not past." Psychology also tells us that the stories we tell about ourselves are rarely historically accurate in every detail, but represent narrative truth.

Narrative truth is sequentially arranged and charged with purpose. It consists of the conflictual, interpretive, and transitional language that gives insight and meaning to the facts. We are the eyewitness to our own story and as such we confront the raw data of our life experience. The story drawn from the data is influenced by the sum of our personal experience up to that moment, limited by powers of observation, and filtered through imperfect memory. Eyewitness accounts are always secondary. The moment a story is told it carries within it the first insinuation of interpretation and is a confounding mix of personal needs and social longings. Human beings live in their stories, and their stories live in them and become the beating heart of their personal, communal, cultural, and societal identities. This confluence of stories in the expanding matrix of our lives affects every decision we make and every action we take. Stories are so significant they require preservation, but memory has all manner of limitations. The next big idea, although it didn't come along for a long, long time, was writing.

3

Writing

"God guard me from those thoughts men think
In mind alone; He that thinks a lasting song,
Thinks in marrow-bone."
—WILLIAM BUTLER YEATS
Poet

WE THINK OF SPEECH and writing as going hand in hand, and they do, but they didn't join hands for about 193,500 years. Speech, as noted in the previous chapter, began about 200,000 years ago. Humans devised ways to preserve speech by inscribing symbols on stone, clay, bone, wood, animal skins, papyrus, copper, coffins, or . . . whatever . . . about 6,500 years ago (4,500 BCE). Writing established the great divide between the Prehistoric (preliterate) and the Historic (literate) Ages. Writing is so pivotal in discussing the story of our race (even though it appeared late in humanity's timeline) that we must examine the foundations and consequences of literacy.

Prehistoric peoples communicated essentially by word-of-mouth, although fires, drums, gongs, horns, and other signals were also used. They conducted all personal business—from courting to quarreling—face to face, so they had to be within, at the very least, shouting distance from each other. As families became clans and clans joined together in tribes, it was important to communicate in ever wider circles. Dispersion of information was critical to social structure. Proclamations, decrees, community business, and history were set to memory and carried from the source to recipients by information relayers called oracles (Latin: *oraculum*, "to speak"). Oracles' work also extended to extracting meaning from something obscure, such as a dream or cosmic event. Altogether, this important work was a valued, ancient vocation and underpinned the preliterate world.

Oracles were granted authority and spoke for authority. Accuracy and trustworthiness were critical. Oracles sustained society, government, law, religion, commerce, war, and founded the entertainment industry. Oracles established oral history, chronicling past events and investing them with meaning. These sagas were not spun from thin air. Modern humans are not the only collectors. Ancient cultures and societies preserved and revered artifacts and used them to glean information and intuit circumstances. The oracular vocation thereby maintained continuity with preceding eras. Story upon story upon story were preserved, passed along, enacted, interpreted, and revered. And so it was, and so it is, that humankind uses story as the fundamental source of communication.

The text of Deuteronomy counseled, "Call together your sons and tell them this story." Jesus told his disciples, "Go into all the world and publicly proclaim the gospel." Shakespeare's Henry V, in his Crispian Day speech said, "This story shall a man tell his sons." At Gettysburg, Abraham Lincoln proclaimed, "Four score and seven years ago." Modern society inclined its ear to Winston Churchill: "We shall fight on the beaches. We shall fight in the streets. We shall never surrender." Postmodern society remains rooted in the oral tradition. John F. Kennedy, in his inaugural address, said, "Let the word go forth from this time and place, to friend and foe alike, that the torch has been passed to a new generation." Neil Armstrong, on July 20, 1969, said these words as he stepped off the lunar module: "That's one small step for man, one giant leap for mankind." Writing has not reduced the importance and power of oral communication. Rhetoric sets words in flight.

Writing was rendered invaluable because of its potential for permanence, portability, and variability. The first writer probably used a stick to sketch something in the sand—plans for the hunt or tactics for war. The message was erased with the swipe of a hand. Pictographs grew from these instructional sketches and a repertoire of symbolic pictures developed. At some point, someone figured out that you could string together a series of signs that would "sound like" what was represented in the picture. Words expressed in phonetic marks replaced pictographs. These symbols had to be permanently recorded to carry their weight into the future. Chisel and stone were precursors of pen and paper, but production was slow and laborious. The stylus and impressionable materials were devised. Animal skins were cured to create parchment. Pulp from plants was processed to make papyrus. Engravings were made on clay tablets, bone, wood, ivory, and copper.

Composition took many forms. The bean counters seized upon writing immediately, so most surviving early documents are merely records of commerce. Prose, poetry, and drama emerged, driven by desire, imagination, and inspiration. Written forms were devised to record scored music, dance, mathematics, natural science, commercial ventures, government, law, and religion. Each form developed its own process, style, technical language, rhetoric, and rhythm. Permanent texts fostered scholarship and criticism. Writing got the word out to a much wider audience over much farther distances. For the first time, every form of societal proceeding could be preserved in script and symbol. The pen is claimed to be mightier than the sword. Ancients didn't grasp the full import of that when alphanumeric script was devised. If they did, they surely knew it was only metaphorical. When a scribe met a brute with a bronze blade, he didn't draw his quill and do battle. He hot-footed it. But over thousands of years, writing gathered momentum and has impacted civilization as much as any other single invention.

Gradually, all elements of society made use of writing for their specific purposes. Kings projected the legitimacy of their reigns and created decrees and covenants. Warriors assured successful wars of territorial expansion through military orders and treaties. Science recorded findings from observations and laboratories in a variety of scripts peculiarly suited to their disciplines. Philosophers wrote dissertations ruminating on the meaning of things. Businessmen wrote contracts. Visionaries declared freedom. Anarchists proclaimed mayhem. Composers devised musical script. Dancers scored the movements for choreography. Poets brought news from the conscience and the heart. Sports scripted plays in symbols. Religion safeguarded its sacred stories and rituals in written texts.

The earliest preserved writing consists of fragments of cuneiform (wedge-shaped characters) that dates to about 4400 BCE and the Sumerian culture of Mesopotamia. Artifacts of Egyptian hieroglyphics (Greek:

hierōs, "sacred," + *gluphē*, "carving," literally, *holy place writing*) were pictographic, enigmatic symbols and date to about 4000 BCE. A clay tablet inscribed about 3000 BCE was found in the Tigris and Euphrates River Valleys. The earliest known script of the Indus River culture dates back to 2500 BCE. Remnants of writing from the Chinese Shang Dynasty date back to 1200 BCE, and are composed of over 4,000 unique characters that represent abstract images or syllables. The Olmecs of Mesoamerica (modern Mexico) used script for writing about 900 BCE. The earliest existing texts of the Hebrew Old Testament are scrolls of parchment or papyrus and date to the sixth century BCE. In every case, the refinement of writing gave those peoples who acquired it an enormous advantage over competing cultures. Most of the records of ancient times were written on perishable goods (wood, clay, animal skins, and papyrus) that either deteriorated or were destroyed, and much of that historical data is lost to us. But what has been recovered is spectacular and of abiding interest.

Ancient Mesopotamian and Egyptian civilizations left a relatively detailed record of their religion by writing on tombs. Such texts, sometimes referred to as "coffin texts," have been found that refer to behavioral ideals and norms in those societies. One such text refers to Ankhtifi, governor of Edfu in Upper Egypt around 2100 BCE, who, the text relates, "Gave the hungry bread, and clothing to the naked. I (Ankhtifi) anointed the un-anointed, I shod the barefoot, I gave him a wife who had no wife. I rescued the weak from the strong, I gave ear to the matter of the widow."[1] A new rhetoric was initiated that had the flavor of theology, and new genres of writing were preserved which have been referred to as "wisdom texts." Ankhtifi's words recount the dispensing of both commodities and justice by a ruler on behalf of his subjects. Ethics were emerging in ancient Egypt. The words attributed to Ankhtifi on the "coffin texts" are close to those attributed to Isaiah some 1,300 years later and to Jesus some 700 years after Isaiah.

The early "coffin texts" served other purposes. They glorified the god and justified the king. Some texts expressed tension between a god of loving care and a god who punishes rebellion. Others referred to humankind as made in god's image. There are texts that emphasized the equality of all persons. These texts developed a dialogue about the nature of god and the connection between god, good behavior, tolerable social conditions, and an afterlife. Scholars claim these "coffin texts" don't reach

1. Assmann, *Mind of Egypt*, 101, 103.

the level of rhetorical theory because they don't include self-reflection and contradiction. But they are certainly based on careful observation and understanding.

Some brief autobiographical texts have been found that date to around 2100 BCE. Those foundational stories are woven into human history. A few texts have been recovered that are religious in nature. The *Epic of Gilgamesh* appears to be the first such surviving epic poem of world literature. It was written on clay tablets dated about 1800 BCE and was unearthed in Mesopotamia within the Tigris and Euphrates River Valley. The *Epic* records Sumerian stories about the King of Uruk, supposed to have lived about 2500 BCE, and addresses one man's search for meaning and immortality. It tells, among other stories, a tale of the gods' decision to unleash a great flood that would cover the entire earth. The protagonist of that story, Utnapishtim, was told by the gods to build a large boat to precise dimensions and seal it with tar. When completed, his family boarded the boat, along with craftsmen and all the animals of the fields. A storm ensued that lasted six days and nights. The boat finally lodged on a mountaintop and Utnapishtim successively released a dove, a swallow, and a raven. When the raven failed to return, Utnapishtim debarked to begin his life again.

The myth of a great, destructive flood, driven by the judgement of deities on a sinful world, is common to various cultures. The *Epic of Atrahasis*, written about 1650 BCE in Akkadian, the cuneiform script of ancient Babylon, records the story of Atrahasis, who was told by his god, Enki, to build a boat and embark his family and animals in order to preserve them from a great flood. A very similar story, preserved on a clay tablet dated 700–600 BCE, was found in northern Iraq near the ancient city of Nineveh, a leading city of Assyria and one of the prominent cities of antiquity. Ziusudra, listed as the last king of Sumer, is the hero of a Sumerian flood epic in *Eridu Genesis*, who learned of the gods' intent to destroy humanity and constructed a boat to preserve the race. In Hindu texts such as *Satapatha Brahmana*, the Matsaya Avatar of Vishnu warns the first man, Manu, of an impending flood and instructs him to build a great boat to save himself. Plato wrote *Timaeus* (c. 360 BCE) a Socratic dialogue in which Prometheus the Titan warned Deucalion that an angry Zeus would initiate a flood to punish humanity and advised him to build a boat to save himself.

Certainly one of the most famous flood stories is found among the Hebraic narratives preserved in Genesis. Believed to have been written in approximately 550 BCE during the time of the Jewish Babylonian captivity, or perhaps even later, we learn that the god Yahweh told Noah of his intent to destroy a thoroughly evil human race by flood. Noah was given specific dimensions for building a boat and waterproofing it with tar, after which he embarked his family and paired species of animals for their common salvation. The storm ended and the ark came to rest on Mount Ararat. Noah released a raven, which went "to and fro." He then released a dove, but the dove returned to the ark. Noah waited seven days and again sent out a dove, who returned with an olive twig in its beak. Noah waited another seven days and released a third dove. When it didn't return, Noah exited the ark. The Hebraic account adds a theological epilogue in which Yahweh places a rainbow in the sky as a covenant with humans that he will never again destroy the world by flood.

These and other ancient flood stories have similarities in plot and certain details. Several conclusions may be drawn from such commonality, one of which is that similarities are early examples of communal memory at work. We may also conclude that a seminal event lies behind common stories. Further, it is entirely probable that the earliest stories provided source material for the later stories. Each of these ancient texts also show variations which were shaped by the culture and purpose of their scribes.

Writing and reading—literacy—was initially the province of very few people in a society. A class of scribes arose who were schooled in the mystery of inscribing and deciphering the strange markings. In addition, a guild of persons who could craft writing materials were necessary to support the undertaking. The entire process was education-based, time-consuming, and costly. It was used sparingly. Illiteracy remained the norm of all cultures for thousands of years. The unlettered weren't ignorant, they just weren't literate and numerate. The illiterate peasant knew he had nine children and two goats, and understood that if he didn't give due deference to the king and his court he would soon have zero. Even kings and aristocrats couldn't necessarily read and write, nor could they perform mathematical functions, but they seized upon the expertise of scribes to authenticate their power through decrees. Writing became more and more authoritative, particularly when utilitarian record keeping gave way to the scribblings of authors, poets, musicians, biographers, historians, philosophers, lawyers, theologians, mathematicians, and scientists.

The development of writing went far beyond the alphanumeric code. Various disciplines in the universes of discourse devised coded symbols to express the notions of their unique fields of study. Coded language was used to compress and transmit information with an economy of scale. These brief formulations represent thousands of years of reflection and volumes of thought, not to mention years of individual study. Pythagoras expressed his theorem of the right triangle as $a^2 + b^2 = c^2$. Einstein gave us $e = mc^2$ to elucidate the nature of energy. Chemistry gave us H_2O to express elements and their combinations. Musicians gave us visual symbols for treble clef 𝄞, bass clef 𝄢, quarter note ♩, quarter rest 𝄽, and hundreds of other musical notations. Computer language uses the digits 1 and 0 in binary code. Other disciplines reduced volumes of information to a word or symbol. Medicine gave us *Syringocystadenoma*. Philosophy gave us *existentialism*. Law gave us *Dominium Eminens*. Christian theology gave us the *doctrine of the Trinity*. All narrative constructs express information and insight. Human imagination, at its best, can be engaged to make narratives soar with uniquely personal discernment, delight, and comprehension. In those moments, all stories are our story. Humankind is diminished with the loss of any. Our species has always needed more than precise data. We longed for life to make sense. *Homo sapiens sapiens* are singularly narrative creatures who use story in all of its manifestations to gain understanding.

4

Stories, Songs, and Poems

"Good art [writing] is an effort to render the world truthfully, to bring speech to that which is often left unspoken because it is too painful, or too wonderful, or too [far] beyond the range of . . . our pitiful powers of description . . . Words are all any of us have to make sense of this world."

—William H. Willimon
Theologian and Churchman

Homo erectus, our most primitive forebear, had some sophistication by Two Million Years BCE. Body and brain size had increased, and *Homo*'s nature evolved from brutish to more gentle. They stood erect, produced stone tools and weapons, used fire, possessed a creative spark, and made sounds. Over the next 20,000 centuries, *Homo erectus* the travelin' man from the Preliterate Age, became *Homo sapiens* the speechifyin' man of the Literate Age. Our increasingly bloviating species, armed with stories, songs, and poems, cohabited, copulated, calculated, and connived its way across continents while capturing fire, fermenting spirits, storing food, domesticating animals and plants, giving up nomadic ways, making love and war, establishing governments, societies, law, science, religion, and art, all the while conjuring crafts and technologies and generally getting on for tens of thousands of years without writing a word.

The fire pits in caves of the Stone Age became hearths in homes of our Postmodern Age. The continuity is palpable and real. Humans have always gathered round the fire with longing and belonging. Stories are shared; poems are read; songs are sung. Narrative prose begins with a single sentence that initiates a web of intrigue.

"Once upon a time..."

"Tell me, O muse, of that ingenious hero..."

"Last night I dreamt I went to Manderley again..."

"When on board HMS Beagle as a naturalist, I was much struck with certain facts..."

"In mathematics, a *function* is used to represent the dependence of one quantity upon..."

"In the beginning, God..."

"Scarlet O'Hara was not beautiful..."

"Dear God, I am fourteen years old..."

Stories framed as poetry piques interest with an initial, bewitching line and has the power of a gut punch.

"The ship was cheered, the harbor cleared, merrily did we drop..."

"For he today that sheds his blood with me shall be my brother..."

"Do not go gentle into that good night..."

"Had we but world enough, and time..."

"Death, be not proud, 'though some have called thee mighty and dreadful..."

"Lying, thinking last night, how to find my soul a home..."

"I can ride my bike with no handlebars, even when the paths are all crookedy..."

Songs use language and music to waft a tale with such emotion as can scarcely be equaled with any other medium. Songs help us "make it through the night." And sometimes, when we "think we have forgotten, the song remembers when."

" I loves you, Porgy, don't let him touch me..."

"Women are fickle, false all together..."

"As I walked out in the streets of Laredo..."

"Oh, Shenandoah, I long to hear you..."

"He said, 'I'll love you till I die'..."

"Amazing grace, how sweet the sound..."

"I'm telling these tears, 'Go and fall away, fall away' . . ."

"Somewhere between prayer and revolution, between Jesus and Huey P. Newton . . ."

This book weaves together hundreds of stories about the cosmos and earth's human civilizations—the *"What?"* of it all. Some stories are drawn from the academic disciplines developed by humankind. These are the *ologies* (suffix from Latin *ology*—the study of), which always have a prefix attached to denote the subject of such study (*bio*—living things; *geo*—Earth's physical structure; *anthropo*—human societies and cultures; *theo*—God). Natural science (at its best) offers well-researched, objective facts about the *"What"* of the cosmos and earth's creatures. There is good science and bad science, attested to by errors of consequence. Sometimes, long cherished scientific facts prove to be erroneous, biased, or even perpetrated as fraud. Further, published texts and journals lag behind advanced research in the laboratory. It takes time to accumulate, analyze, and verify data. Scientists and scholars play catch-up and argue details. The avalanche of accelerating scientific knowledge in the past 100 years is astonishing. For purposes of this book, we have attempted to coalesce a reliable representation of scientific materials as reference points for musing on the cosmic story and life on planet Earth. The fine details of these disciplines are often disputed among experts, but we have made a good faith effort.

This book also gathers together stories that recount some of the notions conceived throughout thousands of years to address the *"So What?"* of the world and its creatures. The stories arise from many continents and cultures. They consist of epics, songs, sociology, anthropology, evolution, poetry, prophecy, philosophy, psychology, preachments, biography, history, and religion. They express humankind's abiding hope of discovering fundamental insights for cosmic meaning-making. These stories are interesting and challenging. Each demands reflection and discernment. Devotees of *"So What?"* stories regard them as sagacious; detractors brand them superstition. Religion occupies a unique place among the *"So What?"* stories. Faithful disciples have died for their beliefs. Skeptics brand religion as blather. To be sure, there is good religion and bad religion, attested to by their outcomes. The lasting lesson of human civilization is that stories have consequences.

In evidence of this fact, the authors include some personal stories within the text. Our stories are not a detour from our general theme of meaning-making, but drive to its heart. In the musical *Oklahoma*, Curly asked Judd, crouching malevolently in his smokehouse, "How'd you get to be the way you are?" Just so, stories that shaped the Hunter brothers might serve as a stimulus for your own introspection. Our stories are not so much to tell you about us, as to tell you about yourself.

Why, you might ask, are these brothers telling their stories now? We are both in our eighth decades—at the very least a middle distance perspective useful to good narrative. During those decades, now gone in the blink of an eye, life has bewitched us by pleasure, blessed us with joy, battered us by misfortune, and bewildered us with the inexplicable. The injuries we inflicted and the wreckage left behind in our wake injured us, of course, but injured those we loved and those we didn't even know. Further, the good we have done seems to have had finite effects. The combined results sometimes seem a discouraging wash. Now in our autumn years, a time of melancholy wisdom, this is a good time to tell the stories and catch the tears.

5

A Long and Longing Journey Through Colliding Narratives

"Leaving home in a sense involves a kind of second birth in which we give birth to ourselves."
—Robert Bellah
  Sociologist

The Hunter brothers were True Believers thrice over. We believed in the Frontier Myth, in the great civil religion of American Exceptionalism, and in the vision of our church. Lanny was born in 1936 during the Dust Bowl days of the Dirty Thirties. Victor was born in 1942 and his name reflects the patriotic fervor after Pearl Harbor and America's entrance into World War II. As boys, we were drawn to a cowboy statue that stood on historic Boothill. The inscription on its base read, "On the ashes of my campfire this city is built."

Dodge City had been sited at a fordable crossing on the Arkansas River where the Great Western and Chisholm Trails intersected the Santa Fe Trail. It was also five miles west of Fort Dodge to comply with a congressional law that made it illegal to sell liquor within five miles of a military installation. The fort—named after Union Civil War general Grenville Dodge—garrisoned the military presence that guaranteed a modicum of safety for the pioneers migrating westward to fulfill their own and America's Manifest Destiny. For about fifteen years, beginning in the 1870s, Dodge City was the farthest western railhead for the Transcontinental Railway. Cattle in Texas were driven north across Oklahoma Territory and loaded on railcars for delivery to eastern markets. The culture that sustained the cattle trade and western settlements was an adrenaline-fueled brew of adventure, escape, desperation, and high expectations, not the least of which were a new start, wealth, and power. A new and different life awaited the immigrants, pioneers, pony soldiers, cowboys, buffalo hunters, muleskinners, gunfighters, lawmen, rail roaders, and yes, even the drifters, grifters, horse thieves, rustlers, bandits, gamblers, and prostitutes who had the courage to cross the Great Plains and seize life's infinite possibilities.

When youngsters, we hiked the five miles downriver from the cow town that became a farming community and county seat to old Fort Dodge, striding thigh-high in prairie grass beside ruts of the Santa Fe Trail that had been carved by thousands of covered wagons. The fort had been maintained as a historical site and a home for military veterans. We walked narrow, cottonwood-shaded streets named Grant, Sheridan, and Kearny. The old parade ground was still there, with Civil War cannon flanking the flagpole. Patriotism was a solemn duty, and the word was never uttered with a sneer. Flying the flag was virtuous, not demagoguery. Standing on the veranda of the headquarters building facing the parade ground, if we listened carefully we could hear the faint echo of bugles blowing retreat. The sandstone building, rock quarried from the banks of the nearby Arkansas River, had a cornerstone with the date 1867 chiseled on its worn face. Dodge City's wild west past was little more than a half century behind us, but our grasp of the timeline of history was so limited it seemed forever ago. But the weight of that past, set in the constancy of a land that stretched to a limitless horizon, attested to unlimited opportunity. Anything was possible for the courageous and adventurous. Not only was it possible to pursue the distant horizon, anything less was a character flaw. God had blessed America, made her great, and there had never before been a nation of such strength, virtue, and preeminence.

True Religion was at the core of our growing up. We took it in with our mother's milk. We are Christians, immersed in water on confession of our faith in Jesus Christ. But there is more: we believed with certitude that our Protestant denomination was the One True Church. Our denomination grew out of the Enlightenment and John Lockean rationalism that spawned, among other things, the religious revivals on the American frontier in the late eighteenth and early nineteenth centuries.

The movement's goal, which we embraced, was to unite all Christians through a correct understanding of an inspired, inerrant Bible. We took Jesus' Great Commission seriously. Our message was that the church, pure in its apostolic days, had been corrupted over the intervening centuries. We offered simple—and pure—New Testament Christianity, but this claim had specific reference points. Gospel preaching encompassed the story of Jesus, certainly, but also included our systematic doctrinal teaching in the manner of doing church. It was a package deal. The convert accepted both theses as equally necessary for salvation. The target of evangelism was certainly the debauched sinner, but we kept our skirts pretty clean. Overall, evangelistic efforts were directed at the unchurched, the disciples of all other world religions, and all Christian folk in doctrinal error (wrong-headedness about faith propositions). Essentially, we called on everyone everywhere to accept our version and vision of the Bible and the church. Our doctrines, traditions, customs, and mores were all equally presented with the eternal gravity of, "Thus saith the Lord." The religious past was to be preserved, and was more important than the religious future. Heaven was the reward for being doctrinally sound churchmen—and as an afterthought, churchwomen—and, of course, being morally upright.

The preceding summation of our church, although it seemed singular to us, surely has a familiar ring to most readers of this book, regardless of religious heritage. That's because the sentiment of singular faithfulness has resided in the heart of Christendom from apostolic times when the apostles thoughtfully considered—and bickered over—the details of doing church. It most certainly rings true after the church crossed the historical boundary from persecuted minority to sanctioned majority. Christian factionalism and denominationalism are testaments to the notion of being the authentic One True Church. Ecumenism, bubbling up from time to time in church history, is a concept of greater currency today. So, we confess: we are the fourth generation of our family to have belonged to the Church of Christ.

Every Sunday morning, Sunday evening, and Wednesday evening our family piled in the old Chevy and drove to our modest building in South Dodge. We crossed Front Street, which fronted the Santa Fe Railroad, and on which our grandfather, Grover Cleveland Hunter, with his third grade education, worked as a laborer when he wasn't farming.

We crossed the Arkansas River (which we pronounced Ar-Kansas) to a small, white, clapboard, one-room church house that was a symbol of unadorned Christianity. The unpretentious building had no steeple and no stained glass. The interior had no icons, no art, no crosses, no statuary, no candles, and no classrooms, kitchen, or nursery. It was furnished with handmade, darkly stained, pine pews, a lectern, and a table. The worship was centered in preaching, prayer, song, communion, and giving. There was a touch of anti-clericalism in the Church of Christ by the time it reached our generation. Higher education was not valued as a prerequisite for pulpit ministry, and some churches thought it wrong to have a located preacher.

The Church of Christ prided itself that it had no creed but the Bible. We claimed to speak where the Bible spoke and to be silent where the Bible was silent. Church organization was local and patriarchal. We were overseen by male elders and referred to ourselves as "the brotherhood." Women were to keep silent (except for singing). They did a lot of the work but none of the public talking. Males occupied the lectern to preach, pray, serve at the Lord's Table, and lead congregational singing. We sang our hymns without instruments, prayed our prayers without prayer books, gave our money without parsimony, and took communion each Sunday. Grape juice was substituted for wine in the sacrament (the temperance movement took precedence over literal scriptural interpretation in this case). Baptism was by immersion at the "age of accountability" and was accomplished in a horse tank full of cold water that waited functionally but uninvitingly beside the lectern.

The Word of God was preached from Genesis to Revelation, treating the Bible as a level book in which every verse was inspired and all had equal significance. The method of interpretation was a form of literalism based on direct command, necessary inference, and approved example. By our lifetimes, the Church of Christ concluded that the work of our early Restoration preachers had correctly teased out the details of doctrine, church organization, and policy. With absolute commitment to our religious positions we boldly declared, "If anyone can show us from the Bible that we are wrong, we will change." Even so, the Church of Christ was not monolithic. There were still doctrinal squabbles and several dissenting strains stood under the Church of Christ banner. There was disaffection, debate, division, and disfellowshipping. Individually, church members were to be faithful Christians and defend our movement's received faith. The purpose of Christian living was to keep "oneself pure and unspotted from the world." Essentially, we embraced a rule-keeping ethic. The subtext of our preaching was guilt, and it promoted a strain of world-denying piety. The body is bad; the spirit is good. The goal of life was to avoid the world (escape hell) and go to heaven.

The decades unfolded and the twentieth century world pressed in upon us in our idyllic, post-World War II, southwest corner of Kansas. Our church, both locally and collectively, generally scoffed at discombobulating theses of natural science and conveniently ignored the social gospel. Modern science forced us to vacuum-seal fundamentalist religious doctrine in an indiscriminating gyrus of the frontal cortex and simultaneously severed the synapses to the motor cortex that would have stimulated involvement in practical issues: civil rights, poverty, the escalating war in Vietnam, growing globalization, economic justice, and the corrupting influence of wealth and power. The sacred and the secular couldn't interact because our movement lacked the cognitive theological underpinnings that galvanize moral outrage and energize public acts of social conscience.

During our youth, something unexpected happened to that small, country church. It became middle-class. By 1945, America had recovered from the Great Depression and defeated fascism in the Second World War. We took our ease in a booming economy. Our church, with a growing membership sharing in the general prosperity, moved uptown. We moved back across the river, across the tracks, and across Front Street to a tree-lined street in Leave-It-To-Beaver country. We sang our faith with gusto, counting our blessings:

> "When upon life's billows you are tempest-tossed,
> When you are discouraged, thinking all is lost . . .
> Count your many blessings, name them one by one
> And it will surprise you what the Lord hath done."[1]

The simple, white, clapboard, one-room building became a physical plant—a multifaceted brick complex, still without steeple or stained glass. The auditorium, still devoid of icons or art except for the painting of a mountain scene (yes, actually, smack-dab in the middle of America's vast prairie) as a background for the heated baptistry, would seat 250 people. The building boasted graded classrooms for Christian education, a nursery, fellowship hall, and a kitchen.

---

1. Oatman, "When Upon Life's Billows," 304.

As life would have it—with its never-ending collision of stories—our home church exposed us to different methods of preaching and teaching. During childhood, we were taught the Bible by teachers, mostly women, who told us stories as we gathered around a utilitarian sandbox. It became the geography for ancient deserts, mountains, and rivers, with miniature people, animals, tents, villages, and cities. We entered the patriarchal world of Abraham, all bearded and Mesopotamian, and traveled from Ur of the Chaldeans to the land of Canaan. We participated in this journey, inching our way across the sandbox with the experience of leaving home in the grip of a faith adventure. We met three strangers by the Oaks of Mamre who might have been angels and heard old Sarai laugh when she heard she would be having a baby in her wizened old age. Fear gripped us when we walked up Mount Moriah with Abraham—knife in hand—while Isaac innocently asked where the sacrifice was.

We put on Joseph's coat of many colors and knew what it was to be special. We knew family rivalry and experienced being betrayed into slavery in Egypt. We watched Moses being rescued from the bulrushes, only to grow up and murder a man. We went on the lam with him and ended up at a burning bush in Midian. We took off our shoes on holy ground and put them back on to go down to old Pharaoh and say, "Let my people go!" The river turned to blood and there were flies and boils and frogs and locusts and gnats—gnats of all things. We had a feeling we were on to something when we thought about slavery and freedom, and maybe, just maybe . . . Then the lights were turned off in the classroom and it was a dreaded night when darkness covered the land of the sandbox and we heard the death angel coming. We knew it was all very important and somehow had something to do with us. We crossed the Red Sea on dry ground and Pharaoh's army got drowned. We ate manna off the sand and drank water out of the rock and felt that the Lord was among us.

Standing beside the sandbox, we stood at the foot of Mount Sinai and experienced the darkness and the smoke, the lightning and the thunder, the terror and the awe. Moses descended from the mountain and delivered the Ten Commandments, only to find that the children of Israel had turned away from God and melted down their gold to create a golden calf. The idol was ground to gold dust and we drank it mixed with water. We wandered in the desert for forty years before the survivors were allowed to cross the Jordan River and enter the promised land. All except Moses. God made him remain behind to die and be buried in an unmarked grave for a moment of impatience when he struck the rock to bring forth water, rather than simply speaking to the rock as God had commanded. The powerful lesson drawn from this story: God's rules were to be followed without variance, and disobedience had consequences—even if you were Moses.

We followed Joshua on his military campaign to take the land of Canaan for the Israelites, beginning with the blaring trumpets and the crumbling walls of Jericho. The stories of prophets and judges led to the first king of the nation of Israel, Saul. We followed the life of David: shepherd boy, sling-shot slayer of Goliath, guerrilla fighter, the beloved friend of Jonathan, the warrior King, poet and singer of psalms, the lover of beautiful Bathsheba, and instigator of the murderous plot against Bathsheba's soldier husband, Uriah. The prophet Nathan confronted David regarding his treacherous deeds: "Thou art the man!" David repented in sackcloth and ashes. His child with Bathsheba died. We were shocked, terrified, and inspired.

The Syrian and Babylonian subjugations of Israel and Judah respectively, turned the sandbox into the Middle East of the Tigris and Euphrates River valleys and cast the Jews adrift in the power politics of ancient Mediterranean world empires. The stories shifted to a Palestine filled with Roman soldiers and the small villages of Bethlehem and Nazareth. The story of Jesus and the stories Jesus told were enacted in the sandbox, ending with three crosses at Golgotha outside the walls of Jerusalem. Except that wasn't the end. There was an upper room and an empty tomb. The sandbox became the landmass of the fertile crescent surrounding the Mediterranean Sea and we followed Paul, Barnabas, and their companions on missionary journeys. It ended with Paul in prison in Rome, pleading with Timothy to bring him his coat because he was cold.

We reached the "age of accountability" and were baptized. As Christians, even though adolescent males, women Bible class teachers could no longer instruct us. We entered Bible classes taught by males and moved from the sandbox to didactic scholarship. We studied the restoration principle, the propositions of faith, and spreading the message of New Testament Christianity to an apostate world. Belief in the Bible came to mean an intellectual assent to a *particular view* of the Bible as completely inspired in every word and detail and incapable of being wrong about anything. Stories were replaced by a pattern-theology deduced from the Bible. Our sacred, Christian obligation was to reproduce the pattern of the first-century church in the twentieth century. This all encompassing theological system was referred to as "The Truth" or "The Faith." In our youthful church lives we often heard the words, "The truth of the Bible," but we never heard the words, "Pending further study," much less, "Pending further experience of the mystery."

Sunday morning preaching was a time for evangelism, although most sermons were delivered primarily to our faithful band of believers. Every sermon closed with an invitation to obey the gospel. Preaching on Sunday evening was generally a time for teaching doctrine and tenets of the faith. One memorable sermon was delivered by a good brother who farmed weekdays and preached Sundays. One Sunday morning, he delivered a sermon from the first chapter of Genesis. He informed us that God began his work of creation at nightfall, October 22, 4004 BC and completed his handiwork in six twenty-four-hour days. Our preacher explained that the date was arrived at by Anglican Archbishop James Ussher, the Primate of the Church of Ireland. Our preacher explained that Ussher had received his Doctor of Divinity at Trinity College in Dublin. He was a respected scholar and published his book on the age of the earth, *Annalium Pars Postierior*, in 1654. He had expertise in the ancient history of Persia, Greece, and Rome, as well as biblical languages, astronomy, and ancient calendars. Ussher reached his date of creation by calculating the genealogies of the Jewish patriarchs in Genesis. Our preacher, a high school graduate, had done enough research to uncover the writings of the archbishop. Had this brother lived one century earlier, he would have been considered erudite. Charles Darwin's *Origin of Species* wasn't published until 1859. The morning our brother delivered his sermon, the Scopes Monkey Trial in Dayton, Tennessee was only twenty-three years in the past. Radiocarbon dating techniques weren't introduced until the following year—1949. We shouldn't sneer—either at Ussher or our preacher. Both worked by the lights of their times and within their own limitations.

This sermon proved to be, in our personal experience, a misbegotten introduction to the Bible as science. It put us in a hard spot for further reading of the biblical texts, because in our schema the Bible was inerrant—incapable of being wrong on any subject across the spectrum of knowledge, from salvation to science. The ubiquitous Truth of the Bible trumped truth from any other discipline. The Bible as science and the Bible as God's plan of salvation were inextricably linked, and neither thesis could be true if both weren't. The two disciplines—religion and science—became competitors for the mind. The way the debate was framed (in our experience) one couldn't have it both ways. It was either/or. But the notion was, we think, deliberately kept vague to lessen the stigma of hayseed provincialism. The church had an uneasy feeling. We were, after all, in the twentieth century.

On the other hand, we were exposed to preaching as lyrical poetry rather than pure pedagogy. This was exemplified by a Tennessee evangelist who regularly visited our congregation. He was a gentle man with a gift of rhetoric that often moved both him and his hearers to tears. The weeping preacher related the Bible in stories with captivating simplicity and power. He might occasionally ask a question, but usually left the conclusions open to the authority of the story. His sermons carried us back to the verisimilitude and enthusiasm of our sandbox days and summoned an echo of discernment that didn't achieve full voice for decades. The Bible characters seemed very much like us. Or we seemed sort of like them. We came to know that stories told to a child will stay with the child forever as foundation, inspiration, and wisdom. Bible stories learned and parsed in Greek or Hebrew take years to master. Intellectual subtlety may be gained, but sheer scholasticism can be barren soil. Desire dies and wisdom withers, scorched by many tasks, mini-crises, mini-quarrels, and mini-aggressions. Stories warm the heart and cast light in the darkest corners of the mind. Certitude freezes the heart and numbs thinking. The tradition of the Church of Christ was both heartbreakingly right and heartbreakingly wrong. We celebrate its strengths while mourning its paucity. We should confront all of life's experiences within that equilibrium.

The previous description of our church heritage may make it sound mean-spirited. And in some ways, when we experienced the nasty infighting as adults, it was. But we also experienced an approach to biblical religion that was undertaken with utmost seriousness, and was prompted by a good heart and carried out with a good conscience, if not an entirely clear one. We spent our youths among God-fearing people who believed God created the world and reigned over it, who revered the Ten Commandments, believed in the Jesus of the Gospels and his church, and who worshiped in faith. These folk dedicated themselves to loving God and neighbor. They embraced Christian principles of obedience, virtuous living, decency, humility, hard work, being nice, good manners, cleanliness, loyalty, patriotism, and taking responsibility for one's actions. If tragedy struck, they would be the first ones at your door with a supportive word, a tuna casserole, and an angel food cake. The tradition was distinct and unambiguous. It was palpably true. Our worldview was circumscribed by our religious view. We had a nagging sense that it had shortcomings, but we thought with age, more knowledge, experience, and wisdom, it would all add up. During childhood, the church provided our religious life, our cultural life, our recreational life, and our social life. What more could we ask? We believed it and we loved it passionately.

As middle-class boys we were ambitious and saw education as empowerment on the way up and out. We left Dodge City to pursue the allure and pedantry of academia, beginning at one of our church colleges. We received a workmanlike education that equipped us to enter graduate schools and follow our chosen professions. College also continued to shape the religious narrative of our youthful heritage. New words entered our consciousness: *come, follow, death, resurrection, community, blessed, disciple, suffer, miracle, life, love, heal, forgive*. Although we didn't have the experience yet necessary, we had a growing sense of awe and mystery. A suspicion that religion might really matter in the life lived, and not just processed in the realm of the mind parsing Hebrew and Greek. The sandbox stories were real.

We embarked on graduate school. Lanny became a physician. He has spent more than fifty years in the consultation room and operating theater. Vic became a pastoral theologian. He has served more than fifty years in the pastor's study and parish pulpit. Lanny experienced the ravages and ruin of the Vietnam War and Vic experienced the ravages and ruin of the Vietnam War peace movement. We have invested ourselves in local church communities since the age of accountability. We have both celebrated our fiftieth wedding anniversaries and have the support and solace of loving, forgiving spouses. We are surrounded by children and grandchildren. We have lived rural and urban lifestyles. We have been relatively poor and relatively rich, knowing neither grinding poverty nor wealthy excess. We have known times of joy and even moments of euphoria and exultation. We have experienced times of brokenness, suffering, and senselessness. We have known moments of healing, and sometimes glimpsed the numinous and transcendent. Struggling with the incomprehensible and the incoherent, we have sometimes succumbed to living compartmentalized, even fragmented, lives. The gift of laughter has enriched our lives, even as it disarmed the unimaginable. We have been lied to by stories that claimed too much, and betrayed by stories that claimed too little. We have done our share of lying and betraying. Our lives are earthy and earthly. Some might say vulgar—and they certainly are common.

We now have over a century and a half of life experience between us, and taken together just under half a century of formal education—all seasoned by experience, braced by fraternal conversation, and buoyed by sibling support. We embrace the foundational stories and songs that are part of our ethos—from Joshua to George Washington to Wyatt Earp; from "God Bless America" to "Home On The Range" to "Rock Of Ages." They called us to this land and the land beyond, but it was all held together with barbed wire and binder's twine. It took the crucible of time and experience to open our hearts to making meaning through desire, narrative, and faith. We are eager to embark on the "What?" and "So What?" of cosmos, creature, and civilization in search of a coherent story.

Before we do, we want to clearly state what we know for certain.

6

Certitude

"Live your questions now, and perhaps even without knowing it, you will live along some distant day into your answers."
—Ranier Maria Rilke
　Poet

We have engaged in brotherly conversation for almost seventy-five years. Watching... and talking... and listening... and talking. And this is what we know for certain: "It's the lower jaw that moves."

7

The Quest for Truth That Makes Us Free and Whole

"From my birth they have hovered over me:
Tradition, authority, patterns, rules, prejudices
I never made, binding me . . .
And in this human situation we all share the same strictures.
Is there the freedom of release for
Faith in the Eternal Presence who will not let me
Lie content in my shackles?"
—Carlyle Marney
    Pastor

SCIENCE IS DEDICATED TO unraveling a mystery. Religion is dedicated to apprehending a mystery. Each discipline uses tools appropriate to its task. Somehow in the long history of civilization, where the stories of science and religion intersected and played themselves out, there was a time when it was thought that the tools in either discipline could be applied to the other. That notion was ill-conceived, but still persists in some quarters. The question in our search for meaning-making should be, we believe, "Is there a coherent narrative that overarches both disciplines that doesn't do harm to either?" In addressing this question, we must first know what each discipline proposes and in what manner.

Life began on planet Earth when the conditions of cosmic evolution reached a propitious state for biological evolution. Life took many forms as it evolved into plant and animal kingdoms, and one form it took was a genus we ourselves named *Homo*. Composed, as Auden imagined of *Eros* and Dust, desire was the foundational emotion of our genus, beginning with the instinctual desire to live. Genus *Homo* rooted for the breast, sucked on the nipple, and thrived—or failed to thrive. It grubbed for nourishment, fought, fled, or froze to survive, copulated to preserve the species, and acquired biological traits that both enabled and energized *Homo* to engage its planet with the brain and the body. One day, when this creature of biological evolution reached a critical stage, it fell into self-consciousness and capitalized on the traits of intellect, spirit, voluminous memory, foresight, an extended hand, an opposable thumb, a discriminating brain, a longing heart . . . and emerged as a human being. Desire for an excess of survivability (fear of scarcity) drove *Homo's* greed for wealth and power. Desire for transcendence refined its hunger for sociability, truth, beauty, and moral clarity.

Even as *Homo* struggled to fill its belly, it struggled to find meaning. *Homo* faced life with the realization that it was a mix of joy and sorrow. Sometimes life was gratifying and sometimes unbearable, but in any case it ended in a death. Death was an inevitable and unsatisfactory conundrum that begged for explanation. All resources were marshalled in the search for understanding, and from the beginning our species spun tales using the fundamentals of all good narrative: What if? How? Why? What? Where? When? Who? Narratives trace the processes of cosmos and creature through natural science and reason. Narratives trace the story of humankind and the civilizations cast forth upon planet Earth through perception. History was both fashioned by humans and recorded by humans. *Homo* consciously and voluntarily—if not wisely and magnanimously—constructed history of its own devices and established for itself social hierarchy, governance, law, religion, science, arts, tools, weapons and other needful things. Narratives arose that linked the known with the unknown. Religion held sway over most of humankind's imaginings as we trekked toward the Age of Enlightenment, during which evidence-based science became recognized as the dependable repository of knowledge. Progress has brought *Homo* to our present moment when we live in a time where humankind can do what neither fluke nor nature has succeeded in doing—destroy most of humanity and irretrievably damage our planet. This can be done through weaponry, poisons, toxic wastes, hate, greed, ignorance, and sheer neglect. What science or philosophy can address these existential facts?

Defining a few terms will be helpful to our discussion. *Evolution*—a word that is emotionally loaded for some—means different things to different people. Meaning can usually be made plain by context, as evidenced by such phrases as the "evolution of biological life" in contrast to the "evolution of art." For the purpose of this book, we use the term *cosmic evolution* to refer to the formation of the planetary systems (multiverse) following what is known of the laws of natural science. We use the term *biological evolution* to apply to change in living organisms that took place on planet Earth over incalculable generations and eons of time—through biochemical, physiological, and molecular processes, to include variance, genetic mutation, natural selection, and other mechanisms—whereby animal and plant life evolved from single-celled organisms to organisms of increasing diversity and complexity. When genus *Homo* appeared, it interacted with its planet and all the species of flora and fauna that had evolved. *Homo*, in its grasping, became the scourge of planet Earth. *Homo's* desires and devisings caused, and will continue to cause, enormous damage to the biological life of the planet and the planet itself.

As Genus *Homo* evolved into *Homo sapiens sapiens* (anatomically modern humans), it also underwent developmental change. We use the term *development* to refer to changes in culture—changes in ways of living, ways of doing, ways of thinking, ways of knowing, and ways of being—driven by the desire and genius of *Homo sapiens*. We use the term *science* to refer to the acquisition of factual knowledge about the natural world through systematic observation and controlled experimentation, a process of theory and proof that can be repeatedly and reliably demonstrated. We use the term *revelation* to refer to something that is "made known" rather than a "laboratory process," and includes the serendipitous "ah-ha" moments we experience. Revelation—ah-ha!—occurs in pursuit of both science and religion. Humankind knows things. Humankind believes things. Humankind has faith in things. *Faith* is always a conviction that there are realities that the mind may not understand and with which the flesh cannot grapple, but upon which we can depend.

Faith is fundamental to life's journey, but is a slippery word used in many ways. We have faith (a mundane example) the commuter trains will run, within reason, on time. But humans (from the beginning of our species) also live lives on a metaphysical plane. Overarching belief systems need not have God-talk in them to take the form of trust that provides a scaffold for living. Whatever the overarching belief or trust or faith consists of, it is a guiding light and the framework for living onward despite the uncertainties of life. As for religious faith, a phenomena encountered in most, if not all, cultures, we are persuaded there is a difference between the academic study of religion and the lived experience of faith. The first is intellectual assessment; the latter is an experience that ventures a life of trust. The life ventured in faith is dynamic and is grounded in desire and narrative. And so, we also want to alert the reader to the term *life-alive* (wholeness), a term used repeatedly throughout this book, seizing upon it because we believe the question "Is there life after *birth*?" is as important as "Is there life after *death*?"

A coherent story is necessary to make meaning, regardless of the subject under consideration. The science fiction genre, for instance, still has a rationale that sustains the story. For centuries, universities provided the table where all disciplines came together for rigorous conversation. Today—the Information Age—this conversation is now scattered throughout institutions, journals, texts, seminars, convocations, and the ether of the internet. But wherever enlightened discussion now takes place, science claims preeminence on the grounds it is indisputable fact. Religious faith, some folk opine (whether traditionalists or postmoderns), is a vestige of a bygone era of ignorance and superstition. We think otherwise. We believe the voice of good religion, as a conversation partner with good science, is ever more crucial in our pluralistic, postmodern world. Science and religion both have something to say to each other in the search for answers to *What?* and *So What?* If these questions are approached by either discipline with conceit, hubris overwhelms discussion. If approached with disdain, the conversations are demeaning. If approached with a closed mind, there will be no conversation. With openness and accessible language, there are grounds for learning and understanding.

We believe desire, narrative, and faith are essential dimensions for coherent living. We are driven by desire to experience, observe, cogitate, and explore the "*What?*" and "*So What?*" of life within a vast matrix of ever-expanding questions. We spin out our personal narratives that intersect with narratives about the cosmos, its life forms, and the prehistory and history cast by the humans who preceded us. Our own personal narratives intersect with others' personal narratives in a never ending succession. Narrative establishes identity. Faith—of our own choosing—in some things and some ones, is a matrix of thought, experience, and feeling that establishes purpose in our living.

We propose that one way to live lives as affirming flames rather than snuffed-out candles is confessional Christian living. We use the language of desire, narrative, and faith as the basic dynamic for a life lived with purpose, inspiration, and hope. We think it possible to acquire enough knowledge, accumulate enough wisdom, and gain enough experience to walk life's long road and at least know when someone is pissing on our umbrella and telling us it's raining.

It's difficult, if not impossible, to fully escape the orbit of our early, doctrinaire credos. The emotional tug of childhood imprinting runs deep. Speaking personally, the authors of this book still hope that we might accumulate enough data, ponder enough philosophy, cogitate enough religion, parse enough language, refine enough ethics, and acquire enough wisdom so that we not only *get it*, but get it *right!* This illusory odyssey for Absolute Truth lingers as a vain siren song of our youth. Life experience forced us to adapt, but the vestigial instinct for certainty still nudges us with longing. Gotthold Lessing, German dramatist and critic, pictures God offering humankind a choice between Absolute Truth and the Quest for Truth. Humankind's response, Lessing believes, should be to choose the quest for truth, acknowledging that Absolute Truth resides in God alone. Lessing's implication is important for scientist and theologian: knowledge is finite.

In the quest for knowledge, some ideas are better than others. In antiquity, it was finally decided that lead couldn't be turned into gold. With modernity, science confirmed that Pb (molecular weight 207.2 grams/molecule) couldn't be turned into Au (molecular weight 196.9 grams/molecule). Physicians finally learned that bleeding (phlebotomy) was bad therapy, until modern evidence demonstrated it was therapeutic for three specific diseases: Porphyria Cutanea Tarda, Polycythemia Vera, and Hemochromatosis. Ancients knew that water could be boiled and turned into steam to provide energy. But, attempts to produce energy through a nuclear reaction at room temperature (cold fusion) has so far resisted all modern scientific efforts. However, uranium can be enriched to release energy. From such non-credible and credible notions, knowledge was acquired and passed along. Some of it proved worthy, even durable. Some of it was merely cultural and was ephemeral. Some of it was foolish and was scrapped. Some was foolish and was perpetuated. Knowledge is not certainty. Facts are not wisdom. The learning curve is nuanced and complex. Reliable data and genuine enlightenment are hard won.

Consider this, for perspective. This book is about one inch thick. If copies of it were stacked one upon another to reach from planet Earth to its sun (a distance of 93 million miles), it would require 5.9 trillion books. If that stack of books represented the age of the cosmos (13.8 billion years), the stories of the approximate 200,000 years that *Homo sapiens* have stood astride the earth could be told in the last sixty-four pages of the last book in the entire stack. The *written* history of anatomically modern humans would fill less than two pages of that enormous stack of books. Everything else, reaching back to the beginning, is increasingly veiled in cosmic mist. That mystery has always been of consuming interest to humankind because we know, even if it's only an inkling, that the vast expanse of cosmic time and space and matter and creaturely existence (of which we have experienced the merest fragment) is still part of our story.

Who or what or where, humankind has wondered, is the center of the universe? How did it begin? Proximate answers to such questions are drawn from humankind's pursuit of science and religion. Both science and religion took shape at the dawn of the earliest civilizations. Both sprang from the same human instinct: meaning-making. Both were refined in the crucible of human experience. Both occupy the common ground of storytelling. Both cast their stories with language, but the methodologies diverged. Formation of the cosmos and creaturely life left data embedded in the natural world. Data is subject to study by academic disciplines in science, from astrophysics to zoology, and tells stories based upon the laws of nature. Academic disciplines in religion, from anthropology to Zen Buddhism, establish stories based on humankind's accumulated experience of how spiritual life works. Both disciplines draw upon human experience from every continent and culture in hopes of establishing trustworthy stories that—in the jargon of modernity— may be referred to as *evidence-based*. This concept is comfortable orthodoxy for modern science. We argue that evidence-based religion is also a credible concept, but not the same as proving a theological point using methods of natural science.

During civilization's early millennia religion was regarded as the foundation of all truth by most, but surely never all, people. In recent centuries, truth has been increasingly expressed in scientific terms and religion relegated to a secondary role. Moderns and postmoderns often regard religion as outmoded and indict it as an impediment to knowledge and even a goad to genocide. Religion, dumbfounded by science's spectacular achievements, envies science its fact-making. Science envies religion its capacity for meaning-making. Practitioners of both disciplines recoil at the amorality that will eradicate populations through germ warfare, Zyklon B, or a mushroom cloud, or who will casually destroy our planet by plundering its resources. Both disciplines occupy the common ground of narrative and spin fact, observation, intuition, and soul-searching as realms of narrative truth.

Fact and narrative truth are different in the same way that DNA identification and personal story are different. Sequencing our genome is a fact grounded in biochemistry, physiology, and engineering, but that fact is orphaned until it spirals into personal narrative. When we want others to know who we are, we don't print out our genome. We tell them our story. We are not Everyman or Everywoman. We have names. Personal story is a narrative of a particular human, set in a particular place, during a particular time, and under particular circumstances. Our stories don't unfold in a vacuum. Stories have distinct historical settings and are shaped by overarching narratives of geology, geography, the life sciences, and culture. Stories are imprinted by civilizations, ethnicities, philosophies, and religions. We can neither know nor remember all of our stories. Ancient, antiquarian stories are lost to our personal experience. Formative, intimate, painful, or traumatic personal stories may not be accessible to conscious memory. Even those stories we recall are not absolutely factual. Jurisprudence has demonstrated that "eyewitness" accounts are almost never faithful in all details, and moreover even their fundamental witness can be tragically wrong.

8

The Atomic Age and the Quantum Universe

"Science means research firmly based upon one or more past scientific achievements, acknowledged, for a time, as supplying the foundation for its further practice."
—THOMAS S. KUHN
    US Historian of Science

PICK ANY PERSON ON planet Earth, from any continent, any race, and any gender, who is alive right now in this technological age, and double-click on them. *Homo*'s computer-like brain, with billions of binary-switch neurons topped off with sophisticated molecular systems and an electrical charge, quietly awaits your stimulus. Turned "on," the neuron downloads its electro-molecular stuff and the resulting cascade sends the entire human organism into action. Double-click on any person anywhere in the world. The humankind-grid dumps you into the African savanna about two million years BCE.

A distant cousin of ours (whose name was Hunter because that was what he did) sat under an Acacia tree. He hadn't eaten for two days. He had tried to catch a gazelle. "Gazelles were freakin' fast!" He had avoided a prowling lioness, also looking for dinner. He had tried to scare a pack of hyenas away from the carcass of a warthog, but he was outnumbered and overmatched. He had narrowly escaped the jaws of a crocodile while crossing a muddy river. His stomach cramped. He wasn't sure he had the strength to make it back to the cave. "I'm a lousy hunter." He reached down and plucked a plant with his facile thumb and fingers. "I'll have to be a vegetarian." He ground the grains to pulp with his molars and stared into the distance. After a time, he buried his head in his hands and groaned, "What's it all about?" In those moments, the proto-language center in Hunter's brain had invented slang, conceived a new word (vegetarian, i.e., *lousy hunter*), and embarked on philosophy. The next night, weary and worn and still hungry, he posed the question to the cave dwellers. They pooled their knowledge, which is often the same as pooling ignorance. "What's it all about?" they cried.

Uncounted millions of people have contributed to deciphering the mysteries of the universe. The effort began hundreds of thousands of years ago by earliest *Homo*, but their successes and failures are unrecorded. They lived in the Prehistoric (preliterate) Era. They had a history, but writing had not yet been devised nor had the materials on which writing could be preserved. They just talked about everything, which is to say, they created oral history. Today, surviving texts give us direct knowledge of men like Pythagoras, who formulated the theorem of the right-angled triangle about 500 BCE. This remains one of the most important theorems of mathematics and extended arithmetic (counting) to mathematics (reasoning with numbers). Copernicus, 2,000 years later (1543 CE) said the Sun was the center of the universe and the Earth circled around it. He created an uproar because his idea was contrary to the accepted notion that it was the other way around, which is perfectly obvious to anyone who has eyes. No doubt, Pythagoras and Copernicus borrowed from ideas formulated by earlier thinkers, but they are credited with these discoveries because they were the first who wrote about them *and* whose texts were preserved.

Writing secured the narrative of humankind. Other modalities, both ancient (cave paintings, arts, and artifacts) and modern (photography and the devices it precipitated) capture and preserve humankind's doings. But writing chronicled humankind's saga and gave it breadth and depth. Writing details the narratives of theoretical and applied science, which is to say musings and the laboratory. Writing also records the imaginings of the mind and the mind's eye, which is to say the humanities. Writing gives an account of people, places, things, civilizations, and events.

Writing records the stories that delivered understanding from ignorance and rescued hope from despair. Writing made sustained scholarship and research possible.

The enormous advances in science during the twentieth century didn't occur because those 100 years produced an extraordinary number of scientific geniuses, but because the many geniuses before them provided the foundation for the increasingly sophisticated theories, tools, and technology that allowed the recent avalanche of discovery. Our giants stood on the shoulders of historic giants who stood on the shoulders of prehistoric giants. Cumulative knowledge and technology has had such an impact that much of the factual understanding of the universe has been done by our contemporaries.

Classical physics explains how the world goes round in terms of atoms. Atoms, science declares, are the building blocks of the universe. We live in the atomic age! Oddly, Democritus, a Greek philosopher living around 400 BCE, proposed matter is composed of minuscule, indivisible particles he called *atomos*. He coined this word from the Greek words *a* ("not") and *témnein* ("to cut"), implying something that cannot be divided. The Greeks proposed atoms were real, but for intervening centuries the notion of atoms was simply a useful theory in discussing matter and energy. Atoms were first "seen" (demonstrated) and their component parts measured and standardized by the cumulative efforts of a dozen or so brilliant European scientists around the turn of the twentieth century. The first atoms were "split" in the mid-1930s and it was conjectured that certain isotopes of uranium might create a chain reaction releasing enormous amounts of energy. World War II began in Europe in September 1939, and those scientists bore the burden of knowledge that, in theory, a horrendously destructive bomb could be constructed. They further speculated Nazi Germany was working on such a bomb because upon annexation of Czechoslovakia in 1938 Germany prevented uranium stores from leaving the country. Several of those scientists composed a letter to Franklin Roosevelt (signed only by Albert Einstein to give it gravitas) that advised the president of the consequence of these matters.

It turned out that Democritus's atoms were as real as ants or azaleas. But concurrent with the work being done by that ensemble of perceptive atomic physicists in the decades bracketing 1900, some realized the science of mechanical physics had many loose ends. The atom story wasn't large enough or detailed enough to explain all of the observed laboratory data. In searching for a bigger story, the theory of quantum physics and the theory of relativity, two pillars of modern science, were born, winning their proponents Nobel Prizes. Max Planck was awarded a Nobel Prize in 1918 for his work on quantum physics, which revolutionized the understanding of atomic and subatomic processes. Albert Einstein earned his Nobel Prize in 1921 for his work on the theory of relativity, which revolutionized the understanding of energy and mass.

Quantum physics claims that *matter* and *energy*, operating at the *scale of subatomic structures,* behave as *both* waves and particles. That is, the stuff of matter and energy (at their fundamental essence) behave like ocean waves *and* machine gun bullets, a phenomenon called wave-particle duality. Using the most modern laboratory techniques, one or the other can be demonstrated, but not both at the same time. Further, waves and particles may also exist in *variable locations simultaneously.* The theory is just plain freaky, but is now considered one of the most important theories in natural science. But it seems *un*natural. It goes against everything we call common sense (as once did the theory of a solar-centric universe). It's as if the physical world we interact with is an illusion. When we kick the tires before we climb into our sports car, the tires, the sports car, and in fact, us, are really fleeting, ephemeral clouds of gravity and electromagnetic charges flowing *and* ricocheting in an expanse of mostly empty space. Postmoderns might feel as though we are back in the days of archaic thought, in which our world was believed to be a reflection of the archetypal (real) world of the gods. We have come full circle and met ourselves face to face. So, we are told, everything we are doing and feeling in our hot little sports car is just waves or particles and electrical charges operating in a duality of ways in diverse locations in a gravitational field. We live in a quantum universe!

The universe of quantum physics has many competing theories—referred to as *interpretations*—to explain how it works. All are messy, mystical, marvelous—and sometimes amusing. All are grounded in story. What is its Ultimate Truth? No one knows—yet. And we may venture such Truth will never be known. Searching for that secure point in our turning natural world may well be deflected by Werner Heisenberg's uncertainty principle. Heisenberg (German physicist, Nobel Prize in Physics, 1932) demonstrated the more precisely the position of some particle is determined, the less its momentum can be known—and vice versa.

The Cambridge University Press summarized the seminal discussions between Albert Einstein and Neils Bohr on the nature of quantum physics in 1949, surely to be considered recent science. But, of course, the field is still being modified and amended. Scientific knowledge has an ever diminishing shelf life. As the knowledge base broadens, there is more to explain—not less. Yet, the world of quantum physics is believed to be largely correct because, in spite of vast areas of disagreement among scientists, the effects of quantum physics may be observed in our natural world, accurately predicted, and made functional. The details can't be explained, but they can be put to work. Quantum physics makes possible—forgive the pun—the quantum leaps forward in (among other things) transistors, lasers, semiconductors, electron microscopes, and magnetic resonance imaging. Quantum physics proceeds and succeeds on the catchphrase, "Stop speculating and start calculating."

Pure science believes there is nothing beyond nature, and sets about to categorize and explain the cosmos. Pure science (but not all scientists) infers that the cosmos has no transcendent purpose. That point of view is worthy of consideration, but is not projected from a discipline based on the scientific method. That point of view is philosophical speculation. Quantum physics is a calling, and may be likened to philosophy or religion. Theologians want to talk about the sacred in our secular world in philosophical terms called God. Theologians believe the world of religion is functionalized and becomes reality only when acted upon.

Science and religion, ancient and modern, rooted in their basic faiths, continue to operate in intersecting narratives. Science has faith that the laws of natural science govern all realities. Religion believes there are realities beyond what can be known through science alone. Einstein wrote a letter to Max Born in 1926 that contained the following statement: "I, at any rate, am convinced that He (God) is not playing dice."[1] Taken at face value, Einstein's words suggest that he believed in a God of masculine anthropomorphism who does not operate by chance. At the same time, Einstein spoke of himself as an agnostic but dissociated himself from atheism. He wrote, "I do not believe in a personal God and I have never denied this, but have expressed it clearly."[2] Einstein's statements are nuanced and don't work as bumper stickers.

The narrative of science is ever unfolding as it expands our knowledge base. Knowledge has been advanced by a succession of lone scientists. Their contribution to our fund of knowledge is staggering. We have already mentioned Pythagoras and his theory of the right-angled triangle and Copernicus's solar-centric universe. Euclid, a Greek mathematician

1. Born, *Born/Einstein Letters*, 88.
2. Dukas and Hoffman, *The Human Side*, 178.

c. 300 BCE, conceived of prime numbers (a number that is divisible only by itself and 1). Dmitri Mendeleev, a Russian chemist, is credited with the remarkable insight that allowed him to grasp the predictable structure of matter and create the Periodic Table of the Elements (1869). He filled in his table with the fifty-six elements known to him, ranked by atomic weight from the lightest to the heaviest, leaving blank spaces within the table where he believed there were elements yet to be discovered. He did this with remarkable accuracy (although he had some misconceptions). Mendeleev's Table—a complex puzzle (with most pieces missing) that he intuited from known facts and imagination—continues to be tweaked as the science of chemistry advances. Elements are still being discovered or synthesized in laboratories. Oganesson (symbol Og) is the 118th element recently added to Mendeleev's Table.

Knowledge has also been advanced by partnerships like that of James Watson and Francis Crick, molecular biologists at Cambridge University, who proposed the double helix model for the structure of DNA in 1962 (aided by the concomitant research of Rosalind Franklin, an X-ray crystallographer at King's College London). Knowledge has been advanced by consortiums, like the scientists at the Large Hadron Collider in Geneva. In 2012, they confirmed Peter Higgs's 1964 theory of a boson particle (nicknamed the "God particle") in quantum physics. All have added, bit by bit, to the fund of knowledge about the natural world.

Multidisciplinary, industrial age science—combining government, industry and teams of scientists, and requiring enormous sums of money—has done revolutionary work. The Egyptian pyramids might be considered the prototype of such an effort, but in our time it was the Manhattan Project (1942–1945) that created Fat Man and Big Boy. A more recent effort produced the Hubble Space Telescope, an apparatus about the size of a school bus, and named for a contemporary American astronomer, Edwin Powell Hubble (1889–1953). The distant focal points of telescopes on earth, even on the highest mountain, are blurred by earth's atmosphere and view objects in space with about the same clarity we see objects when looking at them from the bottom of a swimming pool. To overcome this disadvantage, the Hubble was put in orbit in April 1990. The launch went without a hitch but when the telescope was turned on the images it returned were out of focus. NASA was understandably embarrassed. The main mirror was improperly ground and polished in the manufacturing process. In a repair mission launched in December 1993, astronauts completed a record-setting five consecutive days of space walks and corrected the problem—an essential part of which was attaching a corrective lens (eyeglasses) to the telescope. In the intervening years, Hubble has provided unbelievably dazzling photographs of outer space, streaming back more than a million pictures. It has changed our understanding of space.

The Hubble not only confirmed the fact of a Big Bang, it established the age of the universe at 13.8 billion years to a tolerance of about 3 percent. It confirmed that there are black holes in the center of every single galaxy. It confirmed the existence of dark energy in space. In July 1995 it was focused for eleven days on a segment of sky no bigger than if we were sitting on our deck looking through a drinking straw. During that eleven days, while Hubble was focused on one/twenty-four millionth of Earth's entire sky, it identified more than 3,000 galaxies. The data gleaned from those eleven days viewing an infinitesimal speck of sky stuns us into silence at the possibilities of what exists in the vast remainder of interstellar space.

Another space telescope, the Kepler, named for Johannes Kepler (a Renaissance astronomer of German descent) was launched aboard a NASA spacecraft in March of 2009. It was designed to detect exoplanets (planets outside our own solar system). As of September, 2017, more than 3,667 exoplanets in more than 2,747 "star systems"—defined as at least one planet, usually more, orbiting in a flat plane around its star (sun)—have been identified. At least ten of these planets approximate the size of planet Earth and orbit their star at a distance that would permit water to exist (referred to by scientists as the Goldilocks Zone: neither too far from its sun nor too close, but just right). Theoretically, this might make those exoplanets habitable, at least for species like our own planet's life forms and . . . who knows what else?

The Hubble and Kepler telescopes are fact machines. When they "see" something, scientists stop arguing and try to incorporate this knowledge into science's database. And there is certainly much more to come. Stephen Hawking, a recently deceased British theoretical physicist, over his lifetime picked away at some of the basic precepts established by Einstein and his magical circle of European contemporaries. The cosmos is immense and the science is complex. The knowledge base is broad and is always shifting and expanding. It's difficult to explain, especially to people like us who have trouble adjusting the chlorine in our hot tub. But, the story is riveting.

9

Space, Time, and Mass

"For small creatures such as we are, the vastness is bearable only through love."
—Carl Sagan
Astrophysicist

A LONG, LONG TIME ago—13.8 billion years, give or take, so far back in time our minds can't conceptualize it—the cosmos consisted of an intensely hot, dense thing that held within it all space, time, and mass. Science doesn't tell us how the hot, dense thing came to be; it just was. Furthermore, science as yet offers no explanation as to why the thing went bang. Science picks up the story a New York second after the thing went off and explains proximately what followed.

The Big Bang sent a shower of the hot, dense thing's stuff flying outward in all directions at unfathomable speed. A cloud of gas, dust, and ice formed. This nebulous structure held within it the energy and matter that formed the galaxies of our universe, together with any life forms. It also included the forces of gravity and magnetism. After a long time this expanding cloud slowed down and cooled off, and its energy was converted into subatomic particles such as protons, neutrons, electrons, and bosons. The protons and neutrons combined to form atomic nuclei (the way they do, you know), and after another really long time electrons joined the nuclei to create atoms. The first element produced in this process was hydrogen so we could make bombs; then helium so we could send up balloons; and after that lithium so we could treat bipolar disorder. In time, all of the other elements of matter that make up Mendeleev's Table fell into line with their characteristic properties.

After a long period of cooling, the massive cloud formed from the Big Bang collapsed in upon itself to form a gaseous sphere. The center of the sphere became suns (stars), and the outer rim coalesced to form planets. Left over space debris formed comets, asteroids, and meteoroids. Comets are small planets formed of space dust, ice, and gas that orbit the sun trailing an incandescent tail which may be a hundred million miles in length. They have predictable orbits and Earth's people came to watch for them and marvel at the spectacle. Humans wove comets into our lore as omens for good or evil—the beginning of astrology—that persists today as a method of meaning-making (check your local newspaper). Asteroids are chunks of rock—as big as the state of Kansas or as tiny as a particle of sand—that didn't suck up enough stuff with their gravitational pull to create a planet or a comet, but still orbit our sun. Meteoroids are asteroids (large or small) that drift into the earth's dense atmosphere and glow from the friction. We call them "shooting stars," but technically they are flaming meteors. Meteoroids not totally consumed by their fiery passage through earth's atmosphere, strike the earth and are called meteorites. The amount of damage from impact is related to their size.

After the Big Cloud from the Big Bang went through the Big Slow Down, a pregnant pause, so to speak; it turned on the afterburners and started expanding again. Rather like the newborn baby who, after a slap on the butt and a giant gasp for air, is on its way. Our universe has been expanding ever since. Pythagoras, a philosopher as well as mathematician, used the term cosmos (Greek, *kosmos*, meaning "order") to describe our world in distinction to chaos (Greek, *khaos*, meaning "disorder"). But he had applied the term to a mere fragment of our world. We now know the term *cosmos* encompasses not just a universe, but a multiverse—a conglomerate of universes. It is filled with innumerable galaxies, a word taken from the Greek word for milk (*gala*), to denote their white appearance. There are an estimated 150 billion galaxies in our universe, with gazillions of planets orbiting billions of suns, with each individual galaxy held together by its own system's gravitational pull.

Ninety percent of a galaxy's mass is made up of an invisible something called dark matter. Dark matter is usually formed when a star runs out of fuel and explodes and that region of the universe collapses to form a black hole. Black holes have an enormous effect on the universe because their gravitational fields are so strong that neither matter, nor radiation, nor light can escape (hence, they are considered not to be visible), and within their boundaries time and space, as we know them, don't exist. Stephan Hawking, again, as well as others, have recently offered revised postulates about black holes. Hawking's genius joined quantum physics and mechanical physics to claim that various light particles can escape black holes (hence, the term black hole is not fully accurate). We can always expect revisions in the knowledge base.

Galaxies are of various shapes and sizes and each contains its own suns, stars, planets, and moons. A star and a sun are identical in cosmic composition, but only stars orbited by planets are referred to as a sun. Each sun-planet complex is referred to as a solar system. Stars are balls of gas (about 92 percent hydrogen, 8 percent helium, and a pinch of other elements) with dense cores and outer rims. Stars vary in size, but range within an upper and lower limit on a stellar measuring rod. The star's dense core of hydrogen undergoes nuclear fusion and converts hydrogen to helium. Enormous amounts of energy are released, rather like serial explosions of hydrogen bombs. Star-shine is energy: light that includes every different wavelength in the electromagnetic spectrum—radio waves, microwaves, infrared, ultraviolet, X-rays, gamma rays, something called terahertz rays, and visible light with its color spectrum.

Stars don't live forever. Eventually the star's hydrogen core is depleted and nuclear fusion is no longer possible. The star, in a desperate attempt to stay alive (an anthropomorphic metaphor for just doing what it would do by its nature), enlarges and burns what's left of the hydrogen in its outer rim. It is then called a red giant and resumes nuclear fusion, burning up its remaining hydrogen. When the star's fuel tank is empty, what happens depends on the size of the star. Massive stars collapse and utilize the remaining smidgen of its elements as fuel for a gigantic explosion that illuminates space in a cosmic light show called a supernova. If the core of the star was also massive, it implodes and forms a so-called black hole. Less massive stars' cores become neutron stars. The larger the star, the hotter, brighter, and faster it burns. Its color is dictated by its temperature. The hottest are blue, the coolest are red, and medium-sized stars, like our solar system's sun, are yellow. Our sun (star) is the heart of our solar system and is the source of its energy, heat, and light.

Planet Earth's sun is a relative newcomer in a universe of suns, having formed about 4.8 billion years ago, or some 9 billion years after the hot, dense thing exploded. Our sun, only a medium-sized star, is predicted to go out with a whimper, not a bang. When our sun uses up its hydrogen and helium fuel, the outer rim will be released as gas and dust to form a planetary nebula that will eventually disperse throughout space. Our sun's inner core will contract to form what is called a white dwarf that will use up the trivial amount of energy remaining in its trace elements and simply fade away—riding off into its own sunset, so to speak, like Shane. That is supposed to happen in about 5 billion years.

Stars, as viewed by the humanities, are as interesting as stars when viewed by science. The mystique of stars fuels many phrases and ideologies:

> "Stars in your eyes..."
> "Wish upon a star..."
> "Hitch your wagon to a star..."
> "Catch a falling star..."
> "Born under a lucky star..."
> "The fault, dear Brutus, is not in our stars..."

The word *star* is often combined with other words for greater impact.

> "Star power..."
> "Star-studded..."
> "Star quality..."
> "Rock star..."
> "Superstar..."
> "Hollywood star..."

Stars presage ancient myth and embellish politics.

> "The Star of Bethlehem..."
> "The Star of David...
> "The Red Star..."
> "Stars and stripes forever..."

The motto of Kansas, our home state, is *Ad astra per aspera*. "To the stars through difficulty."

Our galaxy, the Milky Way, a tiny speck perched way out on the edge of the multiverse, is just one among all of the rest. The Milky Way is a long ellipse that is 100,000 light-years wide (a light-year is 5.9 trillion miles) and has a bulge at its center that is a huge "black hole" with a mass equal to three million Earth suns. Our sun, together with planet Earth and its moon, our seven sister planets (Pluto, you recall, was demoted), along with some space rubble, form our solar system. This system is set like a jewel in its own galactic necklace of stars. When we gaze upward on a clear night at the glittering bits of light that make up the Milky Way, we must realize that we stand cheek-by-jowl with them in the plane of just one galaxy. Humans bear the consequential knowledge that we are infinitesimally small creatures who inhabit a tiny spinning rock as it orbits in a huge solar system that is part of an immense Milky Way galaxy that, nonetheless, is finite in size as it spirals in an unfathomable light-year-matrix of interstellar space containing innumerable other galaxies in a possibly infinite multiverse. We are awed by this realization. Yes, but . . . in our gut, we don't think of Earth as *a* planet, but *the* planet—which is the center of the universe. And if we admit it, we think of ourselves and our kind as standing at the center of our planet.

Humans used to be ordinary folk sitting in a rocking chair on the front porch of our world, smoking a pipe and reading the evening newspaper. Now we are postmoderns, fully connected on the internet, whirling on a polluted planet that we use as a launching platform for nuclear weapons, chowing down at the top link of the food chain, and trying to figure out how we can leverage the global economy to get more stuff. The science story overwhelms and intimidates us because it strips away the elemental conceit of our own importance. We have a sinking feeling that we are inconsequential and insignificant.

The remarkable counterpoint to this feeling of insignificance is humankind's resilient hopefulness. In 1977, human traits of optimism and imagination, plus our unquenchable desire for social connections, inspired America's industrialized technology apparatus to launch Voyager I. Today, the spacecraft's technology would be dissed by any self-respecting techno-geek. It had an eight-track tape recorder. Current low-end cell phones have 240,000 times the memory of Voyager's onboard computers. A gold-plated copper disc carried recordings of sounds and images of life and culture on Earth (along with presumptuously condescending instructions to possible recipients on how to use the thing). Sounds include surf, wind, and thunder; the calls of animals, birds, and whales; musical selections of Beethoven, Mozart, Blind Willie Johnson, and Chuck Berry; spoken greetings in fifty-five languages; and images ranging from landscapes to animals, insects, foods, architecture, and people of various races and cultures. NASA received public criticism of its intention to include photographs of a nude man and woman, so silhouettes were used instead. Nevertheless, this craft has now journeyed across space for forty years, is more than 11 billion miles from Earth, has exited our solar system, and entered interstellar space. It is still sending back messages and a small group of scientists at Jet Propulsion Laboratory in Pasadena, California, decipher the contents.

Voyager I is a technological marvel handcrafted by descendants of the human who handcrafted the first tool, blasted aloft by energy distilled from Earth's fundamental elements, and streaks through the frigid darkness of outer space because humankind is imbued with enduring imagination. It was infinitely more than an act of space exploration. It was a serious and symbolic attempt to find a responsive form of life somewhere in the universe, with whom Earth people might communicate and combine our unknown with theirs. If Voyager I continues on its trajectory and if another civilization were to encounter it, astronomers tell us it will most likely be a star designated AC+79 3888 in the Ophiuchus Constellation and the fly-by will take place about 40,000 years from now. Voyager I is a hopeful, earnest, technological prayer offered by science. If the Earth is still present in that far-off epoch, and if that prayer is answered in some futuristic manner, it will be a remarkable accomplishment. The database of scientific knowledge will be substantially expanded, and human garrulousness will be at least momentarily stilled because *Homo sapiens sapiens* will be standing mouth agape. Still, the trove of knowledge from such an awesome achievement will not answer humankind's fundamental question—*So What*? That is a question of a different order.

Meanwhile, our planet, significant to us because we came to inhabit it, has undergone phenomenal transformation. Earth consisted of a molten core some 4.8 billion years ago at the time its sun formed. Over intervening geological ages the planet first accumulated a huge quantity of water and a then a solid, crusted landmass developed over the molten core. The landmass, stewing in the planet's water, went through cycles of formation, separation, and rejiggering. Three hundred million years ago this process forged a planet with one mega-continent located more or less on the equator and surrounded by one mega-ocean. Scientists called the mega-continent Pangaea—formed from two Greek words, *pan* (entire) and *gaia* (earth). Pangaea, as geologists have reconstructed it, looks a little like a humongous, perched vulture. Then, two hundred million years ago great rifts formed in Pangaea and the mega-continent began to break up and drift apart. These giant fragments (tectonic plates) crept along, collided, broke up, coalesced, fell apart again, and continued moving in different directions and at different speeds. Sixty-five million years ago the fragments settled into the seven continental land masses we know today. The continents are still on the move, creeping along about the speed our toenails grow in a process called continental drift. When we look at a world map today and take note of the shapes of the various continents, it takes very little imagination to see them as pieces of a jigsaw puzzle we could piece together and recreate Pangaea.

Planet Earth finally reached the current state of rock, minerals, water, and air with which we are familiar. During those 4.5 billion years a remarkable thing happened. As geological evolution advanced, biological evolution advanced along with it. Earth became a habitat for life, creating and sustaining an infinite variety of animals and plants that could live in its water or on its land, and even some that could do both.

10

Molecules, Cells, and Creatures

"Is there more to life than molecules? There's more to life than meets the eye."
—Keith Ward
    Philosopher

PLANT AND ANIMAL LIFE are composed of earth's simple elements such as hydrogen, oxygen, and nitrogen. Complex molecules such as amino acids and nucleo-bases, essential to form deoxyribonucleic acid (DNA—life's genetic blueprint), were delivered to Earth in the meteorites which bombarded our planet over the eons of its development. Water was vital to life, which began as our young, planetary laboratory boiled, froze, washed, basted, suffused, steeped, homogenized, and hydrated these elements in the broth of Earth's primeval ocean. This alchemy—over time, unimaginable time—produced salts, acids, bases, proteins, and carbohydrates. With even more time, there arose generations of mitochondria, enzymes, DNA, RNA, hormones, and chlorophyl (a molecule in plants and certain bacteria that uses sunlight energy to extract nutrients from carbon dioxide and water by photosynthesis while releasing oxygen into the atmosphere—key to sustaining life on Earth).

Through incessant transformations, reductions, and recombinations, primitive cells formed that possessed tiny organs (organelles), biological fluids, and an electrical charge. At some point, the developing single-cell forms separated into two kingdoms. One was destined to be plants (algae) and one to be animals (amoeba). Algae and amoeba possess a metabolic arc called "life" that includes a beginning, a lifetime of taking in nutrients, discharging wastes, and reproducing, followed by death. Reproduction among single-celled animals is asexual, whereby the species maintains itself by dividing and streaming out identical, cookie-cutter replicas. Over thousands of millions of years, under the influence of genetic principles (including mutation) and environmental stimuli (natural selection), single-celled organisms progressed into multi-celled organisms of ever greater complexity. Predecessors of the blue-green algae were the first organisms to reproduce sexually. Male and female genders established themselves and have endured as reproductive units. Two was the magic number, except for the French. It worked. Sexual reproduction combined one half of the basic life-stuff of the male and one half of the basic life-stuff of the female to birth another creature of their species. There is a phenomenon called parthenogenesis (Greek: *parthenos*, virgin + *genesis*, creation), whereby many plants, some invertebrates, and a few vertebrate animals reproduce from an ovum (egg) that has not been fertilized by a sperm. But in sexual reproduction wherein a sperm fertilizes an egg, species are defined by the biological reality that members can breed only with its specific kind and no other.

Breeding among species has been called coupling because it requires individuals of male and female gender whose sexual organs are complementary. This coupling populated planet Earth. Sexuality drove the instinct for preservation of the species, and the act itself was psychologically satisfying and physically pleasurable beyond description. Sexuality is a one-two punch for survival and for fun. The genetic recombination of sexuality produced diversity—size, shape, color, markings, habitat requirements, and behavior. Diversity drove evolution at an accelerating pace. Adaptation mediated species change. Genetic mutations introduced heritable variables. Survival of the fittest promoted quality and capability. Alpha males don't fight to kill; only for the right to impregnate the female. Over millennia, more and more complex creatures evolved. Animal life took form through the differentiation of organ systems such as heart, blood, muscle, alimentary canal, lung, liver, kidney, glands, bones, and brain.

Human evolution is heavily invested in the brain—the organ which defines our species. The brain, of course, is not the mind. The mind is the sum total of what the brain projects, and is certainly greater than the sum of its parts. The brain is both an organ for thinking and an organ for action. The adult brain only weighs about three pounds, but when compared to both animals and preceding Hominids the *Homo sapiens* brain isn't just bigger, it's qualitatively different. It expanded not just in mass, but in functionality. The human quality of appreciation is distinct from instinctual satiation. The brain has areas given over to instinct, insight, foresight, planning, speech, and uniquely human muscular control—for instance, touching the tip of each finger precisely to the tip of the thumb, using both hands simultaneously and equally well, a facile maneuver independent of right- or left-handed dominance. It wasn't always this way.

In the beginning, the brain was the amygdala. Even the name sounds ominous—although it got its name innocuously enough from a Latin word that describes the shape of an almond. The amygdala sits atop the spinal cord where it responds to external stimuli—sight, sound, smell, taste, and touch. It's the seat of primitive emotions (rage, fear, and desire) and primitive responses (sucking, rooting, and lashing out). The amygdala, bathed in hormones, epinephrine, norepinephrine, dopamine, serotonin, and acetylcholine, is crackling with energy and waiting to strike. Its fundamental purpose is to protect the creature from danger—fight, flight, or freeze enhances survival of the species. The amygdala doesn't think. It's hardwired. It shoots first and doesn't even ask questions. This nub of neural tissue is a witch's brew of pure reflex that arcs out, lightning fast and hard as nails, to activate the entire biological apparatus—heart, lungs, bowels, blood vessels, muscles, adrenal glands, eyes, and ears. The entire organism is jolted into action. The body is flooded with adrenaline and hormones. The heart pounds, the pulse races, the lungs inflate, the pupils dilate, and a surge of fuel (sugar) is blasted into the system. Nonessential services—digestion and sex drive—are shut down. The amygdala is on red alert twenty-four/seven/three-sixty-five.

The amygdala is the foundation of every creature's brain. It's the complete brain of the rattlesnake, but remains alive and well within every animal, including *Homo sapiens*. The mouse brain is the rattlesnake brain (the amygdala) with a little bit of topping: the cerebrum, cerebral cortex, cerebellum, and temporal lobes. In every iteration of advancing species the topping becomes larger, more elaborate, and more complex. The topping is there to keep a lid on the hair-trigger device at its core—the amygdala. Without the topping, the universe of creatures would be a grotto filled with pit vipers. Perhaps twenty-first-century humans don't need this emergency crash cart like our ancestors who faced the sabertooth tiger, but we have it nonetheless, and it's still part and parcel of our survival. It's critical for climbing ladders, hiking a steep mountain trail, moving through underbrush in rattlesnake country, lighting the gas-jet in our barbecue grill, and searching out the odd sound in the dead of night. The complex evolution of brain function and anatomy reached its zenith in the species *Homo sapiens*, where this marvelous organ of gray and white matter is able to perceive, remember, interpret, conceptualize, plan, multitask, create, emote, and act rationally and purposefully. Yes, but how does it actually do it?

Science currently understands the function of the human body at the molecular/cellular level. Advances in chemistry, biology, physiology, pharmacology, genetics, and mathematics awaited the engineering of new tools before the life of a cell could be explored. Cells are microscopic creatures with minuscule, cellular lives and hark back to those single-celled organisms eons ago. Cells are enclosed in a cell wall (their skin). Cells have a brain (a nucleus with chromosomes and genes). Cells have a body (cytoplasm) that is 90 percent water and contains tiny organelles (organs)—like mitochondria—which have specific functions for cellular life. Cells have chemicals—acids and bases and salts. Cells have enzymes. Cells have hormones. Cells have an electrical charge. Cells require and take up nutrients. Cells excrete wastes. Cells beget children (more cells like themselves). Each human cell type essentially performs one task carried out through its complex biological processes. Muscle cells contract. That's all they can do. Gastric cells secrete gastric acids. That's all they can do. The same, single-task dedication is carried out by red blood cells, kidney cells, skin cells, bone cells and on to include every human cell-type. Even stem cells have one task—to retain the potential to morph into other needful cells. The countless cells that make up the entire human organism exist in a particular environment, live in societies, have jobs, and go to work. "Hi ho, hi ho, it's off to work we go."

Cellular life is a molecular extravaganza beyond imagining. Every cell has a biological clock that causes it to function (work, rest, take in nutrients, and eliminate waste) in a rhythm dictated by their private clocks. Further, there is a master clock in the highest brain centers that regulates the "timing" of the entire bodily organism so that bodily processes occur naturally in a twenty-four-hour cycle. This is called a circadian rhythm (Latin: *circa*, around + *dies*, day). This night-and-day rhythm was established in the long evolutionary process that resulted in *Homo sapiens*. Whether the sun is shining or not, whether we work the graveyard shift or not, the fluctuation of light does not affect the timing of our organic selves. Nor does night and day make any difference to individual cells operating according to their personal clocks. This has enormous implications for understanding health and pathology in humankind.

The functional cell of the brain is the neuron (gray matter). There are 100 billion neurons in the brain sustained by one trillion supporting cells. The entire system is awash in various chemicals and hormones. The neuron's "job" is to make, store, release, and recover certain chemicals. These chemicals (dopamine, serotonin, acetylcholine, and others) are called neurotransmitters because it is by the release and uptake of these chemicals that neurons communicate with each other. Neurons may communicate with a single neuron or with innumerable neurons, and do so through a projection from the cell called an axon (white matter). Each neuron hums along, quietly busy with its cellular life, ready and waiting for a stimulus to turn it "on" so it can "go to work."

The stimulus comes from the body's receptor systems of sight, sound, smell, taste, and touch. Remarkably, a thought can also stimulate neurons. Radiographic visual imaging of the brain at work (burning sugar) reveals that specific functional parts of the brain light up, rather like a pinball machine, when thinking of something or someone—a baseball, tennis, a song, an airplane in flight, mother, or the boss. It has been found that when a word is whispered in the ear of some comatose victims, specific parts of their brain light up in a similar fashion. But whatever it is, when a specific stimulus from the exterior or interior world is delivered to its go-to neurons, the branching axons release neurotransmitters that, in turn, stimulate all of their network-neurons to release their neurotransmitters to signal their target neurons. Every part of the brain and body is set in motion. The result is a finely tuned, coordinated cascade of responses that creates purposeful human thoughts, emotions, and actions.

The system is complex beyond comprehension. The miracle is not that the brain sometimes misfires or works poorly. The miracle is that it works at all. It is estimated that 70 percent of the messages neurons try to send don't get through, so the backup system is massively over-wired. It all runs on biology and chemistry. There is no tiny geek in the brain. No skinny little nerd wearing a T-shirt silk-screened, "I think therefore I am." No Zuckerbergian genius outfitted in high-watered jeans, sweat socks, and sneakers, sitting in a cubicle in an ergonomic chair, face eerily lit by the glow of a computer monitor and giddily running the show. No humanoid thing at all. No Wizard of Oz behind the curtain. The anatomists, biochemists, microbiologists, and cellular physiologists with all of their tools didn't find a geek. They found something even more strange and marvelous—molecular biology and chemistry.

Molecular science teaches us that the brain of a human organism is—at a cellular level—an organ just like, for instance, the stomach. Our response to this idea is probably, "Well, of course!" So, when the stomach is filled with steak and potatoes, the cells churn out chemicals and enzymes that digest the food and (together with secretions of special cells in the small intestine, liver, and gall bladder) transport nutrients through the digestive organs where they are converted to sugar, proteins, fat, and elements that are carried in the blood stream and nourish the body. It all makes perfect sense. Likewise, the stimulated brain releases neurotransmitters that flow and recede and . . . civilization occurs. Our response to that is, possibly, "Whoa!"

Yes, civilization flows from this dog's breakfast called the brain because a tiny, electrolyzed cell called a neuron makes and takes up chemicals and is bathed in hormones. This is both simple and complex. Also humbling. And somewhat, to use the phrase, unnerving. Molecules released into the gaps between neurons make possible devoted love and homicidal anger. Sexual desire and a sonnet. But, no two human beings possess identical physiology and biochemistry, not even identical twins. No two human beings, even within the same family, experience identical circumstances and influences during their development. Thus the anatomical, biological, neuropharmacological, genetic, hormonal human being interacts with its environment. Persons, clans, tribes, nations, and populations interact with each other and with a plot of ground, a state, a nation, a continent, and a world with its specific weather, geography, geology, germs, weapons, and the age in which they live. Humans are influenced by nature and nurture. Boundaries are always established. Boundaries are always crossed. Those are evolutionary and developmental principles.

The result is Rameses II, Abraham of Chaldea, Attilla the Hun, Cleopatra, and Leonardo de Vinci. Martin Luther King and Richard Speck. Also the Norman conquest, the antebellum South, the Holocaust, and the National Football League. And the wheel, a bronze sword, the pyramids, the Sistine Chapel, the San Francisco Bay Bridge, and the transistor. To say nothing of Gilgamesh, the Bible, the Mahabharata, *The*

Brothers Karamazov, The Jupiter Symphony, Hamlet, and *Mien Kampf.* Human beings tell stories, sing songs, paint pictures, craft tools, plant gardens, and build cities, cathedrals, hospitals, bath tubs, and battleships. And human beings develop personality disorders, depression, anxiety, schizophrenia, psychoses, and phobias. Human beings also commit heinous acts. We can hardly say inhuman acts, because they are committed by humans. Nevertheless, in the long span of human endeavor, we have come to pronounce certain acts and thoughts as good or bad. We make *moral* judgements. Judgements are driven by desire. By a burning aspiration for better behavior conforming to higher thoughts. By a hope for a better life. Humankind, with distinctive traits and unique accomplishments, exists in comity with the animal and plant kingdoms, but these same attributes set it apart from these kingdoms.

Human animals are multi-cellular organisms that are the end product of single-cell organisms that became the *fauna* of Earth. We reached our current state through the laws of natural science, a discipline that seeks order through classification. The animal kingdom is classified on the basis of defining physical attributes. Humans are creatures of the animal kingdom, phylum chordata (vertebrates), class mammalia (warm-blooded vertebrates who possess hair, whose young are birthed live, and whose females secrete milk to nourish the young), order primate (having extremities that terminate in hand and foot-like configurations), family hominidae (humans and their fossil ancestors), genus *Homo* (Latin: "man"), and species *sapiens* (Latin: "wise").

However, classification is mere description. It doesn't address specific *creaturely animalhood*—self-consciousness and purpose. Animals, in their specific habitats, are both propelled and constrained by the laws of natural science and the principles of biology. They "become" and "do" what is dictated and allowed by their specific creatureliness. The rhinoceros exhibited strength and the cheetah was swift, but neither trait took them out of the Serengeti. They were trapped by their nature in their natural habitat where they have remained ever since (except when humans captured and transported them).

What is the specific animalhood/creatureliness of *Homo sapiens*? Our lineage runs through the family hominidae, which split off from the order primate about seven million years ago. The primate, *Pan troglodytes*, or common chimpanzee, is our closest living animal relative. The DNA of humans and chimps differ by less than 4 percent. But that difference is incalculable. A chimp can be taught to light up a smoke, but deprived of a cigarette the chimpanzee has never shown any inclination—let alone made progress—in cultivating tobacco, making cigarette paper, or producing a match. Chimps have groomed one another for millions upon millions of years but have never created the simplest comb. Cascading, cognitive human thought is something else again, and in spite of modern humanity's erudition cannot be fully explained—only observed and described.

Humans are still intimately connected to water. From a cellular beginning in a primeval ocean, water was vital to life. And so it is today. The expectant mother waits for her water to break. That's what we say, but any fool knows amniotic fluid isn't water. And a fool also knows that when a woman's water breaks it's the end of something and the beginning of something. Fertilization occurs after a moment of orgiastic bliss driven by desire that enables a single human sperm (from a pool of millions) to encounter a single human egg (released from an ovary stuffed with eggs) and penetrate it. The chromosomes align, deoxyribonucleic acids churn, and the egg is fertilized. Incubating in a liquid solution of blood and nutrients and hormones, this fertile cell divides into two cells. These cells, in a spontaneous, precipitous rush, cascade through billions of divisions and iterations while the pulsating mass differentiates into skin, eyes, ears, nose, mouth, heart, lungs, kidneys, bowels, bone, muscles, and brain of the human species. After some nine months, following a completely natural, but *gestaltistically* miraculous, biological process, an infant is born in a rush of blood and water.

The baby immediately follows the primordial, life-sustaining instinct to nurse at the mother's breast. The baby's brain and body carries the weight of billions of years of cosmic evolution, two million years of prehistoric human existence, and some two hundred thousand years of history as *Homo sapiens sapiens* (anatomically modern humans). The baby is the product of an infinite succession of couples, families, clans, tribes, cultures, nation-states, and empires. It is shaped by geology, geography, and climate. It is influenced by a plethora of indescribably unique plants, animals, parasites, and germs. It is infused with countless generations of culture, history, art, science, religion, conflicts, and wars. A baby is driven by biological drives, some of which come without thought, and other instinctual and acquired urges that await the influence of civilizing forces.

Homo belongs to the biosphere of Earth. Driven by instinct to survive and achieve, *Homo* was free to engage the biosphere. The biosphere has shaped humans and we have shaped the biosphere. This led to a lineage of Hominids that stood erect, freeing both hands. Hands could shade the eyes to scan the horizon. Be raised in recognition or salute. Make a fist. Gesture in deference or defiance. Fold in prayer. Each hand had a thumb with which to grasp the world. About two million years ago, *Homo erectus* trekked out of Africa and set a course that took humankind around the globe, creating their own habitat as they migrated. In time, *Homo sapiens* became imprinted with incalculable physical, mental, and spiritual realities, a discerning self-consciousness, and became aware of its mortality. Everything else we revere about humankind developed in the millennia to follow. *Sapiens* acquired a passion for knowledge and was driven by unique traits such as foresight, critical thought, and artful ways. We created civilizations and cultures. When the first of our species hunted dangerous game, cognition overrode instinct and that specimen conquered fear. *Homo sapiens* moved from prey to predator. No person, no creature, and nothing on earth or within our universe was safe from our depredations. We became the terror of the biosphere. We are beneficiaries and victims of our own handiwork. Our tale, spread across the globe, gets very mixed reviews.

11

Narrative and Metanarrative

"The practice of narrative and argument does not lead to invention, but it compels a certain coherence of thought."
—Jean Piaget
   Swiss Psychologist and Epistemologist

Humanity's craving for meaning (reasoned justification for the way of things), as noted in the prologue, carries with it the force of instinct. Narratives attempting to establish that meaning emerged through stories characterized under the rubrics of science and religion. Both were practiced in some form by *Homo* from the beginning, and the speculative ruminations of both were intertwined and almost indistinguishable. Primitive science observed nature with a probing, mechanistic eye. A technical discipline evolved over thousands of years. Religion observed the world with a contemplative heart and ransacked language to capture the inscrutable. When language was not fully adequate to express beliefs, virtually all religions used symbol and ritual to amplify concepts. This took the form of washings, fire rites, feasts, offerings, sacrifices, signing, sexuality, and other modalities including totems (a naturally occurring animal or object believed to have spiritual significance). Above all, meaning-making expositions by primitive and archaic peoples were steeped in the origins of each individual culture, and accounts for the divergence of conceptualizations. This is particularly useful in that world observed by Rudyard Kipling (1865–1936): "Oh East is East and West is West and never the twain shall meet." But it is more complicated than a contrast of West and East. Different concepts arose in the West: Mediterranean, European, Slavic, and the New Worlds of the Americas. Just as different concepts emerged from different parts of Asia: South Asia, East Asia, Southeast Asia, and island landmasses of the Pacific Ocean.

In the West, common threads appeared in antecedents of Western cultures; to wit, the cosmos was thought to be composed of three layers—heaven above (the celestial place of the gods), earth (the dwelling place of humankind), and beneath the earth (the dark place of the dead, evil spirits, and punishment). Focus was often on the heavens, whether as a source of astrological fatalism or the abode of taken-for-granted gods. Gods of the West were anthropomorphic, often combined iconic traits of both humans and animals, and were understood as cosmic and local, plural and singular, male and female. In Eastern cultures, philosophical concepts arose to address time, life, death, and the decisive goals of humanity. Asian religious/philosophical concepts cannot be understood using Western abstractions—God, Trinity, salvation, sin, heaven, and hell. Westerners drift off course in thinking an *equivalency of language* applies when conceptualizing Western and Eastern . . . what? The word *religion* cannot be used here because Western and Eastern conceptualizing words cannot be used interchangeably in philosophizing. Both East and West have conceived metanarratives to sustain *Homo* on life's journey, but the conceptualizing language is distinctive.

We again emphasize that metanarratives of meaningful order are humankind's safeguard against chaos. Ancient efforts to comprehend the "*What?*" and "*So What?*" of our world addressed four fundamental issues—all intimately related. First, humankind attempted to understand sovereignty—who and/or what was in charge of their world. Second, humankind attempted to understand time in relation to history. Third, humankind attempted to cast mythology in relation to sovereignty and time. And fourth, humankind grappled with the terror of historical life and certain death.

SOVEREIGNTY

Polytheism (Greek: *polu*, many + *theos*, God) was probably the earliest prevailing theory of world sovereignty, and is a legacy of Mesopotamia, Indo-Asia, Greece, and Rome. Cosmic gods created the world and possessed ultimate control over triumph, catastrophe, tragedy, the fortunes of war, and the end of the world. These celestial beings established heavenly archetypes to serve as exemplary models for earthly creatures and earthly things. This was especially important for archaic societies, where peoples attempted to shape their civilizations in conformity to the primal myths of their archetypes. Human constructs (events, architecture, government, law, religion, and social hierarchies) as well as virtues (love, mercy, courage, justice) were vested in archetypes. Local gods—intimate gods—managed the affairs of daily life: birth, puberty, marriage, fertility, household, kitchen, fire, rain, seedtime and harvest, death. The goal for archaic peoples was a harmonious relationship with both cosmic and local gods. This was accomplished through philosophy, religion, and ritual. The greater part of archaic humanity believed that *history* did not have value in and of itself.

Monotheism (Greek: *mono*, one + *theos*, God) developed late in the progression of human thought on world sovereignty. The Hebrews were not the only monotheists among archaic societies, but were possibly the first people to invest so fully in monotheism and of whom extensive records have been preserved. Their concept was a single God who was distinctly and supremely separate, but also personal and present. The Hebrews were called to faith in this God who would bless them, sustain them, and provide deliverance in a troubled world. For the Hebrews, history was theophany (Greek: *theos*, God + *phainein*, to show). That is, God was shown to humans through the progression of events in history. In this manner, historical events took on sacred significance and time and history acquired value. Understanding also came through personal epiphanies (Greek: *epi*, upon or very near to, + *phainein*, to show), which carries with it the idea that individuals within history were accorded moments or periods of revelation or insight.

TIME

Two theories of time arose in archaic cultures: cyclical and linear. Observation suggested that the world, inanimate and animate, operated in recurrent cycles. Day and night occurred in continuously repeated diurnal and nocturnal cycles governed by the sun and moon and consumed twenty-four hours of sixty minutes each. The moon had predictable phases that repeated themselves monthly. Ocean tides advanced and retreated predictably with phases of the moon. Celestial bodies churned in cycles and astrology arose to plot their effect on life. The year lasted 365 days, which could be divided into twelve more or less equal months. The seasons rolled reliably around and there was seedtime and harvest. Creatures of the animal kingdom returned seasonally and replenished food resources. Mountains were at rest; mountains erupted. Rivers flowed; rivers dried up. Annual floods renewed the alluvial plains. It was all so perfectly obvious that calendars were established to anticipate annual cycles and timepieces were devised to mark the passage of the minutes and hours. Life itself was bounded by birth and death and lived in cycles of infancy, adolescence, adulthood, old age, and senility. Archaic theorists of cyclical time believed humans were indissolubly connected with the cosmos and its rhythms and that human life and history went through repetitive cycles. Periodic death and rebirth was a process that was infinitely repeated. There was no assumption that time ended.

The second theory proposed that time was linear and encompassed an irreversible span of human history. This linear span was suspended between two timeless eternities—a beginning and an end. As such, linear time could be considered no more than a longer fragment of cyclical time. Linear-time theorists made the distinction that at the end of an individual life or of planet Earth itself, time and history doesn't roll over into cycles of infinite repetition, but simply enters the new age.

WORLD MYTHOLOGY

World mythology, across all cultures, contains remarkably similar images and narratives that became foundational for each society. Polytheism and monotheism share creation stories that commonly spoke of a beginning linked to supernatural gods who created the cosmos, and where humans and gods existed together in a plentiful, peaceful paradise. Such stories often shared a motif in which humans alienated themselves from the gods by wicked deeds that resulted in humankind's banishment from paradise and the gods withdrew into heavenly realms. A mythical hero appeared in many stories, shaped by the society's culture, but sharing common features of a divine parent, a substitutionary death, a journey to heaven or hell or both, and a return to life. Joseph Campbell explored this idea with his book *Hero With A Thousand Faces*. Finally, many myths foretold a final catastrophe of fire or flood that would destroy a corrupt humanity and a blighted world.

THE TERROR OF HISTORICAL LIFE

Life—when viewed as a series of personal catastrophes ending in the entombment of a depleted body—was meaningless, absurd, and terrifying, most particularly if suffering was unprovoked. The general philosophical solution proposed for this terrible burden was that humans suffered because they had done something wrong and were being punished by the gods. Suffering that was understandable was suffering that could be addressed.

Polytheist philosophy generally accepted a world where time was cyclical and subject to archetypes. Repeating archetypal rituals originated by gods, heroes, or ancestors (prayer offerings, substitutionary sacrifices, scapegoating, expulsions, extinguishing and rekindling the fire, water purifications, quests, and other rites) would annul time, erase memory, ease suffering, and sustain people and their acre of geography. Cyclical time set life in a timeless present in which, *this time around*, they might be better attuned to the cosmic cycles and the archetypes (exemplary models) that were the true reality. Connection to an archetypal past delivered them from the terror of history and allowed them to begin primordial time all over again and restore things to the way they once were and the way they ought to be. In this schema, they did not lose touch with their origins or themselves, and both creatures and cosmos could be cyclically renewed into infinity.

Monotheists generally believed philosophically that history progressed uninterrupted through continuous time. This is exemplified in the Judeo-Christian story in which God liberates humans from the terror of history by investing time and history with authority and power. The experience of the moment may not be clear, but it is not inexplicable. Yahweh, the God of Abraham, Isaac, and Jacob, makes everything possible. The God of the New Testament amplified this concept with the advent of Jesus of Nazareth. Christians claim that the Christ event is unique because it need not be repeated to extend its power throughout a history which is Messianic, whereby past, present, and future are linked and history will be consummated as the new age advances toward us. Together, Judeo-Christianity proposes that faith—absolute trust that all things are possible with God—inaugurated a mode of confronting the terror of history that was new and unique. Faith that can move mountains is proposed as a category of reality that carries history through time, across time, and beyond time. Beyond the metaphorical power in this concept, there is the kernel of an idea that liberation from what we call natural law is possible. Faith is the new factor in the equation for humankind's collaboration with God.

Certain distinctions can be made between monotheism and polytheism.

1. Religion/philosophy first addresses the question of the existence of authority or deity, and then the deity's nature, which together profoundly affects the understanding of time, life, and death.

2. Monotheism and polytheism both stared history in the face and tried not to blink.

3. Monotheists live in relationship to a single god *of* all and *for* all and the operative thesis is faith. Faith holds together in a unique way (cosmically and personally) the past, present, and future.

4. Polytheists had many gods, some universal and some local, and all ranked according to a hierarchy. The goal was to appease the gods with prescribed rituals and resolve the crisis of the moment right then and right there.

5. Monotheism regards humankind as a fallen race. Evil is more than acts of reprehensible behavior. A long-term, faithful relationship was required.

6. Monotheists came to believe God was no longer connected to locale (certain geography, tribe, nation, empire), but universal.

7. Monotheism and polytheism both established celestial archetypes which prevailed over human institutions, but for monotheists the archetypes were not to be repeated until the times were accomplished in a new age, while polytheists set about to repeat more faithfully the archetypes with each cycle of dying and reincarnation.

8. Monotheists believe God is passionately involved in the world and history and the cosmosphere has purpose and value.

9. Monotheism expounded the extraordinary proposition that living in a relationship with this God, in whom they had absolute trust and an ongoing dialogue through historical time, assured a triumphant resolution to the terror of historical life and certain death.

Narrative Assumes the Burden of Historical Life

Narratives recount the stories of people and peoples, their times and their civilization's progress, make claims to rational purposes and justifiable and equitable endings—or not. Narratives draw upon many motifs: entertainment, information, inspiration, puzzlement, comedy, tragedy, pleasure, pain, horror, shock, revulsion, tears, and laughter, but finally narratives aspire to establish a satisfactory resolution.

Narrative beginnings devise a circumstance of tension that must be solved or resolved. The middle portion provides relevance and establishes parameters that justify the ending. Without the beginning and the middle, the end would be a declarative statement with no rationale for its support. In this manner, the princess turns the frog into a prince and they live happily ever after. The screw-ups bumble through and win their war. The angst-ridden Hero discovers the Meaning of Life. Or, the angst-ridden hero discovers that life has no meaning. The mad scientist perversely pursues a demonic theory and destroys the world. The test pilot, as his plane spins into its death spiral, maintains a running commentary with his radio contact: "I've pushed X. I've tried Y. I've turned off ABC. The Whatchamacallit quit!" This end-of-life narrative is the starting point for the narrative of the next test pilot.

After everything, narratives instruct and make meaning. They may trace fact or fantasy, foolishness and fear, or inspiration and hope, but at their core they inform us about some things and some ones. Narratives teach us about our world, ourselves, and "the other." Narratives are the means by which we answer questions of personal identity and existential values:

> "Who am I?" (personal identity).
>
> "Where am I?" (in relationship to others, to culture, to geography, to history, to the cosmos, to the divine mystery).
>
> "Why am I?" (in relationship to meaning, purpose, values).

Narratives engage the mind, heart, body, and soul, and are the fountainhead of cognitive, emotional, physical, cultural, and spiritual discernment. Ancients called this a quest. A quest for general knowledge, for self-knowledge, and for the ending of its own story. Narratives take the stuff of daily life and transform it. The transformation, for good or ill, embraces hope because it opens up the heart to reflection. The narrative helps the hearer go on. In these ways, narrative truth can be more stable, more profound, and more true than desiccated historical fact. Therein lies the power of heroic myth, a tale strung together on the odyssey of its hero.

The word *myth* has been assigned many meanings over the ages, but originally the word referred to an overarching, profound, clarifying, meaning-making story that was recalled and appealed to through ritual. In modernity, myth acquired a patina that cast it as fanciful or farfetched, and judgment was passed on its veracity. One thing is certain, humankind's experience taught a hard lesson: myths and their rituals often failed to deliver on what they betokened. The tribe appealed to their war god and lost the war. They did the rain dance and suffered drought. They performed the healing ritual and did not get well. A provident life and a good death could not be assured. Nevertheless, coherent metanarratives (myths, overarching stories, rituals) are still the conduits that invest life with value, contribute understanding and insight, provide perspective and hope, and are absolutely foundational for community.

Metanarratives are rooted in the past, encompass the present, and project an ideal of unification into the future. Metanarratives have the scope to enfold other stories. Metanarratives have the power to disclose authority and consequences. Metanarrative's intellectual, emotional, and experiential purpose is to provide information, inspiration, and transformation. Metanarratives divulge information, but properly leavened by mimicry, ritual, and the rhetorical language of poetry and song, also disclose counsel from the conscience, inspiration to the heart, and empower action. They lead us to the place of visceral knowledge, creative insight, enchantment, and engagement. Metanarrative inaugurates a foundation that perceptively links the mind, heart, senses, and experience with an element of intuition. Metanarratives are not a precursor to natural science nor do they take the place of science. Metanarratives do propose a model for the human in their universe. *Homo sapiens sapiens*, through metanarrative, engaged the miracle of life on a living planet constrained by birth and death, set in the context of our species' interaction with each other and the cosmos, while burning with desire for meaningful life-alive and wholeness on the road into the future.

In this postmodern era, which favors particularity, diversity, perspective, and the local over universalist metanarratives, storytelling is still central to understanding our humanity. Storytelling is the link between us and our ancestors. It began at the primitive fire pit, and is present with us today at the campfire, in bedtime stories, the back porch confab, the dorm room bull session, dinner table conversation, the hearth, national convocations of scientific and humanities disciplines, and local religious services. Storytelling has now expanded to the world of the internet. The internet, pervasive and ubiquitous, provides unlimited access but is also a depersonalizing and isolating phenomenon. Its influence on community is yet to be fully assessed. Personal stories are still derived from the stories we are told and learn to tell, and from personal experience—all impregnated with racial, gender, social, political, national, geographic, and religious themes. These stories give structure to our understanding of the world and our place in it, but also establish how we feel about things. We are imprinted with deep-seated values, commitments, and attitudes. Metanarratives continue to mold our concepts of right and wrong, reveal what is expected of us, and shape the orthodox view of our world. Beyond that, metanarratives empower us to challenge and change orthodoxies that do not make room for life-alive and human wholeness. We are culturally adapted, and discover our world and our place in it through life's experiences. Personal experience makes us aware that life as we know it is both a *given* reality and a *shaped* reality.

Sooner, rather than later, we encounter other stories (ideas and ideals) and other socially constructed realities (human institutions). The universe of orbiting stories intersect, merge, collide, clash, explode, and implode. There are new suns and "black holes." The result is a progression of crises, large and small, in all aspects of life and living that challenge meaning-making.

12

The Human Tribe and Its Planet

"Man is a bundle of relations, a knot of roots,
whose flower and fruitage is the world."
—Ralph Waldo Emerson
Transcendentalist and Poet

During planet Earth's long history, it went through recurring cycles of cooling and warming that created a series of Ice Ages. Continental ice sheets advanced southward from the Arctic and northward from the Antarctic. One-third of Earth's surface was covered. Arctic ice formed as far south as Kansas in North America; France, Germany, and the Balkans in Europe; and northern Russia and China in Eurasia. The fifth, and last, Ice Age began about 2.6 million years ago (600,000 years before *Homo erectus* evolved) and ended about 12,000 years ago, by which time *Homo sapiens sapiens* (anatomically modern humans) had evolved and established themselves as the dominant *Homo* species on earth. Propitiously, fortuitously, miraculously, mathematically, the geological events that produced the last Ice Age coincided with the evolutionary events that resulted in *Homo sapiens*. This era presented *Homo* with unique opportunity.

Glaciation used enormous quantities of water. Ocean levels dropped as much as 350 feet and created land bridges between continents and oceanic islands. *Homo* had access to more than contiguous land masses, but could utilize the stepping stones that appeared across previously impassable water barriers. Humankind had also developed traits and skills that allowed it to begin to shape the world to its needs. Humans were no longer held in the grip of nature. They could adapt and survive in all climates under almost any circumstance. There was an opening for global migration. Anatomically modern humans interacted with the geological period that produced modern geography and ecosystems.

Some of our tribe, perhaps more curious or adventurous, perhaps persecuted or pugnacious, decided to travel. They packed their meager belongings, fixed their eyes on a distant horizon, and started walking. *Homo* spread first to the lands that formed a horseshoe around the eastern end of the Mediterranean Sea. This area, referred to as the Fertile Crescent or the Levant, reveals evidence of *Homo* by one million BCE. *Homo* had migrated into southeastern China, Indo-China, the Malay Peninsula, and Indonesia by 900,000 BCE. They had spread into western Europe by 500,000 BCE. Polynesia, New Guinea, and Australia show fossil forms by 40,000 BCE. *Homo* moved from Eurasia into northeastern Europe and the Siberian Peninsula by 20,000 BCE. *Homo* crossed the Bering Strait into Alaska by 12,000 BCE and infiltrated the North American continent, trailing the retreating ice sheet. There are two other probable sources of migration into North America. Archeologists have found stone tools and weapons in the eastern portions of North America that are similar to those used in northern Europe some 25,000 years ago. This raises the question of whether Europeans, particularly Scandinavians, made their way to North America, leapfrogging along the retreating edges of the glacial ice pack even before the Asiatics pushed across the Bering Strait. In addition, artifacts have been found along the western coast of what is now Mexico that appear to be from the Malay Archipelago. The Vikings may not have been the only adventurous sailors. However that may be, by 10,000 BCE *Homo sapiens* had traversed North and Middle America and reached Cape Horn at the tip of South America. The globe had been populated.

At the close of the last Ice Age, as the glaciers melted and the ice retreated northward and southward to their place of origin, ocean levels rose and the land bridges were again submerged. Migratory passages were closed off and the provident moment had passed. Small groups of *Homo sapiens* around the world were isolated, inhabiting, if you will, several separate gardens of Eden, and left to pursue further cultural development according to their own unique abilities and their environment. Not every strain of the species of *Homo* that evolved in those millennia had equal opportunity for success on a planet that had become hospitable to life.

Paleoanthropologists present an array of proto-human skeletons that have been discovered and categorized over the centuries. Science and the humanities have struggled to establish exactly what it is that defines "human." Subtle distinctions, still debated, are used to characterize the full flowering of modern humans. Diverse lines of hominids arose, interacted, and crossbred. Many strains, through the selective process of evolution, were dead-enders or became extinct. Most recently, skeletons dubbed *Homo naledi* were found in a narrow cave in South Africa. No doubt similar discoveries will be made. The Swedish botanist, Carolus Linnaeus (1707–1778), devised the biological classification system of taxonomy (Greek: *taxis*, "arrangement" + *nomia*, "distribution") still in use. Based on advances in the "-oligies," particularly DNA typing, molecular chemistry, cellular biology, and sophisticated dating techniques, science has divided the genus *Homo* into three major subspecies: *Homo neanderthalensis sapiens*, *Homo sapiens* (early modern humans), and *Homo sapiens sapiens* (anatomically modern humans). The phrase early modern humans (EMH) is used to designate early peoples who didn't possess the full complement of humankind's characteristics. Anatomically modern humans (AMH) is used for those who do.

All three species occupied Europe and Western Asia over the past 200,000 years and coincided with or overlapped one another. Genetic typing shows evidence of interbreeding within the three subspecies, which is one of the defining characteristics of a species. Each *individual* human alive today possesses about 2 percent of the Neanderthal genome. Almost 70 percent of the Neanderthal genome is represented *collectively* within today's human population when all of those small, varied individual snippets of DNA are tallied up. So it is that anatomically modern humans can trace their roots to these archaic species of the genus *Homo*, who were both rivals to and foundational for anatomically modern humans.

Homo neanderthalensis sapiens, popularly called Neanderthals, carry that name because their initial fossil remains were found in the Neander Valley in Germany. The subspecies date as far back as 300,000 years, and have been found in western Europe, the Balkans, east into Ukraine and Siberia, and southeast into the Indus River Valley. Neanderthals seemed better suited to these colder climates. They used fire, made crude stone tools, hunted small animals but did not fish, and cared for their sick and buried their dead. They seemed to disappear from the fossil records about 25,000 years ago. The Neanderthal brain was larger than the brain of modern humans, but the subspecies made little progress beyond a Stone Age existence that allowed them to eke out a living on the tundra below the last great, glacial ice sheet.

Homo sapiens (EMH), popularly called Cro-Magnons, are named for the rock shelter in France where fossil remains were first found. They lived alongside Neanderthals at the end of the last Ice Age and date to about 40,000 years ago. They made a variety of stone tools, needles, spears, bows and arrows, hunted larger and more dangerous game than the Neanderthals, made nets and fished, produced clothing and jewelry, created cave art, statues, and musical instruments, and buried their dead. So, why aren't Cro-Magnons called "human beings"? They looked a lot like us and did a lot of the things we do. Some scientists, in the interest of being precise, regard Cro-Magnons as lacking a variety of traits requisite for full humanity. This is a subtle, subjective judgment and many investigators believe there is not enough difference between Cro-Magnons and modern humans to warrant a separate species designation. A taxonomical compromise was reached among paleoanthropologists and an additional *sapiens* was inserted for emphasis in the nomenclature of our race. The term anatomically modern humans (AMH) was appended to designate "us," and the term early modern humans (EMH) was appended for the Cro-Magnons. This subtle nomenclature equates Cro-Magnons with our own species, but still nudges us phlylogenetically beyond our cousins.

The category *Homo sapiens sapiens* (AMH) is reserved for peoples surviving into the last 50,000 years. Very fine distinctions mark the tipping point when humanity crossed an indelible threshold and attained its full capacity. No single distinguishing trait marked the full flowering of "human beings," but the accumulation of numerous anatomical and behavioral traits, when combined with a substantial long-term memory and the full linkage of the amygdala to the frontal cortex, propelled our surge into full humanity. Humankind embarked upon the journey that led to the establishment of the great world civilizations of antiquity, modernity, and postmodernity.

In this manner, *Homo sapiens sapiens* (AMH), as revealed in their fossilized remains and artifacts, massed into tribes enabled by their commonalities and conformities, cooperated through altruistic group behavior, produced superior tools and increasingly formidable weapons, and fired by desire and the narratives of religion inspiring faith, won the battle of the species. The last iterations of *Homo sapiens sapiens* (AMH) out-thought, out-fought, out-produced, and out-organized other archaic groups. The Neanderthals and Cro-Magnons suffered extinction while *Homo sapiens sapiens* (AMH) flourished. Was our species just lucky? Foreordained? Chosen? That is a question of ontology (Greek: *ont,* "nature of being" + *ology,* "study of"), but approximately 100,000 years ago *Homo sapiens sapiens* (AMH) had carved out a niche for themselves that led beyond survival to supremacy. The entire modern human population at that time probably numbered no more than 10,000, which was the population of Dodge City, Kansas when we were young. The species lived on the brink of extinction, surviving natural disasters, starvation, animal predators, disease, and clan conflict. That band held in trust the protein-coded sequences of the human genome that has benefited all humanity. We are all part of that groundswell of anatomically modern humans who swept all others of our genus *Homo* aside.

Human differences are caused by both nature and by nurture. As literary critic Robert Polhemus says in reflecting on the characters in James Joyce's novels, "any human being is a weird, individual collective—a biological, linguistic fusion of unique psychology, natural matter, thousands of years of history, countless lives, any number of languages, and the residue of all sorts of books, myths, dirty jokes, and sacred writings."[1] From the beginning (which is not a line drawn in the sand), with common biology and biochemistry, this mix of humanity was coerced, propelled, shaped, guided, and transformed by gender, race, ethnicity, and geography. Not to mention different diets, clothing, mores, languages, education, values, religion, and culture. Diversity was the result. Self-preservation was the stimulus that impelled diversity to seek commonality.

1. Polhemus, *Lot's Daughters,* 7.

13

Societies and Stratification

"Society does not consist of individuals but expresses the sum of interrelations, the relations within which these individuals stand."
—KARL MARX
Economist and Philosopher

THE HUNTER BROTHERS GREW up, as did most of us, with a story that was partly true, partly false, part illusion, part delusion, and part fantasy. As a coherent story, it was unsustainable. Our distant Hunter cousin, perched on a rock under a Acacia tree on the Serengeti, chewed grains as he cogitated his prospects. The Hunter boys sprawled in lounge chairs on a deck in Arizona, drank libations of grains, and also tried to make sense of it all. "What's it all about?" One thing is certain, neither our ancient forebears, nor we brothers, nor our clan, nor any of our race, began life as blank slates.

Every unique human begins life *in utero*. Modern technology demonstrates that the fetal brain and other organs are functioning. Something is happening within the fetus and to the fetus developing inside the uterus. After birthing, the world impinges on the neonate in a cascade of feeling and knowing. The infant is a "given" and a "given-to." The selfish, egocentric infant's world is virtually the mother's breast and the initial moment of nursing is a profound maternal communication. From that mammalian appurtenance, the infant's world expands outward into the unknown. By the accident of circumstance, by nature and nurture, through opportunity and choice, as well as the terrible constraints of necessity, the extent of every individual's life journey varies. The child's world may never expand beyond maternal care. The world may stop at the county line. Or the journey may circumnavigate the globe or shed the bonds of gravity and explore space. The journey may be peopled with persons unrecognized and unsung, or the cast of characters may include the powerful, the famous, the distinguished and illustrious. Virtually all individuals encounter the beautiful, the gracious, and the loving. But also the unpleasant, the villainous, dastardly, and perhaps even the heinous.

The journey usually allows each person to witness and participate in moments of family and clan, state and nation, or even world events. Persons may experience marriage and children of their own. Some experience peace and some experience war, but everyone, in some conscious manner, experiences both. Many participate in education, business, commerce, trades, professions, the arts and sciences. The journey may be a daily slog through the mundane. The journey may be the thoughtless outward-bound or the discerning inward-bound. The journey may be from the local to the universal and back again; but for every individual, whatever the journey and its cast of characters, it's their universe.

Whatever life's scope, it's always too provincial. There is no doubt that some have greater opportunity to expand their horizons, but good fortune may have as much to do with it as latent ability. A Native American friend of ours expressed it this way: "We all grew up on our own reservation." Ah . . . recognition compounded of insight and humility. We must understand that whether our experience is Harvard or Community Vocational Tech, every education is too parochial. Whether we trod urban concrete or prairie sod, the encounter is too provincial. Whether we explore space or explore caves, our experience is too narrow. The polymather and the pot-holer need each other, but much more than that, they have things to learn from each other. Inevitably, every person must fall into self-consciousness, or they have never left their personal garden of Eden to join the human migration. We all stand on the shoulders of our literal and cultural forebears, but ultimately every individual must make sense of life for themselves.

Civilization is categorized by whether you use stone, bronze, or iron for the cutting edge of your blade. Or whether you use fire, steam, electricity, or nuclear energy for power. Culture is marked by whether you wear a bikini or a burka. Or whether you use red ochre or L'Oreal for body paint. Sophistication is the ability to differentiate deer and elk sign. Or to distinguish between a cabernet and a pinot noir by taste. In humankind's long journey through civilizations, cultures, and acquired sophistications, some few people may have experienced only giftedness, good health, and effortless prosperity. Many others have been overwhelmed by mean circumstances and deprivation. Most face a confounding mix of life's good and bad. In the reality of the ordinary, no one gets out unscathed and everyone dies at the end. Individuals can live life imprisoned in cynicism or nihilism, or mewl on in one great, carping whine, or journey toward life-alive and meaning-making.

Humankind's journey from clan to tribe to nation to empire is a story of migration, colonization, the subjugation of peoples and lands, use of resources, the development of cultures, the acquisition of education and technology, the establishment of institutions, and a messy mix overall of brilliant accomplishment and tragic failure, of productivity and destruction. All societies had to negotiate a path between domination and nurturing that would serve both individual and community. Hierarchies were inevitable. Hierarchies had aristocrats, who laid claim to lineage, and commoners, who were simply present and accounted for. Historians have identified the rare man or woman whose unique personal attributes aligned perfectly with specific circumstances to cause a watershed moment in world history. Every social structure, great or small, has ambitious and creative outliers. Those whose urge for something else—or something more—effect change. Some yearn for knowledge, others for skills, some remain stubbornly ignorant, some intent on violence, and tragically some are congenitally lacking in wholeness of body and mind. The aristocrat may flee responsibility; the persecuted seek retribution; the subjugated seek freedom; the needy seek sustenance; and the disenfranchised seek power. The wealthy usually want more of everything. Occasionally a true philanthropist puts the robber baron to shame. For some, the realization dawns that just because things are the way they are doesn't mean they must remain that way. Conflict results; the trajectory of change can be beneficial or ruinous. Nearly every civilization has stood on the rubble of its predecessor.

Societal governance has two categories: those in charge and those under control. In some manner, the rulers and the ruled. The glue for this state of affairs is a class of responsible citizens expert in the broad range of societal skills. In the history of civilizations, those genuinely oppressed have only one decision to make: submit or not. If unwilling to submit, violence—civil war—ensues. Civilizations and societies that avoid catastrophic civil violence and endure must hold out the hope—the possibility—that all citizens, regardless of rank, have the opportunity to rise to a position of freedom, self-determination, and responsibility, and that both rulers and ruled submit to societal law and custom. This is exemplified in the roles of parent and child. Children quickly learn that if they cooperate, they will someday become adults and assume a position of autonomy—power. The next generation succeeds the preceding generation. This is important in the family: it's important in society.

Three things are necessary for citizens to accept their social status in a hierarchy. First, generosity expressed in openness, empathy, and a willingness to negotiate with others. Second, freedom and aggression balanced by an all-inclusive justice that allows individuals to conduct their affairs as they wish. And third, without which the first two will not succeed, a self-authenticating metanarrative to sustain widespread solidarity. Metanarratives must be sheathed with moral authority, provide transcendent justice, and articulate an achievable dream mediated by religion and ritual.

The price of the narrative dream is constant vigilance on the part of society. Social orders are fragile and can be subverted by neglect, demagoguery, and evil intent. History acquired an unending procession of successful upstarts. Some few are of historical record: Ghengis Kahn, Alexander the Great, Julius Caesar, Cleopatra, Jesus of Nazareth, Siddhartha Gautama, Henry the Eighth, Washington and peers, Napoleon, Marx, Mussolini, Hitler, Stalin, Mao Tse Tsung, Ho Chi Minh, Mahatma Gandhi, Che Guevara, Martin Luther King, Caesar Chavez, and Malala Yousafzai. How did they do it? Brute force, generally. Even the nonviolent were swept up in violence. But at the onset, each one presented an overarching, convincing, consummate narrative that transcended existing narratives. Political revolution was usually accompanied by religious revolution. Only in that way will those dominated, the subjects, invest themselves in the new regime. Stability is provided, as previously noted, by the older generation who nurtures the younger generation through their endangered childhood and teaches them the narrative and the rituals—the laws of society. Even the largest society rests on patriarchal and matriarchal authority. From generation to generation the story is told, the songs are sung, the rituals enacted and the dream sustained.

Metanarratives evolved as societies progressed. Early narratives revealed gods with human traits who were sometimes whimsical, not always reliable, not always benign, and sometimes (by today's common standards) not even moral. Those cultures that didn't have gods they worshiped, adopted overarching concepts that conceived of supra-normal or fanciful beings with which they attempted to align individual and societal mores. Cultures with god-narratives attempted to understand the nature of a reality where ordinary humans occupied a world in which the gods held all the cards and humankind's lot was struggle followed by certain death. One response was rage and rebellion against the way of things. Lash out and get everything you can and keep it by the unrestricted use of violence. At the other extreme was deference: acquiesce to a subservient role, acknowledge your superiors (both cosmic and immediate), and fit yourself into the system in a manner that allows survival and possibly even prosperity. With the passage of archaic societies and the ascendance of postmodern societies, this cultural conundrum changed only in magnitude, not in the politics. Ancients and postmoderns have observed the oppression of the many by the few. The "elite few," holding the reins of power in unrestrained oligarchies, theocracies, monarchies, dictatorships, and democracies—whether through overwhelming brutality, divine right of lineage, capitalism, Marxism, fascism, or forms of representative government—have the power and the disposition to use it to keep "the many" in compliant submission. The postmodern caveat is that weapons of mass destruction have the means to substantially destroy humanity and its history, and "the few" can force the "many" to endure what the elite unleash. The "many" may be soporifically marginalized with their puny voice, their paltry vote, and their meager status, but it still remains that genuine stability in social constructs is only assured by renewal of the narrative dream.

Cultures, progressing from the primitive, to the archaic, and on through the historically traditional, were the seedbed of new narratives, new rituals, and new dreams that forged new ideas and ideals. The arc of those ideas and ideals—depending on content—might be beneficent or cruel. In either case, storytellers proclaimed and perpetuated the narratives that held societies together. In essence, the human family got religion, and religion infused every aspect of ancient, archaic, and modern societies. The storytellers increased in social stature, became increasingly important, and rose to the upper ranks of the culture. Initially, there was little distinction between sacred and secular stories or sacred and secular power. Chiefs became priests and priests became chiefs and lineages became important. The narrative established an age of gods. There was an age when gods and humans walked the earth and interacted. There was an age when gods gave birth to men and lineages were established. There was an age when gods returned to their abode, usually in the sky, sometimes under the earth. The gods still intervened in the affairs of men: perhaps through cataclysmic events, or natural disasters, or the result of judgments by alien nations. Sometimes the gods called certain humans and elevated them to be intermediaries between gods and people. Calling upon the god's name, faithfulness to the god's enduring narrative, and performance of the god's rituals allowed humankind to find favor with the gods. These primal events occurred at the headwaters of the river, or on the summit of a mountain, near a burning bush, or at a foundational light, or at the dawn, or in the quest, or at the call, or at the graveside, or in the beginning.

During prehistory, with no more definitive authority than an oral tradition, there were many narratives and many gods. Some gods had cultural crossover and the same gods were referred to by different names. Ritual became the link to the gods. Repeating the names, singing the songs, playing the music, and making the sacrifices were critical. Initially, in small, primitive, egalitarian societies, the rituals were enacted by the entire community. As lineages of leaders and priests were established, as societies enlarged and specialized, the chief or a priest became the enactor of the rituals and the intercessor between the people and their gods. The narrative and its rituals defined the relationship and became the basis for societal order—the law. Rebelling against the chief, pharaoh, or king was to rebel against God.

14

Civilization in Contention
Tensions Between Civil Power and Religious Authority

> "Civilization began the first time an angry person cast a word instead of a rock."
>
> —SIGMUND FREUD
> Neurologist and Psychoanalyst

CIVILIZATION REQUIRES SOCIAL STRUCTURES: coupling, companions, and continuity. Making babies (or restricting making babies) is essential to maintaining the civilization. The word *companion* (Latin: *com*, "together with" + *panis*, "bread") literally means, "come together with bread." The phrase implies intimacy and shared nourishment. In the most primitive culture, and even today, a single individual might attempt to meet his or her needs and construct a personal, micro-civilization. It would be lonely, difficult, and perilous, and the civilization would be doomed because it takes both genders to make babies. Human history is an endless story of desire: birth, breathe, feed, and breed. Historical continuity is furthered.

Evolutionary principles are in play. The rudimentary is incorporated into the next higher iteration. The vestigial organ is assimilated by the complex. Anamnesis, a term for a peculiar virtuosity within the mind, allows modern humans to hark back to ancient memory and instinct to reinforce a subtle intimation in the present moment. The amygdala is older than the pre-frontal cortex. Aggression is older than kindness. Sex is older than love. Aggression and sex extend back to the beginning of the human pedigree. The final evolutionary linkage of the amygdala to the frontal cortex was the anatomical basis for the genesis of *humane* in humanity. Love evolved out of mating cultures where parental care was necessary for offspring survival. Only animals who care for their young establish connections and remain in close-knit groups. Cherishing precedes empathy. Empathy crosses species lines. Most humans are touched by the suffering of animals. A dog will care for a cat. *Companis* led to civilization.

Individuals were drawn to other individuals of similar physical traits, like-mindedness, common interests, common purposes, and common needs. Humankind, in ever larger collectives, constructed their own, small civilizations that identified and met the needs of the group. The family, clan, tribe, nation, and empire developed over the millennia. Society evolved from the primitive to the archaic, then through increasing cultural complexity to multiculturalism and globalization. It must be noted that postmodernism has seen a retreat from multiculturalism to tribalism in many societies, but the pattern of progressive globalization has, nevertheless, required new forms to codify membership, institute religion, govern, establish class or caste, and to determine hierarchies of wealth and power. After propagation (making babies), two instincts drove socialization. The first was a disposition to dominate. The second was a disposition to nurture. The two were always in tension. One cannot nurture without dominating. Nurturing is an expression of dominance and receiving is an expression of submission. It may be "more blessed to give than to receive," but both parties know who has the power. The history of human society is the history of the accumulation of wealth and power through greed (dominance), resisted by humane instincts (nurture). The result was stratification of societies with social hierarchies.

In small societies different levels of status were minimal, but not absent. There has never been a completely egalitarian society. Even among the hunter-gatherers, the most egalitarian, it was better to be a man than a woman. It was better to be a powerful man than a weak man. It was better to be a woman or a weak man than a child. It was better to be a boy child than a girl child. Within this limited, societal, egalitarian, hunter-gatherer hierarchy, *Homo* societies revolved around distinctive reproductive units to create a nuclear family with male and female bonding. Adult males in small tribal societies formed a loose confederation to prevent any one member from dominating the group. A peaceful, egalitarian society requires hard work, discipline, and a bonding narrative. It also requires the application of violence, even if limited and restrained, to suppress the natural human disposition to accrue power. Shared equality requires the application of shared aggression. Egalitarianism incorporates aggressive behavior, even violence, into its culture to maintain allegiance to the ideal of a society of equals. All societies, even the most transparent and benevolent, use violence to maintain stability and the social order. The advantage in democratic, enlightened societies is that violence became more predictable and relatively constrained. But when force was deemed necessary, it was no less violent and just as lethal. Imprisonment, even if humane, is still violent and lethal.

A clan or tribe is not just the family with a larger population. The tribe is necessary for the family to exist. Tribes convert the *excess of everything* produced by individual diversity into more power. But if a tribe is to function, it must have an ethos for social conformity and a willingness to sanction those who break the rules. A pattern arose—no doubt a mix of reflective thought and trial and error. Members of the tribe who broke the rules were probably initially counseled. They were successively shunned, ridiculed, fined, cast out, and if necessary, killed. Egalitarianism is not the absence of power, but carries with it a defined policy that employs force to eliminate potential despotism. A developing moral community was incorporated into every developing social community. Nazism had a moral code; it was just diabolical.

Societies, from the beginning, were engaged in the never-completed process of building a lasting, meaningful culture. It was a funny business. First, the larger the society, the smaller the proportion of tribal members who had significant input into the proposals. Stratification was already in progress. Second, the people who did formulate the societal rules were the only ones to have a say in what constituted the common good, although ideally the rule-makers listened to the "others." Third, the rules by which all citizens were expected to live were established in a process external to the society and done by negotiation, fiat, and force. In effect, an idea (ideal) was proposed. "Hear ye, hear ye! This social contrivance *out there*—outside of all of us—that we thought up, is how we all are going to live." Every citizen had first to comprehend the institutions, mores, behavior, and roles the cohort of their society had created, and then each had to accept those ideas (ideals). The social construct had to be internalized, taken for granted, and adhered to as a matter of conscience. Society's most important function was (and is) to instill the rules by which it expected all citizens to live. Each generation had to be introduced to the expectations of the society, and then socialized to accept the range of tolerable behavior and submit to society's response to transgressions. Through this negotiated bargain, the citizen became the citizen ruler with a court and sycophants. The pieces fell into place: the citizen priest, the citizen bureaucrat, the citizen medicine man, merchant, craft-person, artisan, laborer, soldier, spy, prostitute, and least and last, not a citizen at all, but a slave.

Societies can cohere only if the individuals accept the society's worldview and rules as meaningful. Only to the extent that a citizen consents to the realities of the society, including their own role in it, is the society genuine and authentic to them. Only then does the citizen willingly submit to the coercion of the group. Societies, even the best, produce a tyranny by consensus. Create a government and it governs, coercing you to follow its rules. Create laws and prepare to be ostracized as a scofflaw. Create tools and weapons and they will bless or curse you. Create a language, and grammar dominates its use. It makes no difference if government, tools, laws, weapons, and grammar are created by consensus, the forces released still hold the individual within their power. Societies are controlled by law and order. Societies flourish when laws serve justice. The glitch in such societal strategy is that humans are not automatons. It's impossible to totally socialize any human being. Our variability drives creativity, but invites conflict. Ultimately, a society functions at no higher level than most citizens are able to make sense of and then accept its self-proclaimed structures. This kind of meaning-making is dependent upon effective communication.

Human communication, we have noted, evolved through three stages: mimicry, ritual, and speech. Mimicry uses the entire body, and is finely tuned with gestures and facial expression. Mimicry combined with repetitive actions establishes ritual ceremonies of remembrance, meaning, and hope. Ephemeral speech was made permanent and portable by writing. Technology resulted in painting, sculpting, printing, photography, and the deconstruction and manipulation of atoms for diffusion of information through the atmosphere. In communication, as in other categories of evolution and development, nothing (or very little) is abandoned or lost. Each subsequent stage absorbs preceding stages. Societies, from the most primitive to the postmodern, have created ever more powerful means of communication. Over the millennia, each society applied the means of communication at its disposal to perpetuate itself. Civilizations, as history attests, have a precarious existence. Society, once created, is always under threat and must be protected and maintained.

Maintenance requires vigilance and hard work. Untended, society falls apart from neglect. The best society declines through entropy. Furthermore, society is threatened from within by each person's self-interest—their inherent complement of greed for wealth and power. Society is threatened from without by other societies, also greedy for wealth and power. Every society strives to protect its precarious social structure by invoking all of its resources to justify the rules and the rulers. The first line of defense is a persuasive appeal to the authority of bloodline, ancestry, race, ethnicity, genealogy, geography, codes, and myths. The rulers and social institutions are presented as a hard fact—a reality of the world. Society's last line of defense is force, and it reserves the right to use it. In such manner, the society attempts to cloak itself with an appearance of durable inevitability. Durable inevitability is a quality ascribed to God(s). Every secular society, virtually at its inception, co-opted religion (in whatever form it took) to legitimize the authority of government by claiming an incontestable realm of jurisdiction—God(s). "It's beyond you, Bud. Take a knee!"

The story of world civilization can't be told without including the story of world religion. Religion (using the word in it's most generic sense) arose within all ancient societies and represented the fundamental assumptions of the culture—their racial characteristics, their ethnicity, their geography, and the sum of their experiences. Religion established an understanding of the universe, defined society, provided a vision for living a beneficent life, influenced politics and education, and was a force in war. Religious intolerance, in spite of lofty rhetoric, was actually a factor that contributed to the civilization's strength. Human beings distrust, and often fear, religious myths other than their own. Other myths threaten our myth. If their myth is true, maybe ours is less true, or perhaps false. Well, damn them! "Our God is more powerful than your God! No prisoners!"

In society, the stakes were raised when a priestly culture seized control of religion (ancient Egypt, Babylon, Assyria, India, Israel, Rome,

Islam). Religious hierarchies were established and centers of worship designated and designed. The keepers of the story assumed significance and power as they took control of the religious rituals. They interpreted the stories, made pronouncements, dispensed religious justice, and enforced religious law. Insights that served unity, peace, and power were codified into moral precepts and doctrinal systems. Religious leaders took charge of the rites of life's passages—birth, coming of age, marriage, and death. In some myths, notions such as eternal life, enlightenment, reincarnation, immortality of the soul, and resurrection were held out to believers. Heaven, paradise, nirvana, a better life, or utopian states were proposed as the reward for adhering to religious rules and exhibiting good behavior. Religious adherents who failed to measure up were punished, some in a fiery hell which tortured but never consumed its victim.

Civil and religious leaders realized they shared mutual interests. One needed citizens; the other needed disciples. Government held sway over citizens and slaves through state terror. Religion asserted control over both believers and non-believers by sealing their eternal fate. Each had fiefdoms to maintain. Both competed for wealth and power. Government isn't interested in religious theory. Government is interested in solidifying its rule and maintaining order. Religion isn't interested in civil bureaucracy. Religion is interested in protection while it pursues its goals. Each institution saw the advantages of joining hands to achieve their individual aims. Indeed, when the ruling hierarchy and the religious hierarchy joined forces, both prospered. But it was always an uneasy alliance. Neither trusted the other. Sometimes the civil authorities had the upper hand; sometimes the religious authorities. History bears out that when religion marries civil power, it's usually religion that assumes the subservient role (i.e., Rome and the experience of Constantinian Christianity; Henry the VIII and the Church of England, Nazi Germany co-opting German Christians; a university church where university policy subverts church life). Religion that stands outside government or other institutions and critiques them may have integrity, but has no power (except a faithful martyrdom). Religion that joins government has some security, but integrity is traded for pieces of silver. The price religion initially paid the state for its security was the doctrine of the divine right of kings. To obey the king was to obey God. To obey God was to obey the king. Each institution had the other's back and both institutions reaped a surfeit of wealth and power. The church might turn the other cheek, but it had a centurion at its side.

In this manner, the two principal guarantors of every society became government and religion. Together they legitimized authority with a force that neither could claim separately. Religion placed the socially constructed government in a sacred, cosmic frame of reference that it claimed had been present from the beginning. Their civilization, religion proclaimed, was immortal and eternal, and citizens of the state participated in the divine order for the cosmos. On the other hand, the government placed the power of the state in support of religion. Citizens were assured both secular and sacred safety. Kinship in the society equaled kinship in the divine order. State authority and religious authority conferred secular and sacred benefits. All society was sacralized.

The challenge for every society is to convince citizens that they have given their consent to being governed, and to believe that the institutional dictates imposed upon them further their own deepest aspirations. The extent to which citizens accept this is the extent to which they are satisfied with their government. State's citizens tend to forget the social structure was established by someone or some group at some time. Religious disciples tend to forget that their religion is a concept drawn from human consciousness and human activity. This concept is integral to understanding society and culture. The pact made by civil authority and religious authority long ago has been subtly transferred to subsequent societies. Humankind today, without conscious awareness, *feels* that by participating in the societal structure they have "come together with bread" with the transcendent God(s) of history—or at the very least, they share in the divine cosmic experience. Even secular societies today appeal to an authority beyond the state that resides in *Tao, Dharma,* ancestors, the solidarity of comradeship, or the fatherland. Their citizens, too, *feel* they are invested in the cosmic order.

Religious myths gave the people for whom they were intended an answer to the question of our ancient cousin, Hunter, and to successive generations, "What's it all about?" Most cultures regarded the answers provided to these ultimate questions by their sacred stories as the Truth, not one explanation among many. This attitude was necessary, because their survival depended upon it. Clans, tribes, and nation-states attempted to create a myth that encompassed their borders in such a way as to unite every inhabitant in the belief that they were the benefactors of a unique, divine, righteous destiny. This conviction—history reimagined—was religious at its roots, and was meant to impart such loyalty that citizens would fight and die in its defense. The sacred story demanded belief and obedience and thereby promoted group cohesion. It gave identity, worth, values, hope, and direction. Witch doctors, shamans, medicine men, priests, priestesses, imams, popes, elders, preachers, and others who attained or acquired power in the tribes' religious hierarchy held the keys to their kingdom. Into their hands came the power to interpret rules, enforce obedience, and dispense blessings. Marrying the culture's myth to the culture's politics was the strategy for existential survival. Believers of the story were pitted against infidels outside the tribe whose stories—and people—were inferior. Wars of both protection and conquest could be underwritten by the story. The fire of the myth's truth burned in the heart and the belly. With time, as each culture became more sophisticated, and as their knowledge base was expanded through the resourcefulness of the human brain and technology, religious myths were scrutinized with increasing erudition until enlightenment rationalism took up the task.

Theology has passed judgment on civil government's attempts to co-opt the power of religion and make society subservient to civil authority. Religion can summon its moral resources to oppose corrupt civil power (confessing Christians in Nazi Germany c. 1934–1945; South African apartheid c. 1948–1991; civil rights in the United States c. 1600s to the present; India Independence, 1947; Tiananmen Square, 1989). Religion can offer alternative stories to societal greed, wealth, and power. Religion can function as a force for social transformation. The challenge to religion is to retain the ability to critique itself as well as civil authority. Is it possible for a diaspora of believers in the foundational myths of humankind to withstand the power of the state? Postmodern, globalized civilization is fraying because governments and religions can no longer appeal to a unifying narrative that justifies a shared dream. A universal story has given way to local anecdotes designed to appeal to a limited cultural audience. Globalization, in certain circumstances, has regressed to tribalization.

15

Pushing the Boundaries of Survivability

"We never stop investigating. We are never satisfied that
we know enough to get by. Every question
we answer leads on to another question. This has
become the greatest survival trick of our species."
—Desmond Morris
    Zoologist and Sociobiologist

THE CREATIVE THRUST IN human nature was present at the beginning, a spark encoded in our genome that was fueled by biological desire. There are many ways to be creative, invention being one, and we are told necessity is its mother. It must be pointed out that humans are not the only tool users. Tool use has been documented in apes, chimpanzees, sea otters, dolphins, crows, and a few other species. The tools were nearly always used to provide better access to food, but animals *selected* tools rather than *created* them. Dipping sticks have been used to harvest ants and termites from their habitats. Rocks have been used to smash open nuts and shellfish. Animals have never been observed devising or extending one of those "access tools" into something more complex. The human brain evidences a unique ability to perpetually ratchet up cognition and creation and anticipate good and bad outcomes.

Humans, as creatures of the animal kingdom, were aware that their first job was to get hold of something to eat. Filling the stomach is driven by desire (from the mother's breast to the vegetable garden to the grocery store to the fast food franchise), but humans didn't invent eating. The impulse of evolutionary biology had long since established a food chain. It's difficult to know if ancient *Homo* was aware that they were, by and large, at the top of the food chain. They knew they had to look out for lions and such, but basically plants and animals were theirs for the taking—if a predatory beast didn't get them first. It wasn't much of a stretch for our carnivorous (hunting) and herbivorous (gathering) ancestors to realize that tools might be useful. It's hard to know what tool they set about to make first. Our guess is that it was a rock for bashing skulls. But very quickly, they must have learned that between killing and eating, the beast had to be skinned to get at the meat. This was hard on the fingernails. They needed something for cutting and scraping.

Archeologists discovered a stone hand-axe in a narrow gorge in the savannah where northern Tanzania borders Kenya. This tool, on display in the British Museum, is carbon dated two million years BCE. One of our relatives *imagined* a tool for the task of cutting and skinning carcasses and set about to make it. The rounded end of this hand-axe was shaped to comfortably fit the palm and the opposite end was knapped to create a blade. This ancient tool, contemporary with *Homo erectus*, was not only serviceable, it was shaped and scored in a manner that made it more sophisticated than was needed for its utilitarian purpose of chopping and skinning. Two decorative grooves were carved where the "handle" joined the "blade." It exhibited pride of workmanship! An impulse toward beauty—form and function. This two-million-year-old artifact nudges us toward humility. But more than imagination and knapping was involved in early tool production by archaic humans. Our prehistoric ancestors recognized and executed a *pyro-technical process* some 175,000 years ago whereby they heated certain stones (altered a raw material) to make it easier to knap into a more effective blade (fabricated an advanced product). By contrast, our radial-arm saw is a clumsy contraption and the computerized plane is a trick.

Once the beast was skinned and the edible parts harvested, the hide, hair, horns, hooves, innards, bones, and teeth were left over. Humans called these remains by-products, and began to contemplate how they might prove useful. This was the beginning of crafts, art, medicine, mechanics, science, and religion, and it all required the human capacity of foresight, conceptualization, planning, and dexterity. At the pre-hand-axe critical moment, a human comprehended that the universe must be actively engaged, not simply contemplated. The cerebral cortex alone cannot accomplish a task. It must use the hand. The interaction of the two was essential. Life must be grasped or life is not possible. It's the hand that completes the thought. Function, classification, sequence, and pattern are the benchmark of human productivity. Even more extraordinary, human action results in empowerment, joy, and satisfaction. So much so, that the feat is performed over and over again. The skill becomes perfected and the human is perfectly pleased. An individual loves to do what she does well, and having become accomplished, strives to do it even better. The child fits the round peg in the round hole. One day that hand plays a violin, and one day it docks a space capsule with an orbiting space station. So began the love affair between humankind and their tools. "Put the hand-axe in a toolbox," they cried. In so doing, they ensured their future . . . and ours.

It was a small step from tool to weapon. A hafted axe can be imagined from a hand-axe. A spear with a stone point can be imagined from the previous two devices. These were the principal implements that served hunters for the next million years. They not only hunted animals for food and by-products, they made war on their fellows. Tools and weapons accompanied humans on all of their migrations and cultural journeys for the remainder of history. In this progression of events, someone finally said, "I know what let's do. Let's create a military-industrial complex!"

A few hundred thousand years after humans invented the hand-axe, they gained control of fire. We can't say they invented fire, for they had observed the phenomenon from the beginning. It was a force of nature. It was destructive and uncontrollable. How did they conclude that it could be controlled and put to use? Who first attempted to lay claim to fire? That took imagination and courage. Fire was of such significance that the Greeks cast it in its mythology as a theft from the gods by the immortal titan, Prometheus. The blessing and curse of fire was within the sovereignty of the gods, and the Fire God was among the earliest of humankind's deities. Fossil campsites with fire pits have been unearthed in Africa that date back 1.5 million years—again, the time of *Homo erectus*.

Humankind's power to initiate and control fire had an incalculable impact on our species. In one stroke, light, heat, and energy were domesticated. The campfire, the ubiquitous image of society, established a site worth protecting—a refuge. It beckoned other members of our species and frightened away members of other species who were unable to control fire. The campfire begat culture. Fire became a rallying point and provided a destination to return with gathered meat and produce. The campfire provided warmth and became a place for safety, companionship, socialization, storytelling, partnering, reproduction, and the rearing of children. Fire changed the dietary habits of *Homo*. Roasted meat and vegetables were more delectable, but also more digestible and the calories were more readily accessible. A smaller quantity of food provided more energy—a bigger bang for the buck. Furthermore, eating together was an enjoyable and bonding experience. The campfire was the primordial, convivial banquet. The after-dinner speaker was invented.

Shared stories were fundamental to the human experience, and the campfire was its communal connection. History was recounted. Tales were told. Myths were spun. Poems were voiced. Songs were sung. Insights were proclaimed. Secrets were entrusted. Revelations were divulged. People were informed, entertained, delighted, and appalled as the stories cast their spell. The storyteller had to have the gift of imagination, insight, memory, and rhetoric. Information educates and informs; rhetoric persuades and inspires. Excellence in both virtuosity and voice was essential. If those traits were lacking, that particular storyteller lost the right of preeminent place at the campfire and was replaced by a storyteller with the better gift. However, merit didn't always win out. Nepotism and cronyism reared their heads. Some big, hairy guy shifted his club menacingly in his hands and told the campfire community, "Yeah, I know Pug Ugly is a better raconteur, but Dumb Ugly is my wife's cousin and I'm making him chief storyteller. Piss off!" Fire was the ancient symbol of home and in the millennia to come became the hearth . . . still the focal point of family life. What is apparent to the human community tens of thousands of years later is that the warmth and glow of a campfire will never be replaced by the glimmer of a computer monitor. Information has been transmitted through the ether, but much has been lost.

Fire, for *Homo erectus*, was also mystical and metaphysical, and it remains so for *Homo sapiens sapiens* (AMH). Fire was magic. Fire melted some substances and hardened others. Fire made liquids hot and became the basis of alchemy. Fire produced steam. Fire was used for communication. Fire was used for offensive and defensive warfare. Fire was a signifier for religion. Fire was a place of revelation (the "burning bush"), necessary for sacrifice (consumed the offering), and it empowered ritual (fire monuments, *c.* 2600 BCE, Indus Culture; candle at the altar, Camp

Fire Girls *c.* 1910, USA; the Nazi political rally, *c.* 1930, Nuremberg, Germany; the college homecoming bonfire). Fire was valuable but transitory. Fire stood for life. The fire you created consumed itself. What happens when the fire goes out? Humankind's primordial desire was not only for a hearth, but for an eternal, and may we say, "*affirming flame*"!

Fire contributed to humankind's survival, thus furthering the survival instinct. The desire to survive is different from the fear of death. Fear of death is a philosophical construct. Survival is instinctive and is driven by the most primitive part of the brain, the amygdala. Fight, flight, or freeze is hardwired, and that instinct spills over into the acquisition of food, territory, sexuality, and meaning-making. Provisions, space, mating rights, and religion are worth fighting and dying for. Living alone is a threatening enterprise. Survival is enhanced by numbers. Human beings are social creatures, both by instinct and necessity. Charles Darwin and others have informed us about the process of "individual selection," a selfish impulse for individual survival. Social psychologists tell us about "group selection," a selfish impulse for the group's survival. Selection connects the amygdala to the frontal cortex (forethought and reasoning). The frontal lobes prompt altruism, empathy, sympathy, compassion, cooperation, collaboration, and reciprocity. The instinctual desire to mate and have children assures species survival, but without the generous attributes of frontal lobe altruism the vulnerable *Homo* offspring would not survive childhood. The endeavor to survive and thrive was facilitated when families formed clans, clans became tribes, and tribes became nations. Each step in forming those social alliances increased the chances for individual survival, which in turn promoted group survival.

The tribe defined the characteristics of its members, established norms, and implemented rules to regulate social behavior. The tribe created symbols of identity, generated pride in the group, claimed superior characteristics over other tribes, and dehumanized and demonized those outside the group. The tribe stimulated loyalty and demanded loyalty. Larger groups need more territory and were able to amass the strength to get more territory. Territory breeds territoriality and necessitates security and defense. The tribe rallies its members, raises armies, and goes to war. This chain reaction of social enterprise is driven by a visceral need for survival of the individual, and that need is ultimately transferred to the tribe. The result is a net loss of individual power and freedom, but it is reinvested in the tribe for a net gain in tribal strength and dominance. Humankind was on its way to more complex and demanding social structures, but with it came competition. Competition for survival was a two-edged sword. Competition inspired our best instincts and unleashed our worst.

In a society where every individual had the same job—get food in order to survive—there was very little division of labor and neither rich nor poor. Survival was the minimum goal. Inevitably, some individuals were better at surviving than others and accumulated excess survivability. But enough was never enough. Innate fear of scarcity was the root of greed. Society began to stratify. Distinctions emerged on the basis of talent, inclination, strength, and wealth. Strength (violence) and wealth (excess resources) were the successful one-two punch that led to power. Every technical advance during the progress of civilization—from the wooden club to nuclear weapons—was driven by the individual's, and thence the tribe's, need to protect itself. Secondarily, violence was the shortest route to acquiring more stuff. As social classes arose, one thing was immanently clear: birthing could only be done by females. Infant suckling instincts were satisfied only by the female breast (even with Romulus and Remus, and that was a god-thing). The male, larger, stronger, and faster (but not more courageous) was a more successful hunter. In addition to social classes, gender roles in the family were naturally assigned and assumed. The mother at the hearth. The father in the field. Stratification was institutionalized. Discrimination was its bastard child.

Societies flourished, and just as with individuals, some societies flourished better than others. When one lives on the brink of starvation, every other need is subordinated to finding something to eat. The accumulation of surplus food was the foundation for everything else society accomplished.

Geography had established variable ecosystems—interdependent networks of plants and animals—worldwide. Ecosystems provided the vital food sources for herbivorous and carnivorous humans. Aquatic ecosystems provided a unique and diverse supply of nutrients and products for humans who lived in proximity to rivers, lakes, seas, and oceans. The world's vast waterways did not, however, provide domesticable creatures upon which humans could base a culture—except in fantasy. During the millennia between *Homo erectus* and *Homo sapiens,* the human brain had evolved into an organ with a fantastic array of instinctive, imaginative, inventive, cognitive, and creative traits. These traits promoted humankind's ability to select, breed, grow, harvest, and stockpile food. Hunting and gathering, which had sustained humans from the beginning, gave way to the domestication of certain plants and animals. This was the next great turning point in the progress of civilization. It had profound implications because the manner of life to be secured on planet Earth was climate dependent.

Domestication of animals meant much more than taming a critter and creating a pet. Many of the earth's great beasts—such as lions, tigers, zebras, giraffes, rhinoceroses, kangaroos, and bears—possessed traits of aggression and unpredictability that precluded domestic use. Such animals have been made somewhat submissive, but it's only a parlor trick. The animals are not serviceable. The horse, cow, donkey, camel, llama, and elephant could be made tractable. More than that, domestication meant that humans were able to breed them in captivity and even create designer species tailored to a specific task. Domestication did much more than harness the animal, it harnessed genetics. Humans discovered, even though the science of genetics was not understood for thousands of years, that they were able to exploit evolution and manipulate a species (dogs that scurry down rabbit holes; dogs with herding instincts; dogs that hunt).

Domesticated animals were invaluable. First, they provided a reliable supply of food. The clan no longer had to be nomads, following the migratory habits of their food source. Nor did they have to take potluck on what they could find and kill for dinner—their menu had choice. Large creatures used for food also provided by-products, from fur to bone. As noted, aquatic creatures could not be domesticated, but provided nutritious food and valuable by-products. Captive creatures became a measure of wealth and were used in commerce. Large domesticable creatures gave their masters an edge by extending human strength, speed, and endurance. Brutes could be used as beasts of burden and reduce human labor. They could even be used for sport (bullfighting), or in sports (polo). Last but not least, brutes were a vehicle empowering war. Humans gained power over animals far beyond utilitarian domestication.

Domesticating plants was equally important in the advance of civilization. Humans, again without understanding the science of genetics as we know it, but through observation and trial and error (a primitive, intuitive science), used genetics to manipulate plants. Initially there weren't gardeners; there were only gatherers. At some point, while gathering in the wild, our ancestors stumbled upon stalks of various grains (wheat, oats, barley, rye) with large, plump, durable heads of greater yield, and with that discovery learned how to reliably reproduce them in both quantity and quality. They manipulated plants to create a permanent, stable food source.

Farming developed about the same time in different parts of the world. It was dependent upon a geography, climate, and a growing season that allowed reasonable time from planting to harvest. The Middle East utilized wheat and barley. Asia exploited millet and rice. Indonesia used the yam and taro (giant tubers). Africa harnessed sorghum. The Americas employed squash, beans, and corn. These individual varieties became staples for those cultures. Every culture identified what plants would be useful and how to alter and transform them to make them even better in the domesticated form than they were in their wild state.

People had to make a permanent home to tend seasonal crops and care for domesticated herds. Hunting and gathering and a nomadic existence gave way to farming and animal husbandry and a settled, community life. These communities became the cradle of civilizations. However, not every tribe on planet Earth had access to favorable resources because geography had dealt them a weak hand. Geography and climate dictated which species of animals and plants could thrive in a particular habitat. Some species were suitable for domestication and exploitation and some were not. Earth, in terms of habitat resources, was not an equal opportunity planet. Humans who had the best geography, flora, and fauna for sustainable domestication were favored in the race to acquire food surpluses. Surplus food contributed to better health, more wealth, greater power, and—an invaluable resource—leisure time.

Jared Diamond, in his Pulitzer Prize-winning book *Guns, Germs, and Steel*, argues persuasively that, "[H]istory followed different courses for different peoples because of differences among peoples' environments, not because of biological differences among people themselves."[1] Racial superiority among hominids was not the issue. Deciding factors were accidents of geography and the environment's cache of domesticable animals and plants. Some real estate, with a diversity of favorable species, was better suited to our *Homo* ancestor's civilizing skills a million years ago. Such choice real estate, ocean front or river bank, actually covered a very small area of the Earth's total land mass. Diamond essentially placed a ruler on a world map across Eurasia. He drew a straight line from

---

1. Diamond, *Guns, Germs, and Steel*, 25.

Portugal's Atlantic coast to China's east coast where Shanghai sits beside the East China Sea. This entire Eurasian landmass is oriented on an east-west axis a few degrees on either side of the northern thirty-eighth parallel. The line runs directly through Spain, the Mediterranean Sea, and north Africa, on through Italy, the Macedonian Peninsula, Mesopotamia, Northern India, and across southern China.

This geographic expanse shares the same temperate climate, the same seasonal variations and day length, the same growing seasons, and the presence of a diversity of wild animal and plant species which lent themselves to domestication. Further, there was virtually untrammeled access across that entire axis for the migration of people and the spread of animals, crops, ideas, inventions and, also quite critical, the spread of diseases. Infectious disease caused epidemics that both wiped out populations and conferred immunity. Immunity bestowed an enormous biological advantage on those who acquired it. Diamond concluded that through these quirky, geographic advantages, the Mediterranean basin, Southern Europe, the Middle East, the Indus, and Southern China had at least a 12,000-year head start over parts of Africa, Australia, Micronesia, and the Americas in the discoveries that led to technology.

Humankind stumbled upon two other spin-offs from nature that, after fire and domestication of plants and animals, had a profound effect on world history—fermentation and mind-altering plants. The biochemical process of converting sugar to alcohol with fruits and grains was known to virtually every culture, and was almost certainly stumbled upon by accident. Alcohol's effects were immediately recognized. A fermented drink was healthier than polluted water. It aided digestion. It was convivial in social settings and contributed to both table fellowship and celebratory feast days. However, the effects of alcohol were observed to be both good and bad, but perspective had a great deal to do with the verdict. Alcohol altered thought processes and perception, usually without improvement in clarity, but sometimes added entertainment value in a social setting. Usually, it degraded social gatherings by releasing constraints normally imposed by the frontal cortex and promoted violence of all kinds, including sexual assault. Alcohol was also found to have certain medicinal properties—anesthesia and antisepsis. Some used it to self-medicate mental anguish and grief. A continual state of inebriation met certain social and personal needs because it mitigated interaction with others. One could drink and drop out, antedating Timothy Leary's advice by hundreds of thousands of years. For others, the alcohol molecule fit neatly into a biochemical reaction in the brain. Something clicked and they knew they had discovered a compelling coping mechanism. Other than suicide, alcoholism was perhaps the first self-inflicted disease affecting the human race. Mind-altering plants were also probably a serendipitous discovery. But the ecosystems of soporific, tranquilizing, narcotic, hallucinogenic, and psychedelic vegetation were geographically delimited. Then entrepreneurs and greed quickly found a way to funnel alcoholic and psychoactive products into the trade routes for worldwide distribution.

Plant and animal domestication and the ability to store foodstuffs were a vital buffer against lean times. No longer required to trail migrating herds, nomads became settlers. Villages and towns developed. New needs required new products and new processes. Pots, pans, tools, implements, gear, and rigs were invented. Fire and fermentation and communal camaraderie encouraged eating and drinking together. Feast days were designated. New and powerful gods arose. There were city gods and country gods. Gods of harvest, fermentation, fertility, weather, and war. The altar, a unique furnishing devised purely for worship, was created for sacrifice and devotion. There was a better life, better food, better sex, more religion, and more time.

16

Thinking About Thinking

"Sometimes I sits and thinks, and sometimes I just sits."
—Winnie the Pooh
A. A. Milne, Author

Thinking developed over time, as did other human characteristics. Deep thinking, critical thinking, thinking about thinking, or theoretical thinking awaited the convergence of biological evolution with human giftedness. Biological evolution provided *Homo sapiens sapiens* (AMH) with a sophisticated vocal apparatus, a brain with language and music centers, a frontal cortex for discrimination, and a capacious memory. Human species were fully invested with this anatomical equipment by about 200,000 BCE. The brain had become a mind that seethed with thought by about 100,000 BCE. Human consciousness had progressed to self-consciousness. Human giftedness invented writing and writing materials about 4400 BCE—which gave permanence to the spoken word—and thinking was no longer ephemeral and dependent upon memory, oracles, and the narrow wavelength of face-to-face speech. The fusion of language and writing created permanent texts that augmented the mental process and promoted scholarship. Human beings, alone or in concert, could return again and again to the same word, sentence, paragraph, essay, or book for critique, revision, reflection, and refinement. Conceptual knowledge could be shared. Humankind's previous intellectual efforts, in general, were more linear and drove survival, exploration, and invention.

But detailed inventory, description, or even abstract contemplation is not thinking about thinking (theory).

Karl Jaspers, a German physician and philosopher (1883–1969), believed a critical shift in human thought processes took place between 800 and 300 BCE, a period he referred to as *achsenzeit*—translated as axis-time or Axial Age. His "axial" metaphor was based on the modern awareness that many things—planets, wheels, cogs, machines, electrons, and other objects in motion—rotate on an axis. Jaspers proposed that axial thought holds within it the knowledge that theoretical thinking includes self-awareness, self-criticism, and self-analysis. Thinkers became lucidly conscious of being part of, and playing a role in, the thinking process, thereby altering and influencing the conclusions reached. In those five crucial centuries, theoretical thought joined forces with writing and history rotated, as if on an axis, and its trajectory was altered. Jaspers believed this axial time occurred independently in Mesopotamia, the Indus, China, the Middle East, and Greece; areas separated by geography, distance, ethnicity, language, and culture. Some cross-pollinization may have occurred, Jaspers concedes, but he contends that this eruption of advanced thought occurred in those regions spontaneously and essentially without collusion. The time was ripe. Thinking about thinking was one of the seminal achievements in human development and progress.

Axial thought—where ideas come from a point in the mind rather than the point of a spear—was not an easy road. Challenging received wisdom was dangerous (even life-threatening), but gradually contrarian ideas were given consideration and not immediately branded as heresy. Theorists and theoretical thought became acclaimed, not punished. Thought and technology intersected with Gutenberg's moveable-type printing press (c. 1440 CE) and pamphlets, tracts, scientific journals, and books could be widely and inexpensively disseminated. The Western Renaissance and Enlightenment (sixteenth through the nineteenth centuries CE) were there in embryonic form. The Royal Society of London was founded in 1660 and established a journal whose motto was *Nullius in Verba*, a Latin phrase roughly translated as, "Take no one's word for it." The same thought could be heard in street-smart vernacular three hundred years later: "If your mother says she loves you, check it out." The printing press was the seedbed for publishing and evolved into the internet, social media, and the fifteen-minute news cycle. Modern technology makes everything said or done around the globe instantaneous news and more or less permanent. The internet can propagate any pants-on-fire twaddle worldwide with impunity, whereas in ages past it was a lone crackpot in the town square whom everyone knew was not of sound mind.

Axial thought underwrote the disciplines of science, humanities, the arts, philosophy, theology, and religion. Science seized upon axial thought to develop a disciplined methodology to understand natural phenomenon, with the liminal understanding, "knowledge is power." Humanities and the arts applied axial thought in the use of all available mediums—prose, poetry, letters, painting, sculpting, drama, music, and dance—to represent the world in literal, figurative, and metaphorical terms, thereby contributing meaning, passion, and beauty to the universes of discourse. Philosophy used axial thought to address the fundamental nature of knowledge, reality, values, purpose, and existence. Philosophy impinged upon every field of human endeavor, as philosophies of science, history, education, economics, mathematics, war, art, and religion—among others—were formulated. Theology used axial thought to posit a philosophical interface in continuum within the universe where divinity and humankind are inseparably connected. Religion chose the ground of philosophy and hands-on experience to perceive transcendent god(s) and foundational principles of a spiritual reality.

Discussion of "world religions" places us squarely in the realm of story. Clarity requires, above all, that each story is understandable. Since words convey the story, precise words with fixed definitions must be used. For example, both Eastern and Western scientists understand $e = mc2$ in equivalent terms that are believed to be fundamentally true. Both speak a common scientific language. But Easterners and Westerners don't speak a common religious, theological, and philosophical language. This alone makes communication challenging, but furthermore, words are emotionally loaded—particularly the word *religion* and the *words religion uses*. Finally, world religions spring from virtually every culture. Cultural differences are impediments to common understanding.

We refer again to the poem by Rudyard Kipling:

> Oh, East is East and West is West, and never the twain shall meet,
> Till Earth and Sky stand presently at God's great Judgment Seat.

This couplet certainly doesn't work as a bumper sticker. It's too long, for starters. And although the first line carries a grain of truth, the second line erroneously enshrines the notion that a God presides at a judgment seat at the end of the world for both East and West. In certain Eastern philosophies/religions, neither gods, nor judgment, nor the end of the world are proposed. Words used commonly in Western theological thought don't have the same meaning, if they are used at all, in Eastern philosophical thought, and misunderstandings are all too common in conversations attempting to bridge "the twain."

Westerners conceptualize "religion" and "theology" as God-related, and it's almost impossible for we who are so acculturated to think otherwise. The two words are often used interchangeably, and subtle distinctions implied by context. Eastern and Western universities, it should be noted, place these academic courses in entirely different categories of study. Theology in Asian universities includes Judaism, Christianity, and Islam—monotheistic systems. The study of Hinduism, Buddhism, and certain other categories of Eastern thought are grouped under philosophy. Most Western universities classify all such studies under theology, or perhaps religion. The English word *religion* is derived from Latin (*relig, religate*), which literally means to "tie back." Ancient usage communicated the meaning of "tying back the darkness." Usage today implies binding, linking, or reconnecting, and includes reverence. Westerners communicate with Asians as though "religion" and "theology" are interchangeable. This discussion is perhaps clarified by asking two questions. "What is the human dilemma?" And, "What solutions are proposed?"

Western religious traditions (with the understanding that denominationalism and sectarianism have created hundreds of distinctive viewpoints), present a creation narrative, with a Creator God at the center, who was personally involved with the world and its created beings. Humans were instructed in certain rules that governed their existence, but through innate pride and willful disobedience broke the rules and were punished by separation from God. Each human being is part of a fallen race, lost in the world and condemned to death. The solution is "religating" the former relationship shared with the Creator God. Humans need to be found, picked up, healed, made whole, or saved. This human dilemma was solved by the Creator God who entered into the creation, a male infant who was fully God and fully human, and birthed by a young woman. By entering history in this decisive act, God ushered in a new age and a new way of living in which humankind's dilemma is solved. Death is followed by resurrection to a blessed, paradisiacal afterlife. Monotheistic religions tend to emphasize a vertical relationship between Creator and created.

Eastern religion's traditions, with the understanding that denominationalism and sectarianism have created hundreds of distinctive viewpoints, usually present a narrative with no beginning point, but describe a unified existence in which everyone was interconnected and immersed in perfection. Unified perfection was shattered by egocentric, proud, individual entities who emerged out of that perfection into the darkness of ignorance. A Western metaphor for this concept might be framed by the nursery rhyme wherein a falling egg is shattered. "All the King's horses and all the King's men couldn't put" the eggness "together again." The purpose, or goal, of Eastern philosophy is to put the egg together again. The solution is the practice of certain *dharmic* rules and customs—stressing nonviolence—and engaging in disciplined meditation to reach *brahman*. Brahman is a comprehensive term that encompasses enlightenment, understanding, and being infused with the ultimate reality of human interconnectedness. Eastern religions tend to emphasize a horizontal relationship whereby individuals are connected to their past selves and all humankind.

The two, previous paragraphs (without unraveling every nuanced thought) make it almost impossible for Westerners not to think in terms of equivalency in Eastern and Western religious thought. But, the human race is not all dancing around the same maypole of religion/philosophy tethered by unique, brilliantly colored ribbons. Subtle distinctions make a profound difference in perception and conviction. We must guard against analogous and homologous use of religion's specialized language or we will miscommunicate. The common thread of this book is that theology, philosophy, and religion is story. Different stories arose that stated their case, made claims, and established metanarratives that became the primal glue holding cultures together.

The author's notion that humankind apprehends the stories of religion/philosophy through desire, narrative, and faith, is undergirded by the theses presented in Jared Diamond's *Guns, Germs, and Steel*, Karl Jasper's, *The Origin and Goal of History*, and Robert Bellah's *Religion in the Axial Age*. We remind ourselves that Diamond identified a geographical landmass on either side of the thirty-eighth parallel from Lisbon to Shanghai with a temperate climate and an environment rich in domesticable animals and plants that gave its cultures a 12,000-year advantage over cultures with less fortuitous ecologies. Jaspers laid a conceptual line across world civilizations from the ninth to the third centuries BCE, in which axial thought and writing serendipitously expedited cultural expansion in every field of human endeavor. Bellah proposed that world "religions" (the word used broadly with regard to belief systems) used axial thought during that same time frame to advance religious/philosophical concepts in permanent texts.

Paul Tillich, one of the twentieth century's greatest theologians, has written, "The universality of a religious statement lies in the openness to spiritual freedom both from one's own foundation and for one's own foundation."[1] Religions must formulate an experience that is universally valid for humanity, while acknowledging that human experience is rooted in the particularity of time and place. Religion must be tangible and accessible to its culture, but its universal worth should be measured against the following criteria:

- It must cast light in the present darkness.
- It must interpret existence toward enlightenment, meaning, wholeness, and salvation.
- It must heal our present wounds.
- It must embody love, justice, and showing mercy.
- It must invest life's journey (our past—who we have been; our present—who we are; and our future—who we are becoming) with humility of meaning and hope.

As humankind developed from the primitive to the sophisticated, the theory and practice of cultural manifestations developed from the primitive to the sophisticated. The stories were captured by literacy and made durable, portable, and dispersible. Scholarship was developed to investigate the content and context of the universe. Disciplines of science and religion arose. The stories of science, developed over millennia, proposed solutions to the "*What?*" of our world. Science bequeathed data grounded in methodology that served humankind with functional knowledge and technical wizardry. The stories of religion, developed over millennia, proposed solutions for the "*So What?*" of our world. Religion bequeathed solace grounded in epiphany and experience that addressed humankind's yearning for a life of meaning and purpose. Do science and religion, with dual onset in preliterate history, have anything

1. Tillich, *Christianity and the Encounter of World Religions*, 79.

of consequence to say to each other, and consequently to us, today? This question requires that we briefly recount the origin, development, and content of ancient religions.

Robert Bellah proposed that eight world religions/philosophies drew inspiration from antiquity and established textual integrity in the Axial Age: Zoroastrianism, Hinduism, Jainism, Buddhism, Confucianism, Greek philosophy, and Judaism. He included Christianity in his discussion, because Christianity arose out of Judaism and the two spring from the same impulse. Islam is a late arrival on the religious stage as far as Axial Age religions are concerned and Bellah excluded it from his book. We have chosen to include Islam here because it draws on Judaism and Christianity and recognizes the prophets of those traditions. Islam has also had a major influence in both the East and the West and is now the professed faith of more than a billion persons worldwide.

A synopsis of ancient religious and philosophical systems is barely an introduction. Experts from each discipline quibble over details of understanding with their own colleagues and fellow disciples. Certainly, our efforts to summarize religions will fall short. But, as in the scientific "*What?*" of this book, our efforts are expended in good faith.

17

Ancient Text-Based Religions

"He who has a why to live can bear almost any how."
—Frederich Nietzsche
Philosopher and Cultural Critic

When writing of other religions, other philosophies, and their foundational texts, we want to represent them hospitably, accurately, and with integrity. We begin by noting that the medicine men, soothsayers, diviners, mystics, oracles, prophets, priests, imams, and philosophers of those long ago centuries could not possibly imagine what was to come. The world shrank as knowledge, travel, and communication expanded and cultural stories intersected and evolved.

ZOROASTRIANISM

Zoroastrianism is a religion with origins in ancient, tribal Mesopotamia. The prophet Zoroaster proclaimed in the name of the god Ahura Mazda (who figured in creation stories) and two other gods, Mithra (the divinity of covenants), and Apām Napat (the divinity of water). Apām Napat is also named in the *Rigveda* as a Hindu God in creation. These three figures are preeminent figures in the Indo-Iranian pantheon. Zoroaster's disciples believe he lived around 1000 BCE in the Asian steppes. Zoroastrianism was one of the first, if not the first, of the world's text-based religions. Its sacred scriptures, composed over several hundred years in the Avestan language, are referred to as the Zend-Avesta. Zoroastrian worship was initially centered in fire rituals. A life of good speech and good actions was emphasized, with the anticipation of experiencing the best life on this earth and life in a coming spiritual world. It taught that time is linear, that the world is a battleground between good and evil, and that time will end with a great judgment. Zoroastrianism persisted into the time of the Parthian (247 BCE—224 CE) and Sassanian (224 CE—651 CE) Empires. Zoroastrianism became modern Iran's state religion and also persists as a diaspora throughout the world.

HINDUISM

Hinduism arose in the ancient Indus and Indian sub-continent. A primitive religion based in monumental fire rituals and sacrifice (believed to sustain the world) evolved within tribal, agricultural societies referred to as the Harappan Civilization (c. 2600 BCE to c. 1900 BCE). More than a thousand years later (sixth to fourth centuries BCE) a great migration of Aryans from Middle Eastern and Slavic lands occurred. The Aryans spoke Pali, an Indo-European language from which Sanskrit was derived. The Indus culture evolved from pastoral to urban, and the Gupta Dynasties built the first cities in the Ganges River Valley.

The Hindu worldview, based on tradition and Scriptures, arose from this collision of cultures. Hinduism embraces a pantheon of male and female gods; Indra, Agni, Soma, Vishnu, Shiva, his wife Parvati, and their son Kumara being most frequently mentioned. Hinduism also speaks of gods or enlightened ones—Vishnu, Krishna, Ganesha, and others—who could return to earth as avatars and encourage individual humans on their life journey. These gods (heroes) became objects of adoration in Hindu society.

Hinduism relies on four ancient texts, referred to as the *Vedas* (originally transcribed in Pali): the *Rigveda*, the *Samaveda*, the *Yajurveda*, and the *Atharvavedas*. Portions might have been transcribed as early as 1000 BCE, but were preserved in Sanskrit texts much later. The texts were translated from Sanskrit into Chinese about 180 CE. The *Vedas* contain Scripture, hymns, philosophy, instruction, ritual, and tradition, and are among the oldest surviving religious texts in the world. Hindu orthodoxy stands on the Aryan *Vedic* tradition, and these texts are claimed to be revealed truth. Along the way, remnants of the ancient *Vedic* texts were collected into the *Upanishads*, and consist of more than two hundred philosophical treatises considered commentary on the *Vedas*.

Drawing on these sources, Hinduism believes the universe began as a perfect entity, unsullied by differences of any kind. This absolute, non-differentiated perfection (termed *brahman*) was shattered by the emergence (somehow) of entities with an overweening sense of self (ego) driven by ignorance. This event produced a finite number of conscious "selves" (not souls), referred to as Atman, that make up humankind. Each "self" possesses the merest spark of the original, perfected oneness, but enough to enable all humans to reach enlightened, indivisible, original perfection (*brahman*), the goal of Hinduism.

Hindu orthodoxy established five social castes, in which persons are ranked, one above the other, in status or authority. Caste is hereditary, and classically each individual must marry within caste to preserve the *dharma* of that caste through generations. Knowing one's caste—the higher the caste, the greater the possibility to attain *brahman*—guides Hindu living and enables individuals to chart their progress through the caste system. The five castes are:

1. *Brahmin*, the priestly caste and highest ranked, have the better understanding of *brahman*—the original oneness of perfection. (Note the difference between *brahman*—a philosophical concept—and *brahmin*—a societal caste.) *Brahmins* read and interpret the ancient *Vedic* texts.
2. *Kshatriya* is made up of sovereigns, rulers, royal families, and protectors.
3. *Viashya*, the citizen class, is composed of producers—farmers, merchants, professionals.
4. *Shudra* is the servant caste.
5. *Dalits*—the remainder of society—are ostracized as outcasts or untouchables. Their understanding of *brahman* is little more than that of animals.

Note: For the Hindu, non-Hindus are to be pitied because, not knowing their caste, they have to attain enlightenment as though going through life blindfolded.

Hindu philosophy is built upon six concepts.

1. *Dharma* prescribes the regulations and duties for each caste, emphasizing a virtuous, proper, moral life. *Dharma* is sometimes referred to as "The Way of Life."
2. *Artha* is a broad concept and nuanced meanings are implied by context, but includes essence, making meaning, having purpose, or a goal. It may be used in the context of means for living, material prosperity, or success.
3. *Kama*, not to be confused with *kharma*, is desire, passion, longing, and wishing. It refers to pleasure of the senses, including sexuality.
4. *Samsāra* carries the idea of reincarnation in a world in which time is cyclical.
5. *Kharma* expresses the principle that actions in this life affect life in successive reincarnations. The "self" (Atman) incrementally progresses or regresses within the caste system.
6. *Moksha* carries the meaning of self-actualization, with liberation from the interminable cycles of births and deaths.

Hinduism provides the philosophy and the mechanism by which Hindus reach life's goal—*Brahman*. The caste system offers opportunity for progression to ever higher status. Reincarnation provides the mechanism. Each finite, Atman-carrying self must endure countless reincarnations with opportunity to follow the *dharma* of each caste with ascending levels of self-realization of the indivisible state of perfection (*Brahman*) in hope of reaching *moksha* (a realm of liberation from endless cycles of death and rebirth).

Serious pursuit of *moksha* generally required a Brahmin male to leave home and family and become an itinerant religious teacher (renouncer). The path of the renouncer was incompatible with the life of the householder. For Brahmins, this created a conundrum. Without householders, the daily sacrifices of a piece of wood, a glass of water, flowers, fruit, and the verbal *om*—possibly vestigial remnants of the primitive fire monuments of Indus culture—would not be offered to maintain the world. Nor could the ancestral lineage be preserved through children. And significantly, without householders no one would be available to feed, clothe, and house the itinerant renouncer. This tension was usually resolved by deferring the "renouncer" role until after the "householder" role had been completed.

With conscientious devotion to the principles of Hinduism, help from *avatars,* and a little luck, human beings may discover ultimate truth within themselves. Full enlightenment will take place only when all persons have experienced all modes of being (caste) through reincarnations, and "all sentient beings realized their interconnectedness."[1]

JAINISM

Jainism's origins are somewhat obscure, but it is considered an offshoot of Hinduism. Its disciples were called *Thirthankaras,* Sanskrit for followers of "The Way." Jainism is another religion of a book, the *Purva,* and textural studies among its scholars are highly regarded. The original canonical texts were lost, but an oral tradition persisted that was transcribed *c.* 700 CE by followers of Pārśva (*c.* 877 BCE to *c.* 777 BCE), who is believed to be the twenty-third *Thirthankara* of Jainism, and the earliest Jain leader for whom there is reasonable historical evidence. Jainism emphasizes self-control, equality between all forms of life, and prescribes a path of nonviolence toward all living things. For long periods, Jainism was the state religion of the varied kingdoms that temporarily arose on the Indian sub-continent, but has been in decline since the eighth century CE because of oppression by devotees of Hinduism and Islam. The Jains remain as a diaspora.

BUDDHISM

Buddhism also grew out of Hinduism, but doesn't speak of God(s). The term *Buddhism* is from a Sanskrit word, *budh,* which literally translated carries the meaning of "enlightened," "awakened," or "to know." This great world religion can be traced to Siddhartha Gautama (*c.* 563 BCE to *c.* 480 BCE), a prince of the Shaky Clan of the *Kshatriya* caste. He lived in the town of Patna on the Ganges River in northeastern India (now Nepal). He renounced his position and left his wife and child to become a wandering ascetic, searching for the means to deepen his understanding of life and death. His goal was to liberate himself from human nature's suffering, greed, hate, ignorance, and self-delusion.

After years undergoing every spiritual practice available to him, he was meditating under a Bodhi tree plumbing the depths of his

1. Webb, "Zen Funerals," 3.

consciousness (distinct from *conscience*). After forty-nine days, he reached (his own effort) enlightenment (not a revelation). In this state of perfected knowledge he became liberated from self and self-delusion and grounded in the interdependence of all things. The illusory "self" reaches a"deeper presence," rather than a "clinging presence." Suffering and sadness will be experienced, but not clung to. Pleasure and joy will be experienced, but not clung to. This is the "way of being." Siddhartha Gautama, the Indian prince, became known as *Shakyamuni* Buddha, an Enlightened One. He continued his wandering ascetic life, attracting many disciples. The *Shakyamuni* Buddha taught that classical Hinduism might be true, but he had doubts and considered it flawed. In the process, he reimagined Hinduism.

Shakyamuni Buddha believed certain philosophical concepts of Hinduism, including an original, perfected oneness that was shattered by ignorance and egoism. He believed humanity's goal was enlightenment, the restoration of perfection, and a realm of life termed *nehan*. Buddha accepted reincarnation as probable fact, admitting that perhaps humans must go through many rebirths to understand the oneness of all beings. But here, *Shakyamuni* Buddha diverged from Hinduism. Classical Hinduism believes *samsāra* (reincarnation) continues through stages according to *kharma*. Atman (the distinctive "self") progresses up (or down) the succession of castes until—after eons and eons of time—all human beings reach enlightenment (*brahman*, the true reality of connected oneness, the original self, a realm of *nehan*).

The *Shakyamuni* Buddha's notion that without a Creator God there is no beginning and no ending brings into focus the horrifying result of *samsāra's* kharmic cycles: *there is no end to it!* Human suffering (our nature) is repeated forever in painful births, tribulation in life, and the anticipation of death. *Shakyamuni* Buddha resolved this conundrum. He taught that anyone, regardless of caste, could reach enlightenment in one lifetime. "I did it," claimed the *Shakyamuni* Buddha, "and so can you." Good news!

Shakyamuni Buddha denounced the *dharma* of the hereditary caste system. He declared any person who consistently practiced Buddhist principles had the highest status in life. This turned the Brahmin tradition on its head, designating the common person who is ethical the true Brahmin. Not only was this an existential threat to Brahmins, the *Shakyamuni* Buddha's denouncement of violence and the killing of any living being was a threat to any religion based on sacrifice and to the culture's warrior class.

The *Shakyamuni* Buddha expressed his teachings in narrative form. He observed that life is full of suffering, including fear of death, which can be traced to ignorance of the self. Selfish ignorance can be transcended and *nehan*, a state of enlightenment, may be achieved through right practice. This included adherence to a path of effort, mindfulness, concentration, resolve, proper perspective, good speech, fair behavior, and following an honorable livelihood. His disciples referred to this as the Buddha Nature or Buddha *dharma*, and sometimes as The Way. *Shakyamuni* Buddha came to the realization that he was a unique, and perhaps, universal teacher—within the context that he was not known to have ever left his region of northeastern India. Buddhist Scripture preserves the saying: "He who sees the true *dharma* sees me; he who sees me sees the true *dharma*."

Shakyamuni Buddha insisted the path to enlightenment was a personal one—a middle path of deep meditation and a life full of compassion toward all creatures. Self-centered concern was reproved and attention to the needs of others emphasized. Individuals are to search *all* Scriptures, and to probe deeply into their own consciousness for understanding. Meditation requires the discipline "to be inwardly quiet, listen to the world you think of as outside of you, and open yourselves to it."[2] Sitting Zen-style in meditation is painfully rigorous, both mentally and physically, and requires years simply to be able to sit for any prolonged time in the lotus position. *Shakyamuni* Buddha taught it would not be easy, but with hard work and discipline it could be done.

No personal writings of the *Shakyamuni* Buddha are known to exist. His disciples began collecting and translating his teachings by the first century BCE. Referred to as the Tripitaka of Rules, they are written in Pali, Sanskrit, and various Asian languages including Chinese. The Tripitaka is the standard collection of Scriptures in the *Theravadan* Buddhist tradition, and is arranged in three sections: *Vinaya* (rules and discipline), *Sutta* (sermons and discourses of *Shakyamuni* Buddha), and *Abhidhamma* (metaphysics and systematic philosophy). Only the compilation by the *Theravada* school of Buddhism survives in its entirety, and the surviving Sri Lankan version is the most complete. Written in prose and poetry, it has existed in its present form since about 400 CE, and contains the *Bhagavad Gita*, the *Rishyasringa*, and the story of *Damayati*.

2. Webb, "Responding to Buddhism," 11.

This great epic is essentially a work of political theory, and some consider it the deepest meditation in all antiquity on the realities of political life. Different denominations and sects of Buddhism rely on specific translations. Serious study of Buddhism requires a solid knowledge of Pali, Sanskrit, and Chinese.

Buddhism became India's state religion under King Ashoka in the third century BCE. By the early Christian Era, Buddhism had spread throughout southeastern and northern Asia and had become the leading philosophy of all Asia and the state religion of many of those countries. Japan adopted Buddhism by the sixth century CE, about the same time Hinduism had a resurgence in India and Buddhism waned. Beginning about the twelfth century CE, Islam reached India and the bitter struggle between Hindus and Muslims began, continuing into the present with the strife between India and Pakistan. Today, Buddhism has almost vanished from the country of its birth.

When discussing Buddhism, one size does not fit all. A Buddhist priesthood gradually emerged, as the Buddha believed the hard work of training for self-realization required specialization. By the first century BCE a priesthood was well established. Some Buddhist priests practiced celibacy; some married and had children. Ultimately two primary forms of Buddhism developed. One is called *Theravada* Buddhism (from Pali, literally, *doctrine of the elders*). *Theravada* Buddhism maintains a firm focus on the historical Buddha and his teachings. Progressive priests began to rely on Buddhist texts first translated from Sanskrit into Chinese (*c.* 180 CE) that contain both the previously mentioned teachings of the elders and the *Prajnaparamita* (Transcendental Wisdom teachings). Their effort was to devise a more accessible way to bring ordinary people into Buddhist practice. This produced the second form of Buddhism, termed *Mahayana* (Sanskrit: literally, *great vehicle*) Buddhism. *Mahayana* Buddhism—which encompasses almost all denominations of Buddhist practice at the present time—is based on a philosophy of peace, nonviolence, and a discipline of deep self-reflection. *Theravada* and *Mahayana* Buddhism have both divided into hundreds of denominations and sects. Three major categories in Japan, each with their own sub-sects, are Tantric, Pure Land, and Zen. Japanese customs play a significant part in the understanding and practice of Zen Buddhism.

Buddhism has evolved into a spiritual, meditative discipline and a complex philosophical code of conduct that is practiced worldwide and may have more followers than any other philosophical/religious group.

CONFUCIANISM

Confucius (551 BCE–479 BCE) was a Chinese teacher, philosopher, and politician who advocated self-control without asceticism, reform without violence, scholarship without dogmatism, and individualism without insensitivity. Confucianism, in common parlance, may be referred to as a religion, but is not about a deity and does not use God-talk. Confucianism is a calling to principled public service in which the state scrupulously embraces high-minded values. Confucius lived during a period of civil wars and believed the state must be the repository of social order (*li*). The virtuous principles he espoused should not only be aspired to by individuals, but were to be the foundation for state policy. Confucian ideology bent toward classical religions when he taught that individuals should strive toward *dao* (*tao*)—the condition with which one merges to attain "saved-ness."

Confucian morality did not appeal to the power of a God, but to the strength of reason. Confucius emphasized peace and harmony as primary personal and social values. Each individual was to find and accept their place in society. Confucian doctrine was dependent on each individual cultivating righteousness and benevolence. Society then wouldn't need punitive jurisprudence because each person would be ruled by the *"right way"* of what was appropriate. The motivating force that would compel such ethical behavior was profound personal shame over failure to live up to these virtues. A collection of Confucius's teachings and sayings were compiled in the *Analects* by his disciples many years after his death. It records his aphorism, "Do not do to others what you do not want done to yourself." Confucianism (which was also shaped by one of Confucius's great disciples, Mencius) has been the nominal guiding principal of Chinese empires for about 2,500 years, and remains a touchstone for scrupulous, secular people.

GREEK PHILOSOPHY

The Greeks established the concept that reasoned thought required clarity and consistency and thereby bequeathed the foundations of science and religion to the world. Greek mythology and ritual were embedded in the Parthenon and its statuary. Greek philosophy believed the world was warped by human greed for wealth and power, was perversely fated by the gods of the Greek Pantheon, and sought a coherent idealistic philosophy (solution) that would underpin societal redemption. There were profound Greek philosophers prior to and after Socrates, Plato, and Aristotle, but these three are revered (almost immortalized) because of their contribution to philosophical thought that influenced the Western world. One might say, when tallying up the number of devotees to the various world religions/philosophies, Greek thought might have influenced the largest number of the world's population.

Socrates (*c.* 469 BCE to 399 BCE), as we noted earlier, sounded one of the world's great summons to reflective action: "The unexamined life is not worth living." He used the power of his rhetoric to inspire rational thought and free speech, and called for moral courage to instigate action in pursuit of truth and virtue. Socrates was tried and sentenced to death by the leaders of Athens for the crime of corrupting Athen's youth and blaspheming local deities. His execution was accomplished by his own hand through a ritual of self-administered poison.

Plato (*c.* 424 BCE to 348 BCE) was Socrates's pupil. He meditated on the eternal way of things, but unlike his teacher, was not an activist. He taught truth, beauty, virtue, and justice. He thought the present world was a dim reflection of a more perfect world; one which all humankind should aspire to create and inhabit. Plato's classic work is *The Republic*, in which he proposed a Republican City as the ideal form of government. Plato established the Academy, a school which is the prototype of free inquiry and education.

Aristotle (384 BCE to 322 BCE) was a student of Plato, and the teacher of Alexander of Macedonia (who later became The Great). While Plato was a meditative philosopher, Aristotle engaged the natural world (particularly zoology and geology) with his reasoned insights. He was both philosopher and scientist. He directed his attention to politics, physics, metaphysics, poetry, and ethics. Much of his writing has been lost. He established his own academy in Athens, called the Lyceum. Aristotle is regarded as a pioneer in deductive reasoning and a founder of the scientific method.

JUDAISM

Judaism is the monotheistic religion of a Semitic middle-eastern people who, out of their nomadic history, forged a nation. Its thrust was a thoroughgoing monotheism which freed them from magic and totems.

They experienced an anthropomorphic, patriarchal God who created, destroyed, loved, hated, became angry and vengeful, but was also forgiving and benevolent. Their god, Yahweh, was known through dreams, visions, miraculous appearances, and the dramatic historical events they experienced in the clash of the Bronze Age cultures of Mesopotamia, the Fertile Crescent, and North Africa. Their story is preserved in the Torah (Pentateuch), the Prophets and the Writings, and considered revelation. These same Hebrew texts are the Old Testament of the Christian Bible.

The narrative begins with the creation of a peaceful, garden paradise which was disrupted by the serpent and dishonored by the two humans, Adam and Eve, whom God created and nurtured. Eden was closed and an angel with a flaming sword guarded against re-entry. The story picks up east of Eden with a life of struggle and dying. There were times of war and peace, power and weakness, captivity and liberation, love and hate, fidelity and betrayal, damnation and redemption, a flood to drown an evil pastoral world and a purifying fire to incinerate a wicked urban culture. A monotheistic faith was established which rang out with hope against perfidy and despair. There are stories of gods, demons, and angels, giants and witches, prophets and spies, kings and shepherds, hardened soldiers and courageous young girls, of friends and enemies, thoroughly dysfunctional families, paragons of virtue, murderers, thieves, and prostitutes. Story, song, and poetry are interspersed with genealogies of clans, instructions for rituals of worship, and regulations about diet and hygiene. All of it is *history* laced with theological reflection and commentary.

The narrative presents Abram (Abraham), a nomadic patriarch of Chaldea in Mesopotamia, who encountered God as Yahweh who called him into an unknown future and promised him a land and a great nation. His encounter drew him into a covenant with Yahweh and he became the founding father of a people who were known eventually as Hebrews, Jews, or Israelites. A patriarchal period of nomadic clan life ended in Egypt when the twelve great-grandsons of Abraham became slaves of an Egyptian Pharaoh (Israel is first mentioned in Egyptian records *c.* 1208 BCE). The Pharaoh released them to the prophet Moses following ten plagues (*c.* 1200 BCE). The twelves sons of Jacob, having multiplied to twelve tribes, fled Egypt with what they could carry. Their escape route was blocked by the Red Sea as Pharaoh's Army pursued them. Yahweh delivered them from destruction by parting the Red Sea and they crossed into the Arabian Peninsula on dry land. They wandered for forty years in the Arabian desert, disciplined and directed by Yahweh, during which time Moses received the Ten Commandments at Mount Sinai and established Tabernacle worship. Then, without Moses, who died and was buried in an unmarked grave in the Arabian desert, the Israelites entered Canaan (*c.* 1160 BCE). By the power of Yahweh and under the leadership of Joshua, they conquered territory and carved out some land in the middle of other Semitic tribes. They were ruled by a series of judges for about 150 years, one of whom was Deborah. The song of Deborah recorded in Judges was written in the oldest Hebrew in the Old Testament and is the only text that can possibly be dated to the pre-monarchical period of Israel (1200 to 1030 BCE).

King Saul ruled Israel from *c.* 1030 BCE to *c.* 1010 BCE. King David (the shepherd King, warrior, lover of Bathsheba, and lyrical psalmist) ruled from *c.* 1010 BCE to *c.* 970 BCE, followed by his son with Bathsheba, Solomon (*c.* 970 BCE to *c.* 930 BCE). After King Solomon, the Israelite Kingdom fell onto hard times, squabbled, and chose idolatry over Yahweh. The monarchy split into two weak dynasties: the Northern Kingdom of Israel (ten of the tribes) and the Southern Kingdom of Judah (the tribes of Judah and Benjamin). The Assyrians conquered Israel in 722 BCE and carried many away into captivity, where they were lost to history as a distinct people. Babylon's King Nebuchadnezzar conquered Judah in 587 BCE, destroyed Solomon's temple in Jerusalem, and deported Jews to Babylon. Temple Judaism virtually disappeared and Israel's dream to be a uniquely chosen world power disintegrated in Babylonian captivity. The Jewish question became, "How do we sing the Lord's song in a strange land?" Cyrus of Persia (now Iran) conquered Babylon in 539 BCE and allowed some Jewish exiles to return to Jerusalem in 538 BCE and begin restoring Solomon's temple.

The sacred texts of the Hebrew Bible are the primary sources for data about ancient Israel. The narrative presents itself as though it were a chronological history from creation to the sixth century BCE. In the modern sense of critical historiography this is not accurate, because every tale is specifically selected for preservation and each text is interpreted with a national and a religious purpose in mind. The preserved documents were crafted to project the story backward in time to creation and forward in time to a universal messianic kingdom. The Torah and the Prophets are generally believed to have been written in the period of Jewish Babylonian captivity (*c.* 587 BCE to *c.* 539 BCE) and in the few centuries on either side of that date. The Hebrew Bible is so foundational in establishing Israel's narrative identity that people of the Jewish faith have recited the core story for the past 2,500 years. They recite it in the *present* tense as if *they were present* in the story: "A wandering Aramean was *my* father and *he* went down into Egypt and sojourned there; *he* became a nation." And then . . . "The Egyptians treated *us* harshly, and afflicted *us* . . . *We* cried to the Lord . . . and the Lord heard *our* voice, and saw *our* affliction, *our* toil, and *our* oppression . . . and the Lord brought *us* out of Egypt." The Jews reciting this story weren't "present," but they "were there." They are in the story and the story is in them. It is the most important story the Jews know, and they believe it is specifically decisive for them. The language contains their foundational faith statement, emphasizing a covenant relationship with their God, Yahweh, and, together with the Writings and Wisdom literature, records the identity-empowering story of Israel. The narrative undergirds who and what they are, and the *story* is of greater importance than any *theological* reflection or rationale. It means, for the Jews, that the limits of the present do not determine the limits of the future.

Israel's challenge was to believe its historical nature, whereby catastrophes and triumphs were to be tolerated because they were part of Yahweh's scheme for a linear, historical timeline which progressed to a messianic intervention that would save the world and its creatures once and for all. The temptation of the Hebrews was always to return to the gods of surrounding polytheistic cultures because those gods seemed more accessible and more pliant. The solution to life's problems seemed right-there and right-now: light the fire, submit to the ablution, bring the gift, make the sacrifice and immediately appease the gods and find deliverance from the calamity.

The concluding fragments of Jewish history in the remaining centuries before the Common Era are not found within the Old Testament. Other sources relate the Greek conquest of Palestine by Alexander the Great in 333 BCE, as his armies swept east and south from Macedonia to conquer the Persian Empire, the Indus, parts of China, and north Africa. The Jewish Maccabees revolted against Greek rule and were able to create a diminished Hasmonean Monarchy in Palestine about 140 BCE. Rome conquered Greece, defeated the Maccabees, and occupied Jerusalem in 65 BCE. Historical Judaism has been a force since its inception. It has persisted and flourished as a worldwide diaspora for two and a half millennia, and established itself as the nation of Israel (recognized by the United Nations in 1948).

CHRISTIANITY

Christianity flowed out of Judaism and continued the historical strain of monotheism that knew God as Yahweh, and maintained the tradition of a religion of revelation. Abraham, a patriarch of Judaism, is honored by Christians as the "Father of the faithful." God's covenant with Abraham is claimed to have been fulfilled in the birth of Jesus of Nazareth, born in Bethlehem of Judea during the reign of King Herod, when Quirinius was governor of Syria and Caesar Augustus was Emperor of Rome. Jesus was also called the Christ, King, Emmanuel, Son of Man, Son of God, Everlasting Father, and Prince of Peace. The primal story is the cross (suffering and death) and resurrection (new life).

The events of Jesus' life and the lives of his early disciples were preserved in a collection of written texts. Just as Hebrew texts are foundational for Israel's identity, Christian texts are foundational for Christian identity. The two testaments together (Old and New) form the Christian Bible, which Christians view as one book with an overarching narrative. The stories contain theological reflection (reason and logic), but there are no proof texts. There is only confessional witness. Christians believe these events happened and changed the direction of history. Humanity's predicament has been resolved by a new story called gospel. The New Testament explains what led to a community of faith formed by those who accepted the invitation of Jesus, a Nazarene carpenter, who said, "Follow me."

Jesus has a narrative identity recorded in a story that is audacious, but straightforward. It is full of local specificity, but moves to radical openness for all people, all families, and all nations. From beginning to end, the Jesus story is about the humanity of God who is for humanity and with humanity, and who loves, heals, forgives, and saves, to keep the promise of love and life. Jesus lived and died with outstretched arms as a commitment of the surprising God of love, whose grace dismisses all self-important, self-righteous human claims to ultimacy and infallibility. Discipleship—the life centered in Jesus—is about living now, loving now, and being fully human now. It challenges all presumed human limitations and crosses all boundaries for the sake of others. It pays special attention to "the least": the hurting, the sick, the outcast, the orphan, the poor, the needy, the prisoner, the disenfranchised. Self-giving love is sacrificial. The paradigm of the Jesus story is death and resurrection. Redemptive life envisions life-alive in the here and now and a life beyond

God's beloved, created world. Not as a payoff for being good enough or pure enough or righteous enough, but redemptive life as a gift—a life from grace, in grace, and toward grace.

The Christian church itself followed a disputatious, divisive historical path. This is evidenced by the New Testament documents themselves as attempts were made to define orthodoxies among the first factions, Jews and Gentiles. Following the New Testament period, the Roman Catholic Church solidified ecclesiastical power with the conversion of the emperor, Constantine. Politics and power led to the schisms of the various Eastern orthodoxies (the national churches of Greece and Russia; the Coptic, Syrian, and Ethiopian orthodoxies, as well as others). Martin Luther, John Calvin, and others protested against what they believed was a dissolute Catholicism and initiated the Protestant Reformation. Henry the VIII challenged Rome and established the Church of England. In the centuries since Luther and Calvin, the Protestants have further divided into numerous denominations, sects, and even personality cults. Continuing attempts to reform or restore more faithful forms of Christianity have occurred in the centuries since the Reformation. The gospel proclaims that the Jesus narrative is large enough and transcendent enough, particular enough and personal enough, to embrace humankind's ultimate concerns in our living and our dying.

ISLAM

Islam is an Arabic word meaning "complete surrender," which is taught as "the way" to God. A follower of Islam is called a Muslim—"one who submits." Islam appeared some one thousand years after the close of what Jaspers called the Axial Age. It began with the prophet Muhammad (c. 570 CE to 632 CE), born in Mecca in the Arabian peninsula. He was a merchant who, when he was forty years old, began receiving a series of revelations from *Allah*, Arabic for God, through visions of the archangel, Gabriel. Persecuted for preaching monotheism and racial equality, he was forced to flee to Medina in 622 CE. Continuing to receive revelations, Muhammad's close followers memorized and transcribed their contents, using Arabic, in the Koran (*Qur'an*). Muslim faithful believe the Koran is the unaltered, final, and literal word of God. Islam is a religion of the Book. Apart from the *Qu'ran*, the *Hadith* is a collection of stories and sayings of Muhammad that constitute a major source of traditional guidance for Muslims. After consolidating his rule in Medina, Muhammad and his followers waged a series of battles in the region of Mecca, and by 630 CE, had conquered the city. By the time of his death in 632, Muhammad had united most of Arabia. The eighth to the thirteenth centuries of the Common Era are considered Islam's Golden Age, during which Islam flourished and underwent geographic, economic, cultural, and scientific expansion.

Muhammad is believed by Muslims to be the last prophet of God, standing in the monotheistic tradition of Adam, Abraham, Moses, and Jesus. Muslims believe that Islam is the complete and universal version of primitive monotheism. Central to Islamic faith is belief in Muhammad's teaching on *Allah*, angels, spirit beings, prophets, scriptures, the Day of Judgment and predestination. The *Shahada* is the core creedal belief of Islam: "There is no god before *Allah*, and Muhammad is his prophet." The *Shahada* is one of the Five Pillars of Islam, the other four being the recitation of prescribed prayers, giving alms, fasting, and a pilgrimage to Mecca.

The Islamic concept of *jihad* is based on Muhammad's claim that he had been commanded by the archangel, Gabriel, to fight until people profess, "There is no God but Allah." *Jihad* is often popularly translated "Holy War," however, linguistically, *al-harb* is the Arabic word for war. Many Muslims believe *jihad* is not meant as a violent concept, and is not a declaration of war against other religions nor an excuse for terrorism. For example, after returning from a military campaign, Mohammad said, "Today we have returned from the minor *jihad* to the major *jihad*." In this declaration, he was lifting up *jihad* as the struggle for self-control and betterment. The Islamic Supreme Council of America says that *jihad* means "struggling" or "striving." This can involve both external struggle and internal discipline to become a good Muslim. It also carries the idea of working to inform people about the faith of Islam. Military action to protect the faith is allowed, if necessary, however, legal, diplomatic, economic, and political means are to be used first.

Islam is considered the second-largest religion in the world, claiming about 1.7 billion followers (23 percent of the world's population). Only the collective membership of all Christianity, Catholic and Protestant, numbers more members. Islam is the majority religion in forty-nine countries and has enormous religious, political, and economic impact. Islam is monotheistic but not historically monolithic. Islam is divided into numerous denominations or sects based upon questions of succession to Muhammad, varied nuanced doctrinal interpretations of the

Qu'ran, and political attitudes on the establishment of *Sharia* law. There are numerous versions of what constitute proper *Sharia* law and how it should be imposed. Most Muslims belong to two Islamic denominations, of which the Sunni outnumber the Shia. Between these two major sects, there are forty or more denominations vying for loyalty. Among them, to name a few, are the Sufi, Khawarij, Nizari, Alawite, Jafri, Akbari, and Maliki.

Still, in the world of Islam, the kinship of blood is the primary bond between individuals. Neither nation, nor tribe, nor sect has the supreme loyalty of any individual Muslim. Brother stands against brother; brother together with brother join against cousin; brother and brother allies with cousin against the world. Tribal differences and disputes go back 1,500 years. These differences were only intensified by the 1919 Treaty of Versailles ending World War I. The victorious Allies, but principally Great Britain and France, divided up the Middle and Near East by drawing lines on a map according to their own political and economic needs without regard to geography or taking into account ethnic tribal needs.

These nine stories demonstrate that the earliest humans, in the mist of ancient times and from the depths of longing, felt their way toward religion (using that word in its broadest Western context). The stories demonstrate that religions were not all centered in deity or based on revelation. Nor were religions inert and static. Further, with the understanding that we should not use analogous thinking when reflecting on these world religions, it does appear each shared common themes, and were feeling its way toward common goals and ideals. There is some parallelism here, even though some speak of divinity as a reality to be reckoned with and some do not. In what manner, then, may classic world religions/philosophies contribute to the understanding of the "So What?" in the postmodern world of meaning-making?

18

Religion
Seers, Sages, Saviors, and Renouncers

"The one who can make you believe absurdities,
may soon have you committing atrocities."

—FRANCOIS-MARIE AROUET (VOLTAIRE)

THE STORY OF HUMANKIND becomes palpably real only through the flow of history. Absent the story of religion, humanity's story is incomplete. Absent human experience, religion would not exist. Religion is an experience. Religion began commensurate with ancient humanity's long journey into self-consciousness. It is one of the narratives of humankind, developed over history with various manifestations, and its story inevitably intersects with all narratives of human endeavor. Religion must be dealt with in the life experience of every individual. It is a distinctive focus of theorizing, philosophizing, socializing, worshiping, experience, and deeds. Some religions speak of God, some don't, and furthermore God-talk is not absent from other areas of human discourse. Religions centered in deity invest God with a unique reality. To say, "Some call it God and some call it Science," misses the point of both. A religion that posits to a sacred cosmos and operates within that construct shouldn't timidly tiptoe around this understanding to get in step with the latest fad—whether scientific or cultural. Such shenanigans obscure and dilute the religious narrative. This is not the fault of secularists; it's a failure of religionists.

Theology, on the other hand, is an academic discipline. It is a course of study relating to God using precise language, logic, and data. Theology uses the natural sciences, paleontology, philosophy, sociology, psychology, philology, anthropology, and archaeology as *relevant* to theology, but *theorizing in all of those fields* is not theology. Theology is also a vocation. A theologian may or may not even be religious or churched. But when *desire* perceives *narratives* that instill *faith*, religion transcends theology and becomes a calling that produces deeds of discipleship.

Religion in its essential nature, we believe, does not exist alongside culture, but is the core of culture. By contrast, the scholastic discipline of theology arose culturally in the context of other academic disciplines. Religions of revelation claim something unique because religion and revelation (something made-known rather than figured-out) go hand in hand and propose a reality other than natural science, whose specific purpose is to explore the natural world. Religion is contained within history, but simultaneously claims to perceive a reality that is beyond history. Religion embraces mystery as distinct from magic. Religion dares to believe that language, the great, culture-building, imaginative tool of humankind's desire, by embracing mystery and using the concept of faith, attained its most far-reaching potential when it articulated stories of a sacred reality.

The word *sacred* comes from the Latin word *sacrare*, which means "set apart." The Greek word *hagios*, meaning "holy," is a related concept enunciating the idea (not the fact) that God (something whole or complete) is not an illusion, but something embedded in the infrastructures of the cosmos. To say that religion is a human construct does not preclude that it is also a meaning-making reality. Humankind cannot declare with certainty what projected human constructs are ultimately true or false until such time as those realities are openly depicted. The realm of verification for both science and religion is always in the future. There is more to come. Both science and religion foretell an ending to humankind's story. Natural science would hardly dare to be a discipline that claims it has all the answers with its mantra of "pending further study." Religion would hardly dare to claim more than a confession flowing out of desire, narrative, and faith, and its mantra should be "pending further experience of the mystery." Science and religion both await an end time when Earth is reduced to a cinder—or the end time when each individual dies. In either case, these end times precipitate a conclusion (cosmically or individually) of history. God-based religions propose humankind will transcend its biological nature to face the mystery-made-known of a God who abides at the interface of cosmos and eternity. Or . . . for those God-centered religions, if God does not abide, we personally, and collectively, will be ashes and dust. For philosophies not centered in God, death may result in a continuum of personal, cyclical rhythms of life, or there may be an unknown continuum, or there may be nothing.

Religion casts the profane as sacred. Profane, a word derived from Latin (*pro*, before + *fanum*, temple), simply means "outside the temple." Religion confronts humankind with the possibility that the cosmosphere (cosmos and living creatures) is also sacred (set apart) and not meaningless. The religious story speaks of a sacred cosmos that evolved out of chaos. The religious story tells of an order of reality that undergirds the Earth and its life-forms with wholeness, well-being, justice, light, and life-alive. Religion envisions the possibility that there are sacred spaces, sacred mountains, sacred rivers, sacred concepts, and sacred people. A religious story assures humankind that everything vulnerable (animate and inanimate) will find a safe space/place within and beyond chaos and darkness where death is abolished. Religious stories summon humankind to perceive the sacred space/place even while existing in the present profane secular world (outside the temple). Religion proclaims that humankind does not stand on the edge of a cosmic precipice unaccompanied. The cosmosphere is safeguarded by the sacred sphere. Some religions posit that in the final analysis nothing (animate or inanimate) is profane (outside the temple).

Science and religion/philosophies were the dominant expressions of meaning-making for cultures; from the primitive, to the archaic, and on to medieval, modern, and postmodern societies. Over time the emphasis shifted. Religion dominated early societies' explanation for the way of things. In contemporary societies, meaning-making has become increasingly expressed in scientific terms and religion often considered, at best, a secondary source of meaning-making.

Science and religion maintain their individual universes of discourse, but still intersect in conversation. What might be the nature of this interaction? The goal is not to produce an abstract theory of religion nor a fusion of world religions. This would destroy the religions of human experience. Distilling science and religion into one, common, linguistic gruel would violate the fundamental presuppositions of both and do harm to both. Both disciplines, however, are irrevocably yoked by the scientific flame-out of our solar system's sun. This conclusion of history—our sun using up its fuel and being extinguished in five billion years—is difficult for finite humans to imagine. However, humans have a unique capacity to anticipate and quantify their own death. The inevitability and proximity of death is profoundly accessible to everyone—terminally inescapable, whether scientist or religious, or both.

Death may take us suddenly and unaware. Or death may gradually squeeze the life out of us in one long, painful, progressive loss of mind and function. We not only lose life, our humanity is debased. These are not abstractions. This isn't theory. It's not philosophical musing. Death—existence followed by the grave—is an ultimate concern. Science, unfortunately, does nothing more than acknowledge this ultimate concern. Science helps the sewage flow downhill and produces electric power grids, but such contrivances are only of proximate benefit. With science we are cosseted, but not comforted. We are amazed, but have no hope. We are enlightened, but not transformed. We enlarge our view of the natural world, but not its cosmic possibilities. Death is the end of life as we know it. There are some few who say, "Fine! So what? Let it come!" But most of us feel a disquieting seed of regret that may ripen into longing, anxiety, or even fear.

No technological discovery has ever addressed *existence* (life) and *non-existence* (death), nor has it established *norms for behavior*. Some technological discoveries—a Hubble photograph of the Horsehead Nebulae, for example—summon us toward the numinous. But this is awe, not righteousness, and adds nothing to our understanding of life and death. Religion posits narratives that are beyond mundane knowledge, mundane experience, and the mundane world. Religion is not the only field of human endeavor that opens us up to a sacred reality. We can argue that human love, poetry, art, music, nature, as well as other modalities, also serve that purpose. But religion offers hope because it not only acknowledges death, but explores the ultimate importance of the mystery of life and death. From the beginning, a corpse was cause for consternation and grief. What had happened? Just moments before, a companion, albeit frail, was warm, breathing, and conversant. Now she is cold, still, and silent, not to be roused. She was here. Now she is gone . . . Why? Where? What now? The story began at the grave site a long time ago . . .

The dead in ancient times were rarely abandoned, although it did occur. Disposing of corpses in some manner was practical, and might have been prompted by propriety or public health concerns. The dead began to stink. Scavengers came prowling. Corpses spread disease. But perhaps . . . just perhaps . . . some sensitive individual came to believe that abandoning (throwing away) the lifeless remains of mother, father, friend, or enemy was disrespectful. It needed tending to and caring for, which included rituals such as the funeral pyre, or leaving the corpse to nature in a ceremonial pallet slung between trees, or in rock crevices or caves. Maybe, someone assumed, the person who inhabited those silent remains had simply departed from ineffectual flesh that could only putrefy. The grave, usually a hole in the ground, became a permanent human institution. Graves were identified and marked by totems. Sometimes, small dwellings were constructed for the dead. Sometimes, elaborate tombs. One thing is certain: graveyards were a hallowed communal shrine.

In what we usually think of as a lowbrow world, early *Homo erectus* had a highbrow existential insight and did something that reveals what he or she was thinking. They interred utensils, tools, weapons, clothing, and amulets with the deceased. Clearly, such things would be needed . . . somewhere . . . beyond the grave . . . in an afterlife. Crude graves were replaced by architectural wonders and elaborate ceremonies as societies became ever more sophisticated. The pyramids of Giza were the tombs of Pharaohs—along with their wives, counselors, personal effects, goods, and animals. The vast tomb of the first Chinese emperor, Qin Shi Huang (third century BCE) contains a clay retinue of 8,000 soldiers, 130 chariots with 520 chariot horses, 150 cavalry horses, as well as other personages and accoutrements needed for his next reign (with more being discovered in continuing digs). Even today, the Montagnard tribes of the central highlands of Vietnam build a small bamboo and thatch hut for their dead. The hut includes a ladder that exits through the roof. For a year, the living tend the grounds, maintain the hut, and bring food and firewood. They then hold a memorial service and the spirit of the deceased climbs the ladder and ascends to a new life. The family abandon the hut and allow it to be reclaimed by jungle. In our postmodern world, many caskets often contain a memento, occasionally something of great value. The mementos are offered as a solicitous gesture, but hark back to the ancient rituals of providing for the dead's future needs. Throughout the millennia, the deceased have been clothed in their Sunday best. Or perhaps in resplendent robes, military uniforms, or costumes. All dressed up ... with someplace to go.

Death was a universal stimulus for religious thought, beginning with the fundamental question, "Where do the dead go?" But other concerns bubbled up from the developing self-consciousness of early humans. Food stores, protection, social structure, and governance were necessities. Sciences, the arts and humanities, mercantilism, professions, and exploration evolved. Everything was interrelated and interdependent, and religion—with its wide variety of concepts and customs, modes and means—was at the heart of it all. Religion embraced revelation, enlightenment, perfection, underpinning a just and peaceful societal order, a coming spiritual world, good news, full understanding, unity of all beings, wholeness, liberation, salvation, fulfilled life, incarnation, reincarnation, resurrection, and paradise. Religion established rituals, worship, prayers, personal devotions, social practices, and traditions. It espoused ethics of love, peace, nonviolence, and justice. Variations on these concepts, customs, and regulations have evolved in all cultures. Religion has never lacked a witness.

Expressions of faith arose within language and culture. Religions occurred within the limitations, hopes, and circumstances of human and historical conditions. Revelations and declamations were constrained by individual human limits. Religion proposed seers, sages, guides, heroes, avatars, and saviors. Special folk—shamans, witch doctors, wizards, medicine men, seers, priests, priestesses, prophets, profound thinkers—went up to the heights and down to the depths, both in geographic actuality and in personal transporting, experiencing dreams and altered states (with or without hallucinogens). The stories were both personal and epic, intimate and fantastical. They recalled natural disasters, floods, volcanic explosions, catastrophic extinction by disease, famine and prosperity, the building and destruction of cities, battles won and lost, peoples enslaved and peoples liberated. They encompassed visions, knowledge, history, intuition, and wisdom. They were infused with discernment, statutes, directives, proclamations, edicts, rituals, stories, and songs. The stories germinated within community memory and were remembered, repeated, revised, improved, amended, and ritualized. They spoke to humankind's deepest longings and held within them the power of their source. They provided inspiration, a compass for the journey and weapons for the fight. They cast lofty visions worthy of the highest aspirations of the human race. They provided insight—inklings—into the age-old question of "*So What?*" Given these complexities, it's a mistake when seeking to understand "religion" and "the religious" to simply make analogies between them. Differences are to be expected and respected.

These received stories—surviving all attempts at suppression over millennia—shone a light into the darkness. But bathed in light, the shadow-side of religion reveals distortions and evils, both in their human perception and in their implementation. Civilization, in its course, has suffered terribly from religion because it can be perverted as a means to an end and used for wicked purposes. One might think, given religion's dark side, and with the ascendency of the scientific method and increasing secularization of our world, religion would cease to exist. But it hasn't.

What kind of creature of biology and spirit is a human being? The religious dimension should stupefy us; like Jonah, when the great fish puked him up in the place where God wanted him to be—a cautionary tale of a mortal too muddled, too fearful, too big for his britches, too proud to kneel.

It makes one think . . . Think with the wholeness of one's being . . .

19

Informed Critique and Rambling Notions

"I hope for the day when everyone can speak again of God without embarrassment."
—Paul Tillich
    Theologian

THE AXIAL AGE ESTABLISHED a unified, methodological pattern of thinking that equipped humankind for the boundless opportunities in the ages that followed. Axial thought was rooted in the concept that the thinker was conscious of playing a role in the thinking process and thereby influencing—by self-awareness, self-criticism, and self-analysis—the conclusions reached. Interpretation based on informed critique became the standard by which every field of human scholarship is refined, validated, or rejected.

The previous synopses of nine great religio-social narratives of the Axial Age are grounded in surviving texts. The texts are complex and nuanced, and though ancient, have had staying power. Scholars have analyzed these documents for thousands of years, drawing on fields as diverse as language, geology, anthropology, archaeology, history, and theology, as well as analytical chemistry and physics. The best scholars dispute academic details. One thing may be noted: the language, ideology, rituals, and symbols found in the texts of the world religions share many similarities.

Archaeology finds no good evidence that Zoroaster, Agamemnon, Moses, Abraham, Homer, Helen of Troy, or Lao Tzu were historical persons. Authentication of their existence comes from within written documents rather than archaeological evidence. Zoroaster is known only from the *Zend-Avesta*; Agamemnon is known only from the *Iliad*; Moses only from the *Pentateuch*. Homer and Hesiod reportedly used ancient Peloponnese stories to construct their written narratives, but scholars debate whether either author was a historical figure. There is evidence that the texts attributed to them may have been written by a series of anonymous poets, or at the very least have undergone later editing. In any case, the gods venerated were those of the Greek pantheon, and the texts became the basis of classical Greek education, the seedbed of Grecian philosophy, and the kernel of Greek drama. The Homeric and Hesiodian stories represent the oldest surviving use of poetic language of *Western* culture. *The Iliad* is about a war far from home. *The Odyssey* is about a post-war journey home. The cast of characters remain some of the most memorable of all literature.

Greek philosophers were revered, but not worshiped, and some, like Socrates, were accused of treason and dispatched by power politics. Knowledge of the historical Socrates is largely a process of deductive reasoning. His ideas were immortalized in the *The Apology*, a work written during the period between his trial and his execution. This great work—held in high esteem but not considered sacred—was edited, and probably supplemented, by Plato or even later writers. Plato understood that Socrates was not just a philosopher, but a significant person with a powerful story. Without Socrates there would have been no Plato. But without Plato there would have been no Socrates.

The primitive tribal stories of the Indus were preserved in the *Rigveda*. The *Upanishads* were added as commentary. Siddhartha Gautama—the historical Buddha—and certainly a renouncer, was the spark for the *Buddhavacana* and the *Suttras*, but neither are believed to have been written by the historical Buddha, nor are they considered revelation. The *Mahābhārata* is another significant Buddhist text. The document is about ten times the length of the *Iliad* and the *Odyssey* combined, and is a tale of the *Kurukshetra* Civil War. Buddha was the Enlightened One, but not a deity, and revered but not worshipped.

Confucius used narrative and ritual drawn from ancient Chinese stories to espouse high ideals and ethical principles of justice that would enhance personal relationships and undergird civil governance. The goal was a good society. He accepted ancestor worship, common to his culture, but did not establish deities. Confucius himself was neither deified nor worshiped. His teachings, preserved in *The Analects*, were not considered verbally inspired or sacred, but were foundational for subsequent Chinese philosophy, which developed as the "Hundred Schools of Thought." Siddhartha Gautama and Confucius are recognized historical figures. The two men were actual contemporaries and shared the same seven decades during the fourth and fifth centuries BCE, dying peacefully as an octogenarian and a septuagenarian one year apart. Their teachings were produced as texts by disciples long after they were deceased.

The tribal Hebrews had patriarchs, prophets, priests, poets, judges, warriors, kings, and queens. They had an oral tradition of foundational stories. There may have been some written documents, but during and after the Babylonian Captivity (*c.* 587 BCE to 539 BCE) scribes preserved their history in the Pentateuch (Latin from Greek for "five books") or Torah (Hebrew for "law" or "doctrine"). Those documents informed the nation of Israel and the worship of Yahweh. The Jews received and revered the Mosaic Law but the eighth-century Jewish prophets expressed the heart of their ethical life. The prophets dealt with the actualities of Jewish historical life in the chaotic messiness of living it. Practical activists rather than theorists, they rode in on their donkey and spoke their piece to prevailing power. Sometimes they stayed and participated in the dust-up they had precipitated and sometimes they continued on their way. Sometimes they were honored, but often were persecuted or killed. Some few, like Elijah, had glorious apocalyptic transformations to paradise.

Isaiah, perhaps the greatest of that prophetic guild, proclaimed in the opening verses of the book that bears his name: "Your sacrifices mean nothing to me . . . Cease to do evil; learn to do good. Seek justice, relieve the oppressed, judge the fatherless, plead for the widow." Micah, a contemporary of Isaiah, taught, "What does the Lord require of you, but to do justice, love kindness, and to walk humbly with your God?" Amos, a prophet contemporary with the previous two, said, "Let love roll down like water and justice like a mighty stream." The wisdom literature of Ecclesiastes teaches, "Fear God, and keep God's commandments, for this is the whole duty of man." Nevertheless, the evidence for the lives of these Hebraic characters resides only in the Old Testament documents themselves and the books that bear their names.

The Jewish narrative was resumed in the New Testament Gospel stories of the life, death, and resurrection of Jesus of Nazareth—a renouncer and announcer. Jesus is considered a historical figure, but there is scant evidence of that. His name is mentioned twice by Josephus (a Jewish historian who defected to the Romans) in his book, *The Antiquities of the Jews* (c. 94–95 CE). The Roman historian, Tacitus (*The Annals*, c. 116 CE), makes reference once to Christus who was executed by Pontius Pilate. Nothing further is known of him from reliable archaeological artifacts outside the Gospels and the apostolic and early post-apostolic writings. Jesus himself authored no texts of record. He once wrote something in the sand as onlookers pondered the moment, but the context of that enigmatic event implies more of a ploy than an offensive parry in his ongoing interactions with his provocateurs. Even so, in spite of the paucity of scientific evidence, Jesus' historical life is almost universally accepted.

Judaism and Christianity are forever linked by their common monotheism and understanding that revelation is made known by a God who interacts in history rather than something humans figure out through striving. The link is actualized by Christian use of the Hebrew Old Testament to claim Jesus is Judaism's messianic fulfillment. Jesus is worshiped by Christians as the Son in a triune God (which created problems during early Christian centuries for those who felt the concept of the Trinity violated monotheism). Modern orthodox Judaism retains a messianic hope, but its aspirations are subsumed in Zionism for many Jews.

Islam shares with Judaism and Christianity a concept of monotheism, and is a religion of revelation grounded in a sacred book that is revered as the Word of God. There is greater archaeological and historical evidence for the life of Muhammad than there is for Jesus. Islam reflects an ethos similar to that espoused by late Jewish prophets through its emphasis on submission and striving for the way of God.

All of the great, overarching narratives alluded to in this and previous chapters share certain existential and ethical insights. They wrestled with the same conundrum: life-its-own-self was unsatisfactory and then you died. They arose under similar conditions of societal upheavals from which the narratives sprang. For instance, Jerusalem and the Temple had been razed by Nebuchadnezzar in 586 BCE and the Jews languished without hope in Babylonian captivity. Athens was disintegrating by the late fifth century BCE following a long, bloody war with Sparta. Neither the gods (the Greek Pantheon) nor the government (the Athenian Senate) had any moral authority. Lawlessness overwhelmed the city, and Socrates, its most prominent citizen, was executed as a pawn in the civil strife. His death ushered in the death of Athens. From this crisis, Athenian philosophers, poets, and playwrights combined to critique Greece's past and draw on its chaotic present to imagine something new, the utopian Republican City.

Or, again, the Hindu *Brahmins* were committed to preserving *dharma*, a "Way of Life" evidenced primarily by duty to one's caste. Confucius was also committed to preserving normative social order (*li*) by appealing to the strength of reason through which individuals would cultivate righteousness and benevolence and strive toward *dao/tao*—literally the *right way*. Chinese *dao* is similar to Hindu *moksha* (salvation or liberation), but also includes the Chinese tradition of "the Way of the Ancestors." Both the historical Buddha and Jesus turned moral life (*dharma*) upside down when they taught that living in "the Way" (expressing righteousness by loving the neighbor and receiving the stranger) was more important than ritual, sacrifice, caste, and race. Zen Buddhism asks the question, "How do we practice the art of living?" Jesus said, "Do this and you will live." Both spoke of salvation, referred to by Buddha as timeless and deathless *nehan*—a blissful afterlife of freedom and total peace of mind—and by Jesus with the images of a messianic banquet at home in God's big house.

An additional commonality among Axial Age religions/philosophies was the idea of the "renouncer." The Hebrew prophets, the historical Buddha, Jesus, and Muhammad all played roles as renouncers. Renouncers essentially stood outside of societal norms and critiqued societal flaws and offered alternative narratives to affect human behavior and effect social change. Sometimes renouncers chose to retreat into the wilderness. Sometimes they were driven into the wilderness. When they reentered society they were often regarded as strangers, aliens, or even traitors to their own kind. Renouncing has been, and remains, a hazardous vocation. This is evident from the historical circumstances surrounding the lives and deaths of the founders of the overarching narratives of Greek thought, *Daoist* Confucianism, Hinduism, Buddhism, Judaism and the prophets, Jesus and Christianity, and Muhammad and Islam. The stories preserved about Jesus elevate him beyond the exemplar of a "renouncer." He was also an "announcer." He created a story in word, deed, and ritual that announced the coming kingdom of God. This story was called gospel (good news)—not good theology, not good religion, and certainly not good law. His contemporaries sometimes referred to him as *rabbi*—teacher. Over time, they called him Master or Lord, and saw in him something more, although they had trouble articulating what that was, and called him Christ (Greek: *khristos*, "anointed") or messiah (Greek from Hebrew: *māšīah*, "anointed").

Grecian philosophers renounced injustice and extolled courage, but did not leave home. Socrates died for his life's work. Greek drama combined poetry, performance, and politics to lead a charge against barbarity. Dedicated *daoists* (*taoists*) showed little interest in the pursuit of ordinary life and were in this sense renouncers, but perhaps with a more secular emphasis in China and a more religious emphasis in India. Classical Hinduism initiated the ideal of renouncing the life of the householder, bogged down in the entanglements of the ordinary, for an itinerant and ascetic life. The Buddhist narrative strongly embraced the concept of the renouncer as one who left home, exemplified in the life of the historical Buddha. Ethical similarities, as previously noted, are juxtaposed in Buddha's statement, "He who sees the true *dharma* (righteousness) sees me; he who sees me sees the true *dharma*," with Jesus' statement, "He who has seen me has seen the Father; he who has not seen me has not seen the Father." Buddha understood that love caused pain when practiced at the level of normal human relationships. He knew that choosing between comparably "right" alternatives created dilemmas that extracted enormous personal cost. Jesus said, "Unless a man hate his father and mother, wife and children, brothers and sisters—even life itself—he cannot be my disciple." These were fiercely demanding ethics. Ethics which were unendurable and unattainable.

These overarching narratives under discussion had differences, of course, but they also endorse similar ideals and teachings, even sharing stories and jargon. For instance, Confucius and Jesus both taught a version of the "Golden Rule" (Do unto others . . .), and Jesus, Confucius, and Buddha expounded upon an ethical life which came to be referred to by disciples of all three men as living in "the Way." Christianity embraced the Suffering Servant motif in Judaism of offering one's self for the good of others. Confucians regarded the state as a repository of the ideal social order and looked to public office and service as their calling. Hindus regarded the social order as independent of the state, although protected by it, and believed their calling was as religious teacher and priest. The state, in both worldviews, was supposed to embrace righteous values. Jesus understood proper societal living as giving to the state what was due the state, and to God what was due God. He was also clear, "No person can serve two masters."

The various sacred texts under discussion also express similar propositions. The East Indian *Upanishads* contain a creation hymn that refers to a beginning that consisted of water and *eros*. Genesis and the Greek writings of Hesiod express similar narrative beginnings. Some *Upanishads* are presented as dialogues, much like Plato's. Hinduism spoke of salvation or liberation (*moksha*). Scholars find similarities between the ethical teachings of the Old Testament prophets, Buddha, Confucius, Plato, and Jesus (in chronological order). "Unsatisfactoriness" in Buddhist thought parallels what Western philosophers, theologians, and mystics refer to as "the dark night of the soul." Buddha and Jesus both used their culture's well known societal stereotypes as foils for teaching: the Brahmins in Buddha's case, while Jesus used the scribes and Pharisees.

Many religions, sects, and denominations embraced the concept that there was something beyond the mundane, material universe that was transcendent. Such thinking led directly to theories that incorporated ideas of the numinous and the spiritual—something-beyond-all-else. The notion of transcendental realms brings something "other" into a discussion that cannot be proven or disproven by empirical methods. In both Islam and Christianity, the narrative projects Muhammad's and Jesus' ascension to heaven. All such concepts required an extension of narratives, or perhaps a different form of narrative. Along with complexity came a simplified and liberating consciousness of what might be possible in the vision quest of mortals.

The ideals championed in the ethics of all of these individuals were lofty and utopian. It's hard to believe they expected them to be realized in the real workaday world by persons inhabiting a real planet Earth. Their ideals established a vivid contrast between what actually was and what ought to be. They all summoned humankind to a higher, better way. Narratives and rituals were established to inform and sustain the ideals. The stories testify that life enmeshes one in trials and troubles, but for each the fate of civilization was not projected as a rising tide of disappointment and bitterness ending with death. Each society produced a narrative that allowed for something beyond—salvation, *moksha, moksa, nirvana, nehan, li,* Plato's Republican City, paradise, heaven, or the messianic banquet.

The authors of this book, standing in both the historic tradition of these narratives and in the shifting sand of a new age called postmodernism, believe it is more human to live in the hope of a meaningful future than to reside in the despair and diminished self-consciousness of nihilism. We affirm a future with one last surprise!

20

Science and Religion

How Do We Know Things?

"The Bible teaches us the way to go to heaven, not the way the heavens go."
  —Galileo Galilei
  Astronomer and Physicist

"The heart has its reasons that reason knows nothing of."
  —Blaise Pascal
  Physicist and Religious Philosopher

"Faith consists in being vitally concerned with that ultimate reality to which I give the symbolic name of God. Whoever reflects earnestly on the meaning of life is on the verge of an act of faith."
  —Paul Tillich
  Theologian

"Science without religion is lame; religion without science is blind."
  —Albert Einstein
  Physicist

HISTORY DOESN'T HAVE TO be written down to be evidence-based, and such history is defined by the term prehistoric (preliterate). Knowledge about ancient times is drawn from artifacts left behind. Artifacts and imagination are the basis of many of the . . . *ologies*. Their observations may be nuanced, but we can't escape the evidence of ancient Earth and its peoples. The historic (literate) epoch is the period captured by the written word. Together, these epochs present a historical record of what has been discovered and explained, what has been done, what has been said, and what has been finally written down and preserved. History (in the abstract) is also what an individual believes to be true (just as in their personal history). This demands that both be governed by evidence and reasoned insight, and also (in the real world) amenable to rectification.

From the stone hand-axe and first altar, science and religion arose side by side in a search for knowledge and meaning-making. Both sprang from innumerable acculturated stories packed with experiences, brimming with discoveries, and infused with inklings, intuitions, musings, and notions. Both believed the universe was alive. Neither distinguished principles of nature from principles of divinity. The ancients came to understand that from a primeval, inexhaustible beginning there was a process of change and differentiation that led to a vast, purposeful cosmos with living creatures. By the time primitive peoples became moderns, evidence-based science nudged religion aside as an unenlightened and unreliable source of knowledge. We must address the question, "How do people know things?"

One method of knowing is the scientific method. We note, to begin with, that there is no such thing as Christian-Science or Science-With-A-Christian-Worldview. Just as there is no such thing as Nihilistic-Science or Science-With-A-Bermuda-Worldview. Regardless of philosophical persuasion, legitimate science would produce legitimate data. Science is just science, a defined discipline of establishing a data base from what is known of the laws of nature. Christianity is a gracious story of hope for humanity mediated by faith. Science and religion are two categories of storytelling with different presuppositions. This is not relativism, but perspectivism, a significant cultural basis of knowing.

Science is the notion that truth can be discovered empirically from the bottom up by taking things apart and seeing what makes them tick. Science's work, in this regard, can be spot-on practical. It pits humankind's intelligence and the five physical senses against the space, time, and mass of the natural universe. Its goal is to understand the natural world and distinguish fact from speculation. In its purest form, protocols are devised to establish truth by conceiving a theory, designing a controlled experiment, making meticulous observations, compiling and interpreting data, and reliably repeating the process. The purpose, at its best, was to dominate and harness nature for the betterment of humankind. It may envision what is unknown, and in so doing such methodology moves us into the near future. Science may predict the middle distance, sometimes imagines a far horizon, and even has its "ah-ha" moments. The narrative of cosmic and biological science is powerful, convincing, and awe-inspiring. The spirit of science gave the discipline wings, but its wings are clipped by its governing maxim: "pending further study."

A second method of knowing is authoritarianism and some believe this is the basis for religion. This is the notion that truth is revealed from on high as dogma and the source of truth holds the power to enforce compliance. Religions that believe in deities point to their God(s) as the ultimate source of authority and imply that such truth is absolute and universal. Authority flows from their sacred texts. Sacred texts must be interpreted, so in actual practice, religious authority defaults in some manner to the religious institutions, structures, persons, and traditions that hold the power. The edge of the abyss looms, regardless of denomination, sect, or ideology, because devoted disciples often claim immunity from erroneous reading of their text. "Not me, I'm not wrong-headed!" And, they will be theoretically correct, within whatever limitations they have assumed, but vexation often is a persistent nag—like a pebble in the shoe.

Most scholars recognize that theological inquiry into the Judaeo-Christian religion is undergirded by four supporting pillars: the Bible, church tradition, reason, and experience. These four pillars provide a stable platform for scholarly work. Some denominations reject the authority of church tradition in decision-making, losing one pillar of support. When scientific facts are removed from scholarship, a second pillar is discarded. Many churches reject personal experience as having any authority in evaluating Judaeo-Christianity. It should be noted that fortification of the disciples' faith after Jesus' crucifixion was the *experience* of his bodily resurrection, not the persuasiveness of their rabbi's teaching. Only one pillar remains standing in the classical system of theological scholarship, the Bible, and its authority is undercut by disputations (from the petty to the profound) over interpretation. Only one thing can be done with a one-legged table. Observe it. It has no use.

Religion and science seem to stand uneasily on opposite sides of a great gulf of reliable knowing. Biblical religion, in its essence, holds out hope for humankind. It expands the vision of humanity's full potential, offers illumination of the mind and inspiration for the spirit, even envisioning a life beyond the grave. It struggles for verification in a world that pays homage to the scientific laboratory for authority. Theological wisdom understands that religion's method is the laboratory of life, not the test tube.

Science has technical genius, but is bereft of morality. When the bombs are made, science has no standard for saying how, when, or even if they should be used. Pure science doesn't give a damn where the bombs come down, it just wants them to go boom. The lesson of civilization from the Stone Age to the Postmodern era is that all of the advances in science *and* religion have not solved, and have only minimally deterred, human being's capacity to lie, cheat, steal, and murder in the greed-driven world of wealth and power. Science envies religion it meaning-making, but recoils because religious tenets are not subject to scientific methods of proof. Religion envies science its theorem-proof factuality and longs to prove that its worldview is true, but cannot do so with scientific tools. Science has neither a vision of hope nor a technique to empower rectitude. Religion loses authenticity when it uses sacred texts to make scientific pronouncements. History has shown there is not only flawed science, but science subverted to evil means. History has also shown there is flawed religion and religion subverted for both banal and wicked purposes.

Dogmas that claim absolute truth have already gone off the rails. The gulf between science and religion can only be bridged when both understand neither works in a realm of Truth with a capital "T." Both disciplines work with partial truth. Greater knowledge always lies in the future for both disciplines. Both disciplines await the unveiling of the next truth or the next surprise. Science has reached the limits of its discipline when it has made its partial pronouncements on nature. Religion/philosophy has reached the limits of its disciplines when it utters the words *God* or *nehan*. The authors of this book believe it is both fruitless and corrupting to try to create a hybrid of science and religion by homogenizing or harmonizing them. There is another way. Religion offers science and philosophers alike a *redemptive* way of knowing because desire, narrative, and faith are basic to human nature. Desire (*eros*)—passionate knowing *experientially* with body, mind, and spirit—is the critical dimension of "knowing" the narratives that create faith. Dogmas of absolute truth must yield to listening to the story. Such knowing is relational and is both rational and visceral—intellect and gut. Relational knowing—whether, for example, knowing God or one's spouse—is propelled by *eros*. It's not necessary to be able to explain everything or answer every question for the "knowing" to have an authentic foundation.

The scientific laboratory and the laboratory of life must be in continuous interplay. Otherwise we pretend—live with the pretense—that making something more concrete makes it more real. This is to believe that dissecting a flower is the same as appreciating it. Or to believe that knowledge and wisdom are the same thing. In the narratives of religion and philosophy, we understand that the characters' experiences in *their* particular narrative are *our* experiences in our particular narrative. However, the only way we can make a narrative our own is by acting in faith—a holistic way of knowing that goes beyond mere cognition. This passionate, experiential, coherent, narrative way of knowing in religion helps us move forward in faith as we live into the future.

Living and loving dimensions are relational and social dimensions. They encompass the body, mind, spirit, the heart and the will. They are mindfully visceral and viscerally mindful. Relational knowing requires dynamic encounter and engagement. The God known to humankind through religion is erotic—passionately connected with our creaturely existence and passionately concerned in our actions. Through religion we acknowledge the past, involve ourselves in the present, while anticipating a hallowed future.

Creating a false dichotomy between science and religion eviscerates humanity of its greatness. Neither science nor religion can denigrate the other without debasing humans and their culture. Knowing must be extended beyond a purely rational examination of our world, or by imposing authoritarian knowledge by fiat coerced by force (whatever the source). This opens the way for science, religion, and all of the humanities to be conversation partners in the search for meaning. Science lost its way when it mistook chemical elements for human beings and wavelengths of light for wisdom. Human beings, in their wholeness, know instinctively they are more than cells with an electrical charge. More than thinking, digesting, hydraulic, ambulating, consuming, and acquisitive molecular machines. Religion lost its way when it mistook sacred texts for science texts. Religion lost its way when it exchanged relational faith for believing in propositions. Faith lost its way when it mistook certitude for trust. The offerings of both science and religion are fragmentary. Science and religion would benefit from returning to the beginning and articulating a coherent story. Full verification for both always lies in the future.

Science and religion do share one common attribute: hubris. This is to their detriment. It is difficult sometimes to determine which one boasts the biggest load of conceit. Science may be pure, but its practitioners aren't. Science has demonstrated bitter rivalries for dominance, competition for government and private money, for research space, and for the academic, industrial, business, and good-old-boy networks that lead to fame and fortune. Sophistication joins with shenanigans to make or break careers. There is not only reluctance to share research for the greater good, but poor scholarship, shoddy work, extravagant showmanship, grandstanding, a rush to publish, and outright fraud. Analytical thinking is the apogee of science, but greed, wealth, and power can easily crowd out evidence-based standards. As for religion, it fights for money, property, power, prestige, numbers, Nielsen ratings, Emmys, and egos. Greed, wealth, and power subverts faith. Both the scientist and the theologian despise the other's cocksure arrogance. Can science and religion, without doing damage to their singular, cultural universes, maintain their integrity when their stories intersect in the vast narrative of humanity? Science and religion must each understand (stand under) the calling of their discipline, rather than set them in conflict or harmonize and homogenize them.

Science and religion need each other, for at the end of the day both are time-warped back to the primitive grave site, seated side by side, heartsick to comprehend the fundamental meaning of life and death. And narrative is still the vehicle for communication. The last conscious thought of scientist or theologian, on their deathbeds, will surely not be the refinement of some arcane bit of academe, but rather upon the great mystery of the moment—living and no longer being alive. If humans can only be weighed and quantified within the construct of science, we are to be pitied above all creatures because we have inklings of other knowledge. *Homo sapiens sapiens* (AMH) of the animal kingdom have profoundly intuitive spiritual feelings. These feelings—deep within us, as yet scientifically unquantified, and we may believe never to be so quantified—inform our being that there is more to us than data. Boiled down in a test tube, a human being is surely more than $3.79 worth of elements in the Periodic Table. We desire . . . ache . . . long . . . for more. But, just aching for something doesn't ground it in possibility. Longing must be measured against what we know of reality.

The Enlightenment, an intellectual movement of the seventeenth and eighteenth centuries, set the stage for the next 200 years of profound advancement in Western civilization. Bracketed by the fall of two walls—the French Bastille in 1789 and the Berlin Wall in 1989—the nineteenth and twentieth centuries were techno-cultural marvels blessed by a cornucopia of plenty and cursed by violence. Modernism bequeathed technologies and resources to address society's pernicious flaws—poverty, disease, hunger, racism, violence, war, xenophobia, and misogyny. There were moments of optimism when it was believed all that was required was the will to act to usher in a new age of prosperity and peace. Two powerful cultural forces—secular humanism and religion—focused their efforts on making this happen.

Secular humanism was a philosophy of optimism reveling in the advances of natural science, social science, the humanities, and technology. The Humanist Manifesto of 1933, setting forth its principles, was signed by Nobel laureates, scientists, philosophers, church leaders, cultural notables, educated elites, and politicians. The original document was updated in content and signatories in 2003 by the American Humanist Association under the title, *Humanism and Its Aspirations*. Secular humanism attempted to uplift the world through high culture—philosophy, literature, poetry, drama, music, science, technology, law, medicine, and education.

Religion was the second force for bringing in the new millennium. We have previously discussed nine text-based, ancient religions and philosophies worthy of consideration as a way of being. The authors will narrow our focus at this juncture to Protestant Christianity—the author's heritage. We acknowledge Roman Catholicism's two-millennia history of charitable work. Protestant churches in America invested themselves in the good works of a social gospel, but many disagreements (doctrinal and institutional) shaped the manner in which it was carried out. The stage was set for a battle over the Bible.

The battle was waged on two fronts. One was between "liberal" and "conservative" wings of the Protestant church. Closely related was the battle between some "conservative" religionists and science. The growing body of knowledge in natural and life sciences challenged long-held assumptions about the Bible. The rise of the historical/critical method for evaluating ancient texts required reevaluation of notions about biblical inspiration and inerrancy. The 1859 publication of Charles Darwin's book, *On the Origin of Species,* undercut a literal interpretation of creation recounted in the first two chapters of Genesis.

The Protestant world split into two groups. Generally speaking, mainline Protestant churches accepted Enlightenment views on natural and social science and this view—labeled *liberal*—contributed to their social activism. The liberal churches took up the abolitionist cause in antebellum America, and went on to address prison reform, poverty, hunger, health, violence, civil rights, and gender and sexual identity issues. The remaining denominations—labeled *conservative*—generally believed Enlightenment views on natural science violated their doctrine of biblical inerrancy. These denominations—among them staunch biblicists, resolute cultural pietists, charismatics, and evangelicals—chose a path in which inconvenient scientific facts were denied or ignored.

The term *fundamentalist* entered the lexicon of religious language at the turn of the twentieth century, drawn from *The Fundamentals: A Testimony To The Truth,* a twelve-volume work with numerous contributors. The collection was serially published between 1910 and 1915 to establish orthodox biblical doctrine. Topics included proof of the living God, proof of the Bible (often using snippets of science), support for literal interpretation of the early narratives of Genesis, and many others—usually leading to identifying markers for the One True Church. If such fundamentals (and the emphases varied) were not embraced, personal salvation was forfeited. During that time, various fundamentalist or conservative denominations chose heartfelt, cultural expressions for their Christianity that served their faith. These cultural expressions often became quite distinguishing, a pattern or process of life or doctrine regarded by the general public as quaint, quirky, ill-informed, or foolish. Still, these expressions of doctrine and piety were humored or ignored. But, when the fundamentalists, conservatives, and evangelicals denied science, it was impugned as a rejection of reality. Akin to believing a stork brings babies.

Consequently, the eighteenth, nineteenth, and twentieth centuries found mainline, liberal Protestant churches linking Christian morality with social justice. This wing of Protestantism and the secular humanists shared similar goals. The accomplishment of social justice would usher in a new age of humane living through self-improvement and societal advancement. Church and secular humanists differed over motivation. Liberal protestant churches believed they were doing God's work. Secular humanists were empowered optimists. For both groups, social progress was evidence that the world was getting better and better. Bertrand Russell (1872–1970), philosopher, mathematician, and Nobel laureate wrote, "Religion is something left over from the infancy of our intelligence; it will fade away as we adopt reason and science as our guidelines."

Two cataclysmic events, one in the nineteenth and one in the twentieth century, destroyed both the secular humanist's and the church's optimistic view of the future. On September 17, 1862, almost 23,000 soldiers (North and South) were killed, wounded, or missing at Antietam, making it the bloodiest single day of the American Civil War. The second event occurred during World War I on the opening day of the allied Somme River offensive in France. On that single day, July 1, 1916, the British army suffered 54,470 casualties (19,240 KIA), while the French Army sustained 1,590 casualties overall. The German Army had approximately 11,000 casualties. Such slaughter made it difficult for either secular humanists or the church to imagine an optimistic future for humankind. The human race seemed on the path of chaos and destruction, in spite of the social gospel of the church or the bright, onward and upward future proposed by secular humanism. The Christian church and secular humanism both found their belief systems inadequate to the realities of their times. Human effort had severe limitations in the face of human nature. Cultural and social challenges since World War II have done nothing to brighten our view of human progress.

Secular humanists and liberal Protestants have been horror struck through World War I, World War II, Nazism, fascism, the Holocaust, communism, the Gulag, Korea, the Great Leap Forward, the Cultural Revolution, Vietnam, the Killing Fields, the negative effects of greed-and-power–driven capitalism, increasing societal dysfunction, purposeful evil, mindless violence, terrorism, the health plague of AIDS and drugs, and the endless wars of the last quarter of the twentieth century and opening decades of the twenty-first, all within the flourishing of an enlightened, scientific era. These hard realities grievously wounded—if not killed—the vision of onward and upward through human effort. Disillusionment and disappointment resulted.

The conservative, fundamentalist, evangelical Protestants faced the same hard realities, and made a stupefying decision: if (their view of) the Bible wasn't true, Christianity wasn't true. The result was denial. They rejected any science that confronted their belief system with inconvenient facts and chose a world-denying piety that retreated from science, culture, and coherence. These churches' views of the modern and postmodern world were rendered quaint. Why should a terrorized and troubled world believe any pronouncements coming from a religious source whose basic conceptualization of the universe was a standing joke? Such thinking germinated into a mind-set that set the stage for a post-truth era where facts were dismissed as falsehoods. Succumbing to purveyors of fake news, a voting bloc formed wherein Christian folk shamelessly traded their moral ethic for the porridge of political power—the oldest sellout in the history of religion. Their Christian preaching emphasized a biblically sanctioned aspiration for personal success and wealth, and preparation for the final, apocalyptic judgement of God through personal salvation.

The damage was incalculable for any religion that included body, heart, soul, and mind. Members of those denominations faced a personal choice. Check their brains and personal experience at the door of the sanctuary, remain with the fellowship, and keep their mouths shut. Or, leave and face the recriminations and opprobrium of their fellowship. A religious narrative of knowing and understanding—*What?* and *So What?*—had to be redeemed.

PART TWO

SO WHAT?

Religion: A Christian Perspective on the Dynamic of Faith

"If seven maids with seven mops
Swept it for half a year,
Do you suppose," the Walrus said,
"That they could get it clear?"
"I doubt it," said the Carpenter,
And shed a bitter tear.
—Charles Lutwidge Dodgson, aka Lewis Carroll
  Mathematician, Anglican Cleric, and Writer

21

Beings of Desire
The Yearning Heart

"If you want to build a ship, don't drum up people to collect wood and don't assign them tasks and work, but rather teach them to long for the endless immensity of the sea."
—Antoine de Saint-Exupery
    Aviator and Writer

Desire is a deep, biological urge that is one of life's givens. Desire is the visceral instinct that fuels our creaturely existence. Desire isn't a philosophical abstraction and is more than a swooning heart. Desire is anatomy and physiology, cellular biology and molecular chemistry, and erotic essence. Desire (the great impulse) drives great thought, great culture, great science, great art, great adventures, great love affairs, and great faith, as well as great longing for beauty, goodness, and truth, and yes, great love between disciples and their God(s).

Without *desire*, humans would have little interest in either the "*What?*" or the "*So What?*" of this world. The scientific language necessary to address "*What?*" (nature's givens) was never far from philosophical musings of "*So What?*" (how we shall live in relationship to everything and everyone). Humankind's inquiring mind not only delved into the nature of the cosmos, but also, in every time and place, posited sacredness.

Religion attempts to characterize how the sacred reality safeguards the secular. Religion is the language of confession—not science. It is the language *of* our lives, not the language *about* our lives. Each individual seeks a place to stand within the infinite cosmos, while operating from the finite experience of their own race, culture, civilization, and geography. Every person inches toward the grave searching for a foothold at its edge. Prehistory and history—era upon era, civilization upon civilization, culture after culture—document religion's tale. Humankind's quest for "*So What?*" emphasizes meaning-making, establishes values, and weighs consequential commitments.

Webster defines desire as "A strong feeling, craving, or yearning for anything, and is often used in a sexual sense." That definition is a starting point, but it leaves us cold. One can see the dust mites scrabbling off the desiccated page. Humans know from life experience that without desire we become, in Einstein's phrase, a "snuffed out candle." His metaphor positions us to see the light and feel the heat, and causes our heart to sink at the thought of the flame burning out—or worse, being snuffed out. Auden sees desire (*eros*) as the combustible fuse that touches off the primal matter (dust) of our fleshy bodies, igniting life as an "affirming flame."

Psychologists have explored the fundamental role desire plays in the development of the human personality. The hierarchy of human needs includes physical survival (food, air, and water), safety (protection), social welfare (connections), sex (species survival), and transcendence (reaching beyond ourselves in all of our aspirations—in science, the humanities, arts, and religion). Desire, inherent to our creaturely life, establishes a hierarchical need for religion. Two million years of evolution and development have neither bred nor refined that out of us. That's curious, because religion has generally tried to stamp out desire. Religion, by and large, is uncomfortable with desire, whether as a fleshly urge or a theoretical concept. Hinduism sees God as a loving couple and sexuality as a sacralized blessing of human activity. The Greeks conceived a sexual pantheon and their mythology incorporated masculine and feminine Gods. Judaism saw their monotheistic God as male, although many feminine images of God reside in Hebrew texts. The historical Jesus of Christianity was male. The mature, Christian theological concept of a trinitarian God was historically expressed as Father, Son, and Holy Spirit. In recent decades, in an effort to move beyond sheer male images, the phrase Creator, Redeemer, and Sustainer has been used.

The historical Christian church from the beginning struggled with human desire, flesh-and-blood sexuality, and a divine savior incarnated (Latin: *incarnare*: *in*, into + *carn*, flesh). This mind-boggling challenge led to the ascetic sects, the withdrawal from society, celibate clerics, monastic societies, and Gnosticism. Gnosticism (Greek: *gnosis*, esoteric knowledge) was an early Christian sect that believed all matter was bad and only the spirit was good. Gnostics embarked on a spiritual dualism that pitted flesh and body against spirit and mind. The creation, they taught, was the product of some distant emanation of a God who would scarcely deign to have anything to do with a physical world. Therefore, Jesus was only a spirit who seemed to be flesh and blood. Gnostics stressed a world-denying piety based on fleshly denial. They exalted esoteric knowledge over material involvement, rationality over passion, spirit over body, and abstraction over incarnation. Much of the early church's energy was directed at what was termed the Gnostic heresy.

Gnostic heresy during the early Christian centuries is what *agape* is to Greek linguistics in recent centuries. Long-standing religious anxiety in the presence of desire (linguistic or actual) requires we take a moment to parse the Greek word *agape*, which scholars note is used for whatever Aramaic word Jesus used for "love." Theological systems and dogma have been formulated throughout Christian history based upon single, nuanced Greek words—often a slippery doctrinal slope. *Agape* is one such word. The Greek language used four words to address the dynamic concept of love: *agape, philia, storge,* and *eros*. We reject a Christian theology that makes any of the Greek *love*-words antithetical.

Scholars tell us *agape* is an unselfish, giving love that seeks the highest good of the other. *Philia* is the love of friendship. *Storge* is the love of family. *Eros* is the Greek word for visceral desire, but is not *epithumia* (Greek for our word *lust*). By itself, *eros* connotes erotic love (and is the name assigned to the Greek God of love), but *eros* is not the same as lust precisely because *eros* is infused with *agape, philia,* and *storge*, just as they are infused with *eros*. When examined separately, the nuanced dimensions of each are instructive. However, strict linguistic distinctions, for all of its academic value, robs each individual word of depth and breadth. The durable, serviceable *love* that could cut it in the workaday world of both the first and twenty-first century is braided of strands from the four Greek *loves*—neither single strand of which stands strong alone. The four must be conflated for any one of the notions to be alive and vibrant. Christian *love* reduced to separate, nuanced categories results in a religion that is merely a matter of feeling (having to do with the viscera), or merely a matter of knowing (having to do with the intellect), or merely a matter of action (having to do with the will). Together, Christian *love* is expanded beyond self-gratification, self-centeredness, and self-interest. Without *agape*, the other three are selfish. Without *philia*, the other three are friendless. Without *storge*, the other three have no society. Without *eros*, the other three are impotent. *Eros* empowers the other three and the other three make *eros* humane. Loving in all its forms is visceral longing. Love cannot exist without desire. Desire is not an outlier to Christianity, but integral to it.

Understanding the four Greek-*loves* as indivisible summons a longing, a visceral desire which quickens the biblical narrative to kindle the faith that empowers life-alive. In this manner, our entire self is passionately invested in authentic, energetic, imaginative, creative, curious, humorous, vibrant relationships. To the degree that any of the Greek-*loves* is deficient or missing, our Christian walk is not just halfhearted (or quarter-hearted), but consists of imposing on others what we define as good for them in a self-interested, domineering, and coercive manner. The conflated Greek-*loves* make possible walking in the Way. Or walking a mile in another's shoes—all circumstance and context. Without that erotic, unselfish, friendly, brotherly/sisterly, all-embracing empathetic dynamic, it would be impossible to fulfill the goal of any of the four nuanced, separatist Greek-*loves*. Without *eros* love is neutered. We couldn't make sexual love, we could only make motions. Without *eros* we couldn't make *agape*, we could only make notions. Without *eros* we couldn't make *philia*, we could only make acquaintances. Without *eros* we couldn't make *storge*, we could only make genealogies. When we extend love in separatist categories (*agape* her, *philia* them, *storge* some, and *eros* one), our love is not just fragmented, but a world-denying antiseptic idea rather than a world-engaging celebration of the love affair between a passionate God and the God's creation.

Just as humans are indivisible persons who are bodily, soulfully, mindfully, psychologically, and spiritually integrated—an enfleshed whole—the four Greek-*loves* are not part this and part that, but a combustible whole that sets life ablaze through an encounter with an inviting, passionate, empowering God. We are saved from the life barely lived by the *Shema*—loving God with the heart, soul, strength, and mind. This is the mature Judeao-Christian proclamation of poets, prophets, wisdom teachers, and Jesus. Jesus' words should startle us out of our complacency:

"I have come that you might have life and have it abundantly." Incarnational encounter replaces isolated theological speculation. Walking in the Way replaces toeing the line. Ethics replace edicts. Future-opening relationships replace closed systems that drain life of vitality. Dynamic engagement replaces pious preachments, sweet sentimentality, and organizational schemes that lay a frost on the soul. The Christian hope is not to escape life, but to prevent life from escaping us. The story of Jesus informs us that if we love passionately, we will suffer. Cruciform love makes it possible to endure tragedy, knowing that love and suffering are linked. But through loving passionately, we will encounter joy.

Desire joined with narrative and faith make the Judeo-Christian experience holy and wholly possible. It is specifically to that narrative and that confessed faith we now turn.

22

Narrative Theology

"Even such is life that takes in trust,
Our youth, our joys, our all-we-have,
And pays us but with earth and dust,
Who in the dark and silent grave,
When we have wandered all our ways,
Shuts up the story of our days,
But from this earth, this grave, this dust,
My God shall raise me up, I trust."

>   —Sir Walter Raleigh
>   Explorer and Writer
>   *Poem, discovered in the flyleaf
>   of his Bible after his death.*

THE BIBLE NARRATIVE IS a love story, passionate to the core. The characters—including Jesus—are reassuringly human. It begins with a creation epic that deity pronounced good: God lives and is the source of life. A patriarchal God the Jews called Yahweh initiated a pilgrimage with and within the creation. God searched out humans for the covenant relationships described in the Old Testament. This was not enough for the fulfillment of divine love. There was much more. The Christian church expresses "*For God so loved the world . . .*" in the language of incarnation, accomplished through the birth of Mary of Nazareth's firstborn son.

The story is not about gynecology, but gospel—a tale of absolute wonder wherein God's fully divine presence was and is mediated through an encounter with a fully human Jesus. A fully human Jesus driven to survive and to thrive (desire hardwired), *of* God and *from* God *to* God, was and is an unbelievably scandalous reality. But, that's the story!

In first-century Palestine, divinity lived life in a flesh-and-blood body like ours and experienced the natural world of cosmic and biological evolution all humanity has experienced. Jesus, like every other human being before and after him, gasped for air and suckled at his mother's breast. Driven by those two primal instincts, Jesus climbed aboard the "Streetcar Named Desire" and was off on his earthly journey. Every step was an encounter with another person, another place, another situation, issue, and challenge. Relationships were grounded in his creaturely existence, drawing on his faith in God and the enlarging vision of his calling. A descendant in the tribe of Judah through the lineage of David, he was circumcised on the eighth day: it bled and it hurt. Spoiler alert—he was squalling; like a baby. He had childhood fevers, tonsillitis, and diarrheal illness under the watchful, worried eyes of his mother and father—Mary and Joseph. He was taught to fasten his sandals, put his robe on right-side-out, and comb his hair. He learned language, the acculturation and socialization of being a Jewish male in a conquered land, as well as his religion, in the care of his parents. In his youth, he worked in his father's carpentry shop. He was instructed in the use of saw and mallet; plane and plumb line. When he hit his thumb with the mallet he hopped around on one foot, squeezed his thumb, and groaned *something* in exasperation and pain. He was hungry and thirsty, got splinters and bug bites, and acquired calluses. He became familiar with the temple built by his forebear, King Solomon, and restored by his ancestors who returned from Babylonian captivity. On at least one occasion, in what must have been a remarkable encounter, he engaged his elders in a discussion of the law and proffered instruction. One gasps at his audacious precocity, if not impudence. It was the opening round in his ongoing conflict with the leaders who spoke for official Judaism.

Jesus read the Torah, observed the Sabbath, and celebrated the Passover. He had a younger brother, with all that entails, and a widening circle of men and women friends. He experienced sexuality as *Homo sapiens sapiens* (AMH) of the male gender. If we deny that sphere of his humanity, we deny the incarnation. A compelling theological insight of modern times is the love song of Mary Magdalene in *Jesus Christ Superstar*,

"I don't know how to love him . . ." It has been assumed, but without substantiation, that Jesus never experienced a sexual relationship. That would have been a choice for him. But all persons of the male gender know that the fully human Jesus had erections and nocturnal emissions. He socialized and he was solitary. He dined in company at open tables and with intimates in closed circles. He went to weddings and funerals, addressed large crowds, and was sought out, sometimes furtively, as a confidant. He had moments of acclaim and adulation. He was famous, you know, in his particular world.

Jesus lived life in all of its humanity, sweating under our sun and bathed in the light of our moon. With growing self-awareness, he dedicated himself to a God mission. Whatever else Jesus was, he was a man of faith. His faith set him on a collision course with the socioeconomic and religio-political realities of his time and place—Roman-occupied Palestine. He was executed on a cross at the instigation of religion and empire. He died a mortal death and his lifeless body was placed in a tomb. But this was not "The End" to the gospel story. The narrative resumes when the disciples experienced Jesus' *resurrection in his body* and witnessed his glorification as *ascension*. In Jesus, God's love affair with humankind bore all the mysterious complexities of life itself—followed by death.

The story surrounding Jesus' life and death in Palestine, and witnessed by family, friends, and enemies, was disseminated throughout the Mediterranean first-century world. The first preachers of gospel proclaimed and confessed the full humanity of Jesus, as did the ancient Christian creeds of later centuries. The full humanity of Jesus was hard for some Christians back then, as evidenced by the Gnostics. It's hard for some Christians now, as evidenced by a secularization of the cosmosphere that allows no room for the sacred. But God outflanked humankind when deity's desire to be one with creation culminated in a narrative of good news made known through faith. God's creative Word was inspirited in flesh and inspirited in text. The tangible, corporeal life of the fully-human Jesus was almost concurrently documented in written texts grafted onto the Jewish writings that set them in context. How should the biblical text—long affectionately regarded by Christians as the Good Book—be read and understood?

* * * * *

The Bible was not lowered down, leather-bound, through a hole in the heavens on a celestial umbilical cord. Although, that idea may work in a theo-poetic sense! Clearly, the two volumes of collected anthologies arose in the context of history. They preserve the written witness to Judeao-Christian monotheism. Judaism reveres the Old Testament (the Hebrew Bible) as sacred stories revealed (made known) through their experience of life. Christians believe the Old Testament is their book too, and from which the Christian Testamentary story arises. Together, the Old and New Testaments make up the Christian Bible, and Christians acknowledge both anthologies as sacred stories revealed (made known) through their experience of life.

Scholarship tells us, as mentioned in the discussion of Judaism, that the documents of the Old Testament were written in Hebrew by scribes around the time of the Babylonia captivity (587 to 538 BCE). Scholarship also tells us the documents of the New Testament were most probably written in common Greek (as opposed to classical Greek) during the first decades of the Common Era, even though the general populace living in Palestine at that time (including Jesus) spoke a Syrian dialect of ancient Persia—Aramaic. We have no autographed copies of any documents in either Testament, and Hebrew and Greek remain the languages of Bible scholars.

The first-century Christian church was a devoted group of disparate confessing believers in the Jesus story. More than a few early Christians—certainly not all—knew Jesus before and after his resurrection. Many early Christians—again, not all—knew certain apostles or other eyewitnesses of Jesus. In nurturing the early church, and particularly as living witnesses died, various persons wrote histories, letters, essays, and other expositions that were accumulated within the early church communities. These highly regarded writings were circulated among believers. We must assume that the documents were here and there, no doubt seen briefly and passed on. Some Christians may have seen one, or even several, other disciples saw and read none, and no one possessed all of them in those early decades. Christians confessed Jesus, lived the Way, worshiped, and proclaimed the gospel that formed communities that persevered as an ever-expanding discipleship scattered throughout the Mediterranean world.

The historical and empirical reality in response to the "proclamation of the Jesus story" was and is the living and growing community of faith. It is expressed boldly in an early letter from Paul the Apostle, who himself experienced an encounter with the risen Christ, which was of such a nature that his own narrative was forever altered. He makes clear that the witness to Jesus' bodily resurrection was not a single incident to a cloistered few, but repeatedly and to many. This is his statement of faith to the Corinthians. "Now I would remind you, brothers and sisters, of the good news that I proclaimed to you, which you in turn received, in which also you stand, through which also you are being saved, if you hold firmly to the message that I proclaimed to you—unless you have come to believe in vain. For I handed on to you as of first importance what I in turn had received: that Christ died for our sins in accordance with the scriptures, and that he was buried, and that he was raised on the third day in accordance with the scriptures, and that he appeared to Cephas, then to the twelve. Then he appeared to more than five hundred brothers and sisters at one time, most of whom are still alive, though some have died. Then he appeared to James, then to all the apostles. Last of all, as to one untimely born, he appeared also to me. For I am the least of the apostles, unfit to be called an apostle, because I persecuted the church of God. But by the grace of God I am what I am, and his grace toward me has not been in vain. On the contrary, I worked harder than any of them—though it was not I, but the grace of God that is with me. Whether then it was I or they, so we proclaim and so you have come to believe."

Paul was unable to leave it at that. He circled back a moment later, driven by conviction and concern, to hammer home his understanding of gospel. His incredulity at the confusion of some Corinthian Christians is obvious—as is his fervor. "Now if Christ is proclaimed as raised from the dead, how can some of you say there is no resurrection of the dead? If there is no resurrection of the dead, then Christ has not been raised; and if Christ has not been raised, then our proclamation has been in vain and your faith is in vain." And one more time for good measure—an exasperated postscript! "For if the dead are not raised, then Christ has not been raised. If Christ has not been raised, your faith is futile . . ."[1] The resurrection is theologically indispensable to the Jesus story. Call it what we like—paranormal, post-nature, supra-natural, a miracle. A resurrection to life is no more or less awe-inspiring than a creation to life or an

---

1. 1 Cor 15:1–14, 16, 17, NRSV.

evolution of life. The story is not over. Life *is* more than molecules. Without the resurrection we are not disciples; we are Christian philosophers.

We cannot escape the fact that the response to the Jesus proclaimed in the core gospel narrative changed individual lives and altered the world. Death, the last great enemy of abundant life, was overcome in Jesus' resurrection. Paul is obsessed with this witness. He was not concerned with a human comprehension of *how* it transpired. It was just the rest of the story. Resurrection is not a proposition but a confession. It is not speculation, but a way of living and dying in faith, hope, and love. It is not a matter of explanation but of encounter. It is not a matter of certitude but trust. It is not a matter of proof, but of possibility. Confession is to live in the whole story. The full dimension of the good news overcomes human limitations that are simply too finite, too unimaginative, and too nihilistic. The Greek word for gospel—*euangelion*—means "good news." If the story is not surprising, it is not "news." If the news is not "good," it is not gospel. Humankind has always lived with a vision of hope in an open future with "more to come."

The early phase of historical Christianity ended with the conversion of Emperor Constantine, who ruled the Roman Empire from 306 CE to 337 CE. He made Christianity the empire's state religion in 324 CE. This phase of church history played out over approximately three and one-half centuries (about as long as it took for the American Colonies to become the present-day United States of America). Christianity transitioned from life as a persecuted minority to being, in some places, a fully accepted majority. During this time, the Christian writings were accumulated, sorted out, reviewed, their provenance debated, until finally twenty-seven documents were sanctioned as authentic in various counsels assembled during the fourth century CE by church authorities. The New Testament canon was declared closed by those historical acts and that historical church. Those sanctioned documents recorded the foundational history of the church to that date and have been a constant reference point for subsequent confessing Christians.

The biblical documents themselves encompass some 1,750 years of specific human history. The narrative begins with a legendary tale of beginnings and ends with a projected apocalyptic image of the end time. The beginning tells of an innocent paradise in which human beings fall into self-consciousness of desire and rebellion to the way things were to be. They are driven from the garden and face death—returning to innocence is not an option. The ending is an apocalyptic story of an open city in an entirely new heaven and a new Earth. The first story is before history. The second story is after history. The first story is before religion is needed. The second story is after religion was needed. In between, the Bible weaves a tale of nostalgia for a home that was lost and an anthem of desire for a home that is yet to be realized.

Religion and mystery share common ground. The Bible, eyes wide open and with a realism that is embarrassing and authenticating, tells intimate stories (Noah's poor daughters) and epochal stories (the trumpets of Jericho). They speak of life and death, war and peace, of empires emerging and disintegrating, of power and violence, bondage and freedom, the lost and found, of love and betrayal, of faith ringing with hope, and of perfidy with death-knell despair. The Bible also contains non-narrative writing—genealogies, dietary restrictions, hygienic strictures, codifications, commentaries, poems, prayers, songs, erotica, and varied cultural emphases and interpretations—but these have no purpose without the fundamental narrative.

The text itself is filled with introspection, analysis, critique, and theologizing. Secondary thinking has created scholastic disciplines such as theology, and together with the study of languages, anthropology, archaeology, sociology, philosophy, geography, and world history shed light on technical particularities, peculiarities, and conflicted details of the Testaments. This is informative and interesting, but may shift the reader's emphasis from a living faith to codification, propositions, doctrinal concepts, proof texts, philosophy, or science. Such emphases can distract from the very nature of biblical faith—those stories that define the relationship between humankind and a God who showed both Godness and human-ness. We find ourselves in those stories and it is always to the narrative—of the Bible and of our own lives—that we return. The story is not just to convey information; rather its function and purpose is human transformation and numinous inspiration.

The biblical literature is grounded in and judged by its primal core narrative. Both Testaments are a witness that point beyond the text to a person—to the God who acts in history and covenants with beloved people for the sake of a beloved creation. The sum and substance of Judaeo-Christian religion is to choose life and to love. We have previously referred to Deuteronomy texts (the *Shema*) that proclaim, "Hear, O Israel! The Lord our God is one Lord; and you shall love the Lord your God with all your heart, and with all your soul, and with all your might, and with all your mind." And again, "I have set before you life and death, blessing and cursing: therefore choose life, that both you and your seed may live." The three Synoptic Gospels record Jesus' reference to the *Shema*: "Love the Lord your God with all your heart, and with all your soul, with all your strength, and with all your mind," adding, "Love your neighbor as yourself. Do this," Jesus said, "and you will live." These recitations claim that despair is redeemed by hope; life is victorious over death. Human consciousness can never again be the same.

Old Testament scholars such as Gerhard von Rad called the core narrative of the Hebrew scripture its *credo*—its confession of faith. New Testament scholars such as C. H. Dodd called the core narrative of the New Testament the *kerygma*—the foundational preaching of the gospel story. Walter Brueggemann, in recent years, has used the term *primal narrative* to speak of the central story of the Bible. He cast the various forms of literature in the biblical canon as concentric circles of a target for simple clarification (illustration used by permission).

Target As Simple Classification of Biblical Literature[2]

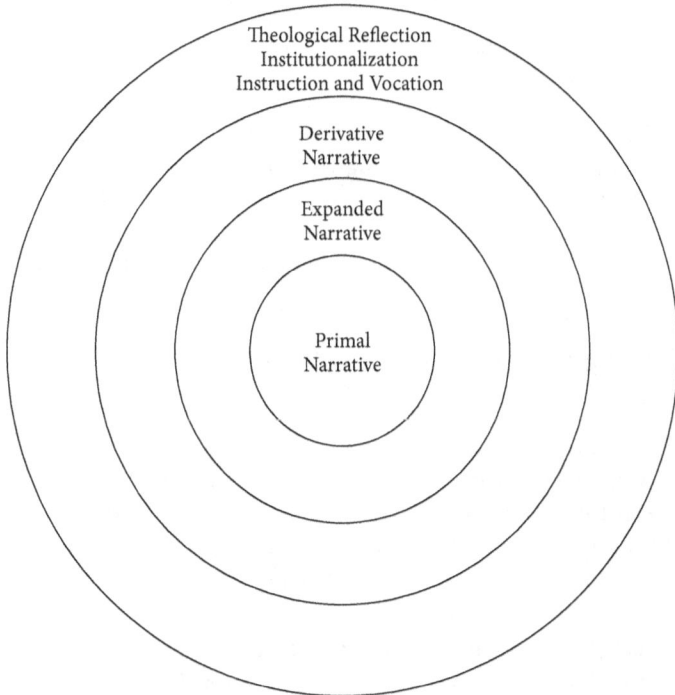

---

2. Brueggemann, *The Bible Makes Sense*, 58.

The Bible stands as canonized by fourth century CE church authorities, and is revered above the literary production of any and all other Christians. Christian literature written before, and all Christian literature written after the New Testament canon was established, is part of the ongoing and developing tradition of the Christian church. None of this belongs in the various rings depicted by Brueggemann's target. Brueggemann helps us visualize that, when reading the Bible, the further removed from the primal narrative we get, the greater the risk of substituting peripheral matters for the core. It's not that expanded and derivative narratives are unimportant, but they are not of primary importance. Some parts of the Bible are simply more central to the life of faith than other parts of the Bible. Science has long since abandoned a *flat earth* view of planet Earth because it isn't sustainable. Good theology abandons a *level book* view of the Bible because it isn't sustainable. Let us briefly review biblical literature, as we understand the narrative, using Brueggemann's target image as a guide.

The primal narrative is represented by the bull's-eye of the target. Other applicable terms are the *credo, kerygma*, core, heart, kernel, or metanarrative of the Bible.

> For Israel: Promises (covenants) of God with Abraham, the Exodus, wilderness wanderings, and settlement in the land of Canaan.
>
> For Christians: The incarnation of Jesus, his death, burial and resurrection, and outpouring of the Spirit in the New Age.

Expanded Narrative is one step removed from the Primal Narrative and expands upon it.

> For Israel: Epic stories elaborating on the faithfulness of God evidenced in the lives of Abraham, Sarah, and Hagar; Isaac and Rebekah; Jacob, Rachel, and Leah; Joseph, Moses, Miriam, and Joshua and other collateral characters through the Exodus, wilderness experience, and occupation of Canaan.
>
> For Christians: The Jesus story is recounted for specific communities in Matthew, Mark, and Luke through the collection of materials, the telling of stories in different ways and with different emphases, and speaking to different questions in different cultures, all elaborating on the meaning of the death,

resurrection, and exaltation of Jesus, and the Way of Jesus and his community in the world.

Derivative narrative is two steps removed from the primal narrative, but derived from it.

> For Israel: The material found in Judges through Nehemiah records how the God of the Exodus still worked in the history of the Israelite nation. It tells Israel's national history through the lens of its religious tradition of judges, prophets, Kings, and commoners as the Jews established themselves in Palestine at the crossroad of empires by the first millennium BCE. These are derivative stories of the primal narrative and don't have the same weight of authority in the believing community, but present how Judaism lived out its destiny.

> For Christians: The Acts of the Apostles records the ongoing story of Jesus' disciples as they carried out his commission to preach the gospel to the whole world. It contains history, establishes tradition, records sermons, and posits theological reflections in understanding the Jesus story. It attributes the dynamic of both personal and communal life to the indwelling of the life-giving Spirit. It explains how a Jewish sect in Jerusalem evolved into a Gentile church poised at the gates of Rome. This derivative narrative does not have the same authority as the primal gospel story, but traces what happened for discipleship within different cultures and under changing circumstances.

The literature of theological reflection, institutionalization, and instruction/vocation is three steps removed from the primal narrative and is a record of mature theological thought. It contains material for instruction and discusses vocation.

> For Israel: Various portions of the writings in Exodus, Leviticus, Numbers, and Deuteronomy are examples of the literature of institutionalization. They record community organization, mores, customs, leadership methods, and varieties of liturgical practices. Passages within these parts of the Hebrew scripture speak of the meaning of their faith, although not necessarily with a strict, systematic, theological method. Many sections, particularly in Deuteronomy, constitute a literature of mature theological reflection. The wisdom literature and writings of the prophets contain instruction, vocational material, and inspiration.

<u>For Christians:</u> Parts of the book of Acts and the pastoral epistles deal with various aspects of institutionalization. Romans is a classic example of mature theological reflection on law, grace, and gospel. The body of epistles instruct and give vocational direction.

Bruggemann's concept helps us evaluate the various forms of biblical literature and move beyond the misperception that every motif or story line in the Bible is as important as any other. We look to the primacy of core narrative, the common ground between individual humans, humans in community, and biblical faith. Just as core narrative holds the Bible together, core narrative also holds human beings together. For "God's sake," just read the narrative.

*****

The first overarching movement of the core biblical narrative begins with a Genesis story of Yahweh's call and promise to Abram, a specific and particular Semitic patriarch who lived in Ur of Chaldea. In the Hebrews' case, its specific narrative did not begin at the graveside, but was a calling. The narrative was expressed as a blessing, not a narrative of domination. Yahweh changed Abram's name to Abraham (Father of Nations), for the covenant intended that through him all families of the earth would be blessed. From the beginning, God's story in the Bible is moving from the "one" to the "all." From *particularity* to *inclusivity*.

The second overarching movement of the core biblical narrative is the story of God's call and promise to Israel. The narrative moves from Genesis to the great Jewish Exodus from Egyptian bondage and the pilgrimage of freedom to Canaan—the specific, seminal event that formed the nation of Israel: "You have seen what I did to the Egyptians, and how I bore you on eagles' wings and brought you to myself . . . you shall be my treasured possession out of all the peoples. Indeed, the earth is mine, but you shall be for me a priestly kingdom and a holy nation."[3] Israel is set apart (made holy) for a specific purpose that is far beyond abstract purity or ethnicity. The defeat of Israel by Nebuchadnezzar, destruction of the Jerusalem temple, and the deportation of Jews to Babylon ended Jewish dreams of empire. They lamented, "How could we sing the Lord's song

---

3. Exod 19:4–6, NRSV.

in a foreign land?"[4] God's response is proclaimed by Isaiah and other eighth-century Jewish prophets: "I am the Lord, I have called you . . . I have given you as a covenant to the people, a light to the nations, to open the eyes that are blind, to bring out the prisoners from the dungeon, from the prison those who sit in darkness . . . See, the former things have come to pass and new things I now declare . . . Sing to the Lord a new song, his praise from the end of the earth!"[5] The whole earth and the produce of creation is from God, and is the object of God's love. The movement is from Abraham to Israel, from person to nation, from the individual of faith to community of faith. God's blessing of freedom and justice is open-ended and extends to *all families* and *all nations*.

The third overarching movement of the core biblical narrative begins in the Gospels of the New Testament with the story of Jesus. Christian confessional language projects this as a story of incarnation. The Latin term *incarnare* ("into flesh") is not found in the New Testament, but the sense of it is central to early Christian understanding of the mystery of the faith. The concept was articulated by Isaiah's use of *Immanuel* (Hebrew: "God is with us," later Romanized as Emmanuel). Matthew, Mark, and Luke cast the narrative as divine love enfleshed in the human Jesus. The poetic prose of John's gospel sings of light, love, and the Word in the beginning with God that became flesh and lived among us. The fast paced, almost breathless, stories of the Gospels are steeped in the history and language and thought forms of the day—son of man, kingdom of God—and reach back into the depths of Judaism. The sermons in The Acts of the Apostles cast the story as Lord and Messiah (Christ). Paul uses language of cosmic presence to express "the power and wisdom of God" in "foolishness and weakness." Incarnation is the church's way of speaking of God's humanity wherein divine presence is a mediated presence through an encounter in Jesus, in persons, in community, in sacraments, in ritual, in cups of cold water, in visitation of the imprisoned, in clothes for the naked, in shelter, in mercy and justice. The incarnation of Jesus invites all humanity to incarnation (enfleshment) of grace, love, and life-alive.

The story of Jesus is the ultimate story of the relational nature of faith—faith as trust through encounter and involvement with God. The God who visited Abraham under the oaks of Mamre. The God who

4. Ps 137:4, NRSV.
5. Isa 42:6–10, NRSV.

confronted Moses in a burning bush. The God who entered the hovels of Egypt for the sake of freedom from slavery. The God who crossed the Sinai to deliver the promised land. The God who sojourned in exile in Babylon for the sake of release and "going home." The God who was always giving up geography (moving beyond geopolitics, imperialism, and dominion) for the sake of history. The God who was so in love with the world that divinity finally joined itself with humanity and entered the world fully by taking on human flesh in the life of a specific human being who lived at a particular historical time, in a particular culture, in a particular place—Jesus of Nazareth.

Jesus' adult ministry began upon his baptism by John, after which he was led into the wilderness by the Spirit where he was tempted by Satan (the adversary). Each of Jesus' temptations attacked his identity as defined by his faith in the One he believed to be true. In the first temptation, Jesus demonstrated he understood faith as "living by the story of God, not by bread alone." In the second temptation, he refused to provide a spectacular religious circus by diving off the temple to be rescued by heavenly luminaries. In the third temptation, he rejected the power of wealth and empire as a means to gain his end. Instead, he took upon himself the role of a suffering servant. He mingled with everyone, served, healed, and exorcised evil. He taught (*rabbi*) with wisdom and authority, telling pungent stories. Jesus' parables beg the question, "*What happens if you live in the narrative of the parable?*" He once gave a sermon on a mountainside that turned the world upside down by contrasting conventional wisdom with godly blessings. He invited all humankind into a relationship with him. Faith in the relationship leads into the way, the truth, and the life.

Jesus' life, and the life to which he called disciples ("*Follow me . . .*"), was and is rooted—we remind ourselves—in the core of the Torah (*Shema*): love God and love neighbor. "Do *this* and you will *live*," he told his disciples. Jesus' life, teaching, challenge, and vision were more than the power structures of politics and religion of his day could bear. He was executed as a criminal in a conspiracy between religious and civil authority. His death occurred in the fifteenth year of the reign of Tiberius Caesar, Pontius Pilate being governor of Judea and Herod being tetrarch of Galilee, while his brother Philip was tetrarch of the region of Iturea and Trachonitis and Lysanias was tetrarch of Abilene, and during the Jewish high priesthood of Annas and Caiaphas. Historical particularity! Not "Once upon a time!"

Jesus had lived for some thirty years as a person who could be interacted with in the ways common to humankind—eating, drinking, working, worshiping, weary and worn, anguished and angry, laughing and weeping in joy and sorrow, surrounded by companions. He loved, forgave, challenged, crossed boundaries, withdrew into solitude, was in your face and by your side and told the truth. Jesus was not observed in evanescent flashes of smoke and fire and bedazzling light, but in the steady flame of a human life who became, *whatever one thinks of the veracity of the story*, a light to all the world. The impact of a man named Jesus upon the world is fact. After he was crucified, Jesus was sealed in a tomb provided by Joseph of Aramethea. Jesus' companions were devastated. Everything was lost! They hung up a sign: "Gone fishin'." But they were reengaged. The story wasn't over. The Jesus story is anchored in his resurrection. In the Christian's case, the story really begins at a graveside.

The narrative picks up again about three days later when women friends of Jesus went to visit his tomb. To their astonishment, they found the stone rolled away and the tomb empty. While they wandered forlorn near the grave site, they saw a man they presumed to be the gardener. Somehow, there was something different about their friend, Jesus. Perhaps it was because they had no intention of seeing him. They went to anoint his dead body. They recognized that it was him only when he called one by name. "*Mary.*" They returned—*the first preachers of the resurrection*—to tell the other disciples. In the New Testament, there was never any doubt that women were included in discipleship. Their witness, however, was so absurdly unbelievable it was greeted with disbelief and fear.

Some time later, Jesus joined the disciples in a room where they had gathered. They were challenged to come to grips with a new reality. Jesus lived! The story goes out of its way to make clear that they entertained no thoughts that Jesus was resuscitated, nor that he survived as an abstract, immortal soul or a disembodied spirit. Christian theology is an anthropology based in a unique understanding of human *nature* and of human *being*, both in life and in death. Just as God experienced bodily life in Jesus, Jesus experienced bodily resurrection in God after the death of his body. The Christian hope lies in resurrection—the redemption *of* our bodies, not redemption *from* our bodies.

An important witness, Thomas, wasn't present for that moment and remained a doubter. He had his own moment of recognition and conversion from doubt to faith on a later day. Jesus and the disciples began to spend time together again, sharing meals and conversation during which he expanded on what had transpired and what was to come. He called them friends, but also must have nudged them with his elbow when he whimsically referred to them as "Little Faiths." The disciples experienced something of what they had shared with him before he was crucified. But, most emphatically, they lived with the knowledge—the conviction—that there was one empty grave in all of the wide world's graveyards. That changed everything.

Jesus left the disciples one day—just disappeared from their sight—with a charge and a challenge to carry the good news into all the world. This part of the story, referred to as the ascension, is not just stage direction: Exit stage up! It clearly has elements of the "three-layer-cake" view of the cosmos that was prevalent in the world at that time. In contradistinction to Jesus drifting skyward—and passing out at 35,000 feet—we should understand the ascension as the theological counterpoint to the incarnation. If one thinks either parameter of Jesus' life can be rationally explained, theo-poetic mystery has been bypassed in favor of the scoffer's unimaginative pragmatism. Exultation or glorification might be more useful language to portray the "ascension" in our twenty-first century. Nevertheless, the purpose of Jesus' disappearing was not to shuffle him off *terra firma* and out of the picture. It was not a cosmological explanation, slight-of-hand, nor science. It was not understood as spooky and apparitional. It was not a conspiracy to defraud. It was the rest of the story. God came to humanity in the flesh of his incarnation; so humanity was taken to God in a fleshly body—*wounds and all*. The wounds of God and the wounds of humanity are joined. This third overarching movement of the biblical story champions love not power, forgiveness not condemnation, freedom not oppression, liberty not imperialism, and life not death. The story's movement now opens up all humanity to life-alive in the present and a life-beyond following our own inevitable death. Universal! A living faith, an alternative hope, and an inclusive love! It is an unimaginable, shocking, offensive, incredible, unbelievable story. But it is the Christian story.

Finally, the fourth overarching movement of the core biblical narrative is the story of what happened to the companions of Jesus after he disappeared from their sight. The account begins with the Acts of the Apostles and continues through the remaining books of the New Testament. The narrative relates how the small community of disciples took the message from Jerusalem to the ends of the earth—from their specific locale to the far-beyond.

23

Christian Identity
From Pentecost to the Present Moment

"Who am I? This or the Other?
Am I one person today and tomorrow another?
Am I both at once? A hypocrite before others,
And before myself a contemptible woebegone weakling?
Or is something within me still like a beaten army
Fleeing in disorder from victory already achieved?

Who Am I? They mock me, these lonely questions of mine.
Whoever I am, Thou knowest, O God, I am thine."
>   —Dietrich Bonhoeffer, Theologian and Pastor
>   Confessing Church in Germany
>   Written from Tegel Prison
>   Hanged by the Nazis, 1945

"Tolstoy once suggested that certain questions are put to humanity not so much that we should answer them, but that we should spend a lifetime wrestling with them. I don't recall Tolstoy listing any such questions, so here's one of my own: 'Who tells you who you are?'"
>   —William Sloan Coffin
>   University Chaplain and Pastor

THE GOSPEL NARRATIVE LIVED and thrived through faith. Thereafter, history unfolded with new light and life-alive. The fourth overarching movement of the core biblical narrative was carried in the flawed, earthen vessels of men and women who were God's sons and daughters, emphasizing that sacred and secular are integrated.

The *Follow-me* community identified with the suffering servant who did not exercise his will to grasp power, and whose faithfulness resulted in his execution by power. They were first called Christians at Antioch of Syria, a term still used in the postmodern world. It is clear that early Jewish disciples understood the Old Testament narratives had been fulfilled in the life, death and, resurrection of Jesus and it was good news! God loved the whole world, not just these few persons, that tribe, this nation, that religion, this institution, that ideology. As the missionary venture unfolded, the Gentiles were included as recipients of the gospel. Crossing this racial threshold caused consternation, even dismay, among Jewish Christians, but some, at least, were led to accept the broad inclusiveness of God's initiative on the part of humanity. The death and resurrection of Jesus made life-alive available in the freedom of the spirit, and was large enough to contain the high joys and the deep sorrows of all peoples. This story has shaped the Christian experience for some 2,000 years, unfolding under the promised guidance of the Holy Spirit. Twenty-first–century Christians are the living extension of the fourth overarching movement of the core biblical narrative. The desiring heart of personal experience engages the expansive narrative of gospel through faith that promises a transformed life in God. Christianity is an open journey.

Christians have no place. We have no Mecca or Medina—no abiding earthly city and no permanent country. We have no holy mountain and no enduring shrine. We have no Wailing Wall to which we repair. Christians are permanent nomads. We have been sent on a journey to the ends of the earth and a city not made by human hands. We are strangers and exiles, pilgrims and sojourners. We are always on the way, with more to come, more to do, more boundaries to cross, more burdens to bear, more gladdening visions, and more far horizons. As the Cotton Patch version of the New Testament puts it, "Faith is the turning of dreams into deeds." Desire (*eros*) summons, invites, and energizes. Our hearts are homesick for the as yet unrealized possibilities. The way things are do not determine the way things can be and will be. Our sojourn is, according to the One whose story has become our story, contextually and specifically in this world and in the embodied flesh of our incarnational existence. This clearly means that authentic Christian existence is not "other-worldly." Christian life-alive is not a life-denying, world-denying piety that rejects this God-created, God-visited, God-touched, God-loved world of nature and grace in which we live from our birth until our dying.

Because we have no place, Christians are free for every place. Every place is a place of faith-affirming, love-generating, justice-orienting, hope-engendering life-alive. We have given up specificity of locale for the sake of a history-making future. Our temporary camp fires and tents, oases and deserts, work places and play grounds, shrines and sanctuaries, tabernacles and temporary dwellings are deeply rooted in the soil of our ever-moving and sojourning contexts. The paradox of incarnational Christian experience is that we are rooted and always moving, ever present and always facing the future, radically contextual and achingly homesick. Our journey is in the duality of life-alive in the *now* and the *not yet*—committed in the world and to the world of God's love in a visionary hope of the new heaven and the new Earth.

Instead of a *place*, Christians have a story, a community, a prayer, and a promise. The Christian's *story* is drawn from the Bible, referred to in faith as a revelation of the Word of God. That Word, first, is "person-in-incarnation" (Jesus) and "person-in-relationship" (the life-alive, affirming flame of faith). The Word, second, is "inscripturated" and preserves the story of God's Son, Jesus, as it germinated from the stories of the Jewish patriarchs and the nation of Israel. The Word includes the stories of the Spirit's work in the experience of the early Church. Without the story, there is no content to Christian faith. But it must be emphasized that when we speak of the Christian story, we are speaking of the gospel as in the opening of Mark's story: "The beginning of the gospel of Jesus Christ, Son of God." Or John's gospel: "In the beginning was the Word, and the Word was with God, and the Word was God . . . And the Word became flesh and dwelt among us full of grace and truth." The gospel is a person, revealed and remembered in story. The story is not simply didactic, and certainly not a schema of propositions. The gospel is relational from beginning to end. The core mystery is Jesus' person. The story is told in four different ways in the first four books of the New Testament. The differences are important. And, as we shall see, the future of our story is tied to the future of Jesus.

The Christian *community* embodies the sacramentally connected disciples of Jesus. The community must get the story straight (theological reflection), celebrate the story (liturgical action), share the story (witness in word and deed), and live the story (walk a journey of life-alive in the Way of faithing, hoping, and loving). Life-alive, in all of its joys and sorrows, is Spirit-animated. It consists of a freedom proclamation, a life-affirming faith, a relationship-affirming love, a justice-seeking ethic, a redemptive generosity, and a healing presence. Without the community, we are lonely and alienated.

The Christian *prayer* is the liturgical "Our Father . . ." that Jesus taught his disciples. His inclusive address to God underscores the unity of humanity in all of its diversity. The prayer vouchsafes each day of discipleship, the eternal now of reverence, the constant embrace of heaven and earth, enough bread for the day's journey, the rhythm of forgiving and being forgiven, and the life-affirming liberation from the death forces of evil. Without the prayer, we haven't got a prayer.

The Christian *promise* is that our earthly body will be filled (incarnated) with the divine Spirit in Jesus' earthly absence. The Christian promise delivers life-alive now, not after death as a reward for being a good boy or girl. The Spirit empowers identity, instills purpose, and gives direction. Our future is filled with hope because this present life is transformed in redemption and reconciliation. We have been freed and equipped for ethical action. This promise to Christians in our life-alive journey is disclosed (a secret made known) by our *experiences* in life as informed by the biblical stories that resonate with our own stories. There are times of faithfulness and faithlessness, development and digression, confusion and clarity. There are times of captivity, idolatry, wilderness wandering, confusion, and abuse. There are also times of freedom, purity of heart, clear vision, meaningful worship, strength of purpose, and times of healing and empowering love.

Christians—people of the word—must attend to the stories, poetry, and songs that weave the dynamics of erotic faith. That inspire and enchant. That spark creative insight and validate visceral knowledge. That release passionate energy to shape the world toward freedom, justice, redemption, healing, and wholeness. We must perceive that a divinity of love energizes creation, incarnation, life-alive, and resurrection on this long journey together through history toward its final consummation when we experience a new heaven and a new Earth. It was so with Jesus and it is so with us. We must find words of integrity in the dialogue between the "... *ologies*" and *religion*.

Postmoderns now have a perspective of Christian church history. The moment Jesus' disciples began to preach on the Day of Pentecost, inaugurating their worldwide missionary effort to fulfill the Great Commission, the development of the institutional and ecclesiastical structure of church began. The Jerusalem church was the mother church, where Peter and the other apostles thrashed out policy within the confines of the Greco-Roman world and its Palestinian protectorate where Judaism gave birth to Christianity. The same policy issues were confronted by Paul and his peripatetic companions while on the road in missions throughout the Mediterranean world. Peter and Paul finally met personally in Jerusalem and argued certain issues of doctrine and policy. It was a long time coming, not occurring until approximately twenty years after Jesus was crucified. We can scarcely imagine the momentous nature of that conference where Peter and Paul went to the mat on doctrinal issues.

The Christian church has now amassed twenty-one centuries of history. Today's community of Christians are the faith descendants of the community of Christians who lived in the first century. There are no first-century Christians today. They are all dead. There is no first-century church today. It ended at the close of the first century. In the words of the Letter to the Hebrews, they are our "cloud of witnesses." We live and serve as twenty-first–century Christians in the twenty-first–century church in a twenty-first–century, globalized world. Each of our faith communities have experienced faith in settings so radically different we can scarcely imagine it—different races, different eras, different cultures, different politics, different economics, different worldviews, different circumstances—all under the guidance of the Spirit. We must not constrict the Jesus narrative by becoming bogged down in the specific details of the cultural issues of church from Bible times to postmodern times.

The Christian church has had both Testaments of the Bible (in Hebrew and Greek) since the fourth century, during which time the New Testament canon was established. St. Jerome, in the late fourth century, was responsible for the preparation of a Latin translation of the Bible. It was referred to as the Vulgate Bible (from Latin, *vulgus*: "common people"). The Bible was generally held within the province of the Roman Church. Priests read it in Latin. A thousand years passed. Ecclesiastical arguments discouraged translation of the Bible into commonly spoken languages. John Wycliffe, an Oxford don and church renegade, oversaw the translation of the Vulgate Bible into Middle English, a project completed about 1395. In the late fourteenth century, English law established the death penalty for anyone found with an English translation of the Bible. A version of the Vulgate Bible was one of the first books produced on Johannes Gutenberg's printing press, and was released about 1455. Martin Luther, during the time period of May 1521 to March 1522, while in hiding at Wartburg Castle under threat from the Roman Catholic Church, translated the New Testament from Greek into German. A French physician and theologian, Jacques Lefevre, published the first French translation of the New Testament in 1522. William Tyndale, an English scholar, translated St. Jerome's Vulgate Bible into English, the first English translation of the Bible to take advantage of the printing press, released 1526. Approved English translations of the Bible began with King Henry VIII's commission of "The Great Bible" in 1535. Queen Elizabeth I commissioned "The Bishop's Bible" in 1568. The most famous translation was commissioned by King James in 1604 and published in 1611. The King James Bible is regarded as one of the most important books in the English language and its prose and majesty of style was a force in shaping the English-speaking world.

This brief history of the collection and canonization of the New Testament documents, and of the progress of translations of Old and New Testament into common language for common folk, and the printing technology that made it available and dispersible, makes it clear that the Christian church existed for more that sixteen centuries before the term "family Bible" became part of our lexicon. How did the church get along? It relied on the story, spirit-filled disciples, a prayer, a promise, and tradition.

The inscripturated Word (the rule book) didn't make it into the hands of common, literate people until around the 1600s and was a force undergirding the Protestant Reformation. In the centuries since Jesus lived and died in Palestine, the church has seen councils, creeds, convocations, encyclicals, confessions, declarations and addresses, songs, hymns, poems, unholy alliances with empire, racist and sexist behavior, confessing churches, religious propaganda, schisms, shenanigans, theologies, cathedrals, buildings, universities and colleges, commerce, television empires, books, tracts, hospitals, movements, denominations, reformations, radical reformations, counter reformations, restorations, purifications, calcifications, sects, cults, venality, bigotry, stupidity, craziness, and downright evil. All are part of the ongoing personal, historical, contextual, political, philosophical, and theological interaction with the story of Jesus.

The church has been overwhelmed with mediocrity in all of its seductive disguises. It has attempted to foreshorten the pilgrimage and settle down *prior* to God's surprising conclusion. Prophets have become fortune tellers. Preachers have become prattlers. Renouncers have become renegades. Activists have become agitators. Some notions and activities have been wildly misconceived and others profoundly insightful. Most efforts have been a mix because *we are a mix*. But in and through it all, the Spirit has blown where it will to invite, sustain, guide, heal, reconcile, transform, liberate, and to keep the story alive. The new wine of the story continues to ferment and will always need new and expanding skins. From Pentecost until the present moment, Christians have added to the complex narrative and sacred language of God's historical people on the Way.

The relationship of the biblical narrative to our narrative shapes our personal and our communal identities. Our best stories, prayers, poems, and songs are said and sung in the hope and belief that the un-nameable might touch us on the shoulder, whispering an enchanting invitation. We wait for a mystery-beyond-solving to melt our icy pride, shake us out of our complacency, free us from our cultural captivity, and heal our deepest wounds. It is our responsibility to understand the nature of narrative in general, of narrative history specifically, and of biblical narratives and narratives about the Bible. We must draw appropriate lessons from the history of the Bible as a text, and we must understand the unfolding nature of the Bible's primal, expanding, and derivative narratives. We, too, must not exchange the Bible's primal narrative for its peripheral narratives. We, too, must comprehend the expanded and derivative narratives of the Bible. And we must also appreciate that we are privy to 2,000 years of theological living, theological reflection, and theological writing on the Old and New Testaments, which has produced a vast literature devoted to thinking about thinking on the faith received.

When Iraneaus wrote *Against Heresies*, Augustine wrote his *Confessions*, Hildegard of Bengen wrote *On God's Activity*, Luther wrote the commentaries, Calvin wrote *The Institutes*, Teresa of Avila wrote *The Interior Castle*, Edwards wrote "Sinners in the Hands of an Angry God," Campbell wrote *The Christian System*, Barth wrote *Church Dogmatics*, Bonhoeffer wrote *The Cost of Discipleship*, King wrote "Letter from a Birmingham Jail," Gutierrez wrote *A Theology of Liberation*, Song wrote *Third Eye Theology*, Ruether wrote *Sexism and God Talk*, Cone wrote *Black Theology and Black Power*, Lindbeck wrote *The Nature of Doctrine*, Frei wrote *The Eclipse of Biblical Narrative*, McFague wrote *Models of God*, Farley wrote *The Wounding and Healing of Desire*, Hall wrote *Thinking,*

Confessing and Professing the Faith, and popes wrote Vatican Encyclicals, they were all contributing to the ongoing conversation of theological reflection in their times, places, and circumstances, and joined the people of God of all biblical time. The vast repository of Christian literature contains material that is insightful, instructive, inspirational, important, and worthy of consideration. It also contains material that has been narrow, self-serving, mean-spirited, and just plain cockeyed. *None are part of the biblical canon*, but are the ongoing Christian witness and reflection produced during the life-alive history of the church.

We today, as well as Christians of the earliest communities of faith and all communities of faith since the close of the biblical canon, are all *equidistant* from the faith confession of the primal narrative. That is because we live in the primal story of Christian faith by an *act of faith*—by the common confession of the most important story we know. But we, like all who have gone before us, live out that primal narrative in a myriad of diverse historical, national, and cultural world contexts. "Tradition is the *living* faith of the dead, traditionalism is the *dead* faith of the living."[1] And we would add, it is traditionalism that gives tradition such a bad name.

The gospel story, in all times and places, is received in faith. Faith is understood as a gift, and received and embraced, rather than achieved. The gospel is witnessed. Witness is an intimate experience of faith walked in the Way within the reality of God. The gospel is confessed. Confession is personal but not private; communal and not separatist. The gospel is love in action. Love is life-alive passionately expressed for the sake of the others, the outcast and the disenfranchised. The gospel is animated with hope. Hope crosses all boundaries of cosmology, geography, race, ethnicity, class, and gender. Hope encompasses all boundaries of religion and all boundaries of creation and extends to the far-beyond—a new heaven and a new Earth.

The gospel has always been translated from language to language. From the speaking of the word (the miracle of Pentecost) to the reading of texts, the message held within the language requires translation. The gospel has always been theologically interpreted. The events spoken and written about were explained and given meaning as God's activity in history. The gospel has always been contextually articulated. The words were given meaning in context of time, place, and circumstance. The

---

1. Pelikan, *The Vindication of Tradition*.

gospel has always been existentially received—embraced fully as a reality. The gospel has always been experientially lived. The Jesus story was not theory; those who heard and received it had to try to live it in order to understand and believe it. We remind ourselves that we spoke of religion in an earlier chapter as voluntarily embracing a distinctive *philosophy and hands-on experience* that serves as a foundational premise for life-alive.

The gospel proclamation and the summons to discipleship over these 2,000 years has been preached and practiced, understood and misunderstood, expropriated and exploited by believers and non-believers alike. The core biblical narratives, particularly the gospel story and the narrative of the church—like all historical narratives—have been hijacked for purposes banal, commercial, and iniquitous. The history of the Christian church is replete with stories of subversion and sellout. The Christian narrative has often been made ugly and cruel. It has been tamed, diluted, and corrupted. It has been permeated with and distorted by the secular culture of every nation. It has been commandeered by classes, races, and nations for selfish or imperial purposes. What was meant to be an alternative narrative to greed, wealth, and power, has been used to promote greed, wealth, and power. The past two millennia have seen the Christian church (both in its individual practice and its communal capacities) sometimes succumb to the *three representative temptations that Jesus rejected*, choosing stuff over story, entertainment instead of worship, and wealth and power rather than service and justice. The "faith *of* Jesus" evolved into "faith *in* Jesus," and has finally metamorphosed into advancing *"propositions about* Jesus." Whenever spirituality withered, the church attempted to muscle up through institutionalization and get with the program *du jour*. In this manner, the overarching narrative of Christian faith segued into—or surrendered to—the dominant cultural motifs of its time.

The monotheistic Christian church, like the ancient monotheistic Hebrews, has historically fallen prey to the blandishments of nearby gods. Postmodern, popular, slick expressions of Christianity can barely abide the Jesus story (and its dimension of faith) in its clamor for religion as entertainment that promises success, self-aggrandizement, possessions, and power.

24

Functions of Narrative for Christian Theology

"We are the sum of all the moments of our lives—
all that is ours is in them: we cannot escape or conceal it."
—Thomas Wolfe,
Novelist

THE OVERARCHING CHRISTIAN NARRATIVE is the gyroscope of a Christian's life. Sometimes, in the course of things, we realize our personally experienced story doesn't work for us any longer. Our gyroscope wobbles, malfunctions, or carries us off course. We don't leave the realm of personal and communal story, but we may experience narrative cracks . . . or even the terrifying experience of something hollow at the core. Our story ceases to make sense or empower. It may be imprisoning, crippling, deforming, or toxic. It may be life-denying or dead-ending. A new light may have appeared in the firmament of our experience. A new song may have been heard. The questions are raised again: "Who am I? Where am I? Why am I?" It's a time of disorientation. A new consciousness is awakened. Personal and communal identity may be revived and reoriented. We enter a realm that is called conversion. We begin to live in a new story. This can be so dramatic, or so traumatic, that it has been referred to as death and resurrection, being born again, or a new creation.

* * * * * *

Christians must attend to the functions of narrative. Coherent, competent living—with the heart (viscera), soul (spirit), and mind (intellect), the wholeness through which we reach for life-alive—depends upon our ability to evaluate colliding narratives and embrace, discard or revise them. We suspect, in fact, that in this reciprocal relationship of stories, we do not so much change the story as the story changes us. This, by the way, is the core of cognitive behavioral therapy. Similar mechanisms are present in Christian confession. These dynamic processes are actually an invitation to transformation and liberation. In some ways, we choose which stories are critical to our identity—which stories make meaning, establish values, and determine the manner in which we choose to live. But we must also be aware that some stories—the *givens* of Part I of this book, as well as the *determinisms* of time and circumstance within which we live—choose us.

Time and circumstance are bound to narrative by memory. Without memory we are unable to weave past, present, and future into a fabric of connected understanding. Deprived of our story (amnesia), we have no identity and are lost in the world. The cruelty of Alzheimer's is losing identity in time and space. Narrative not only involves words, but participation in the rituals that surround the narrative. Narrative can then progress to intimacy, rather than mere acquaintance. Lovers introduce their beloved to other members of the family. They participate in family dinners and family outings. They look at photographs, handle heirlooms, artifacts, treasures, and memorabilia. They visit homesteads, schools, churches, and graveyards. They listen to mundane stories that have shaped the *mundus*—the world—of their lover. They experience the immediacy of the present, but also plumb past experiences of personal and family dynamics in all of their nuanced subtleties. They enter each other's story. These powerful bonds establish a rhythm that enables imagining a future.

Beyond narratives that bond individuals in personal intimacy, communities share narratives that create bonding identities. All social communities—families, tribes, races, villages, cities, nations, clubs, colleges, churches, armies, political parties, and on and on—are grounded in the stories they tell. Participants are plunged into the mystery—something beyond comprehension—of their existence. The perception that God's grace precedes human action is a biblical insight that theology refers to as prevenient grace (God is the initiator of any relationship with the world). God is the one who pursues the creation and the creatures in creative, redemptive, and sustaining love. Some personal and communal narratives can be so definitive for our lives that they assume overarching power and are regarded as inviolable—sacred.

Sacred narratives, whether of a person or a community, provide identity, an understanding of place, a sense of belonging, and coherence in life. Sacred narratives have depth and breadth beyond story line, and we *awaken* to them in a *lived* experience. Sacred narratives make meaning, but also empower and transform. They function in the present by recalling the past, but also anticipate the future. Past, present, and future are in tension. The past cannot be undone but it can be reinterpreted. The present can be shaped. The future is open, held within the boundaries of the sacred story.

The sacred story of the Judaeo-Christian faith—the written narrative preserved in the Old and New Testaments—must be understood. Since the church began dealing with written texts in the absence of the eyewitness apostles, two scholastic disciplines of theology have been central to the church's interpretation of its sacred texts—*exegesis* and *hermeneutics*. *Exegesis* (Greek: "to lead out") is the task of leading out *what the text said and meant in its original context*. Stories do not take the place of exegesis and exegesis does not replace the story. Story belongs to faith. Exegesis belongs to textual scholarship. Exegesis belongs outside the target Brueggemann has posited. Theological reflection is not faith. Its language is secondary to the primary language of narrative and confession. Exegesis uses the tools of language, historical and literary criticism, and contextual and cultural insight to prevent a text from being made to mean anything anyone wants it to mean. The opposite of exegesis is *eisegesis*—leading one's own meaning into the text. For example, the popular mantra, "What would Jesus do?" (WWJD) is easily warped if one doesn't know what Jesus actually did. This is explored with the tools and methods of exegesis.

Hermeneutics (Greek: "to interpret") has to do with *what the text means today* in the current context of the life of the Christian community in its various world settings. Numerous interpretive hermeneutics have been proposed throughout Christian history. An *apologetic hermeneutic* has often been concerned with proving the truth of the Bible. A *puzzle-solving hermeneutic* has been concerned with putting together biblical commands, examples, and necessary inferences in the manner of assembling a puzzle, where every perfect piece fits in its perfect place to arrive at the perfect solution. A *patternist hermeneutic* attempts to create a blueprint for religious life and church organization that is categorically absolute and where theology consists of arguing over the details of the pattern. The *propositionalist hermeneutic* has been concerned with codification of abstract truth claims to which devotees pledge allegiance.

Apologetic, puzzle-solving, patternist, and propositionalist hermeneutics establish strict foundational dogma for denominations, including the church in which we grew up. These hermeneutics cannot do justice to the narrative nature of the Bible nor to the narrative nature of human experience. They cannot properly assess the difference between ancient worldviews and contemporary ones, nor between the fundamental questions of exegesis and hermeneutics. What the text *meant* is not always the same as what it *means*. Certainly these hermeneutics can't capture the nature of the personal and confessional aspects of Christian faith. Nor can they capture the power of narrative in creating a story-formed faith community. And finally, we must note, they are completely foreign to the nature of faith as trust, risk, commitment, and engagement with God in life-alive.

A *narrative* requires a *narrative* hermeneutic. If the primal narrative is replaced by conceptualizing doctrinaire credos, faith is euthanized. If reason is abandoned, the gospel is stolen—made vulnerable to ignorance, prejudice, self-delusion, and self-interest. If faith is co-opted by greed, wealth and power, faith is assassinated. Theology certainly needs all the critical tools that are available to academics—historical, literary, sociological, psychological, practical, cultural, and contextual analysis—to establish integrity of language, history, and culture. But a narrative hermeneutic enables us to read the entire Bible as intentional story. A narrative hermeneutic recognizes that some parts of the Bible are more crucial to the life of faith than others, but also recognizes that we must not randomly pick and choose from disconnected texts and piece them together in a story that suits us. Rather, the narrative itself illumines the power and purpose at the primal core of the Judaeo-Christian story. Narrative functions to critique, challenge, and correct our own personal stories and values, as well as to bring comfort, consolation, and inspiration. A narrative hermeneutic gives meaning to Judaism and to Christianity—individually and communally. Our concern is the actual life of faith, hope, and love depicted in biblical narratives—not simply ideas about

God and religion. The goal of a narrative hermeneutic is not to prove God but to portray (depict) God.

Ultimately, questions of faith and doubt, decision and commitment, apathy or passion will not be resolved by appealing to the power of naked authority or to the proof of propositions—no matter what the power, what the authority, what the means of proof, or the contents of the propositions. We are dealing with another dynamic entirely. Christians don't confess:

> "This is the most important proof I have believed."
> "This is the most correct pattern I have deduced."
> "This is the best proposition I have accepted."

The Jesus story is foundational because it launches an alternate narrative that sheds new light on humankind's search for meaning. Christians confess a relationship. Through confession of our faith in Jesus, we have entered the story as a participant. We become characters in the Jesus story and Jesus is a character in our story. The Christian's life is embedded in a narrative-in-time. The past still lives, rather than simply being past. The present is crucial and filled with passion. The future, though not yet, is present in desire and potential. The viscera of our fleshly body and the vitality of our soulful reality seize the day—our moment, our time—to encounter mortal life-alive that is in our present being and in our resurrection. The purpose is not to embrace some past golden age or to await a future golden age, but to enable our living in the here and now.

The world thinks life is lived from the past into an unknown future. The gospel story raises the possibility of living Christian faith's promised future into the present. This is the logic of the beatitudes. Jesus—the incarnation of the prophetic Word, and whose story is preserved in the inscripturated Word—spoke about the way things are and the way things will be. He combined the present with the future tense in the beatitudes: "Blessed are . . ." And, "You will be." "You shall be." "It will be." He penetrated the delusions and confusions of the present moment to not only *reveal* God's purposes, but to *live* God's purposes. He invited disciples to experience the same great reversal of realities—to live the story of future promise into the present moment. The gospel is not an opiate to narcotize people's brokenness and oppression. Rather, it is life-alive through transformation, healing, freedom, and empowerment, and carries the dual promise of life redeemed and death defeated.

Narrative is the foundation for ethical action. "Character is destiny." This aphorism from the Greek philosopher Heraclitus has not only been used in discussions about ethics, but is the foundation of good fiction. A character in a novel must act "in character." She must be true to the beliefs and experiences that make her who she is. In life, as well as in fiction, the narrative of a person's life shapes her character, and a person's character shapes actions, and actions have consequences. Ethical choices are revealed by what a person *does*, but grow out of who a person *is*. Ordinary ethical challenges are usually resolved by ordinary ethical choices. Common rules commonly work best. But sometimes ethical choices, like people, are complex and nuanced. We are faced with the ambiguity of "lesser evil" and "greater good." These issues demand serious reflection in the halls of philosophical and theological academe, but our purpose here is simply to argue that ethical action can't be separated from the narrative that shapes character. Rational objectivity is an illusion. Legalism is inadequate. Relativism is warped by self-interest. Good intentions are ineffectual. Narrative is crucial to ethical action because narrative frames context, shapes perspective, and either energizes or compromises the will to act.

Narrative theology allows Judeo-Christian religion to be a natural conversation partner with all other fields of endeavor. Wherever questions are raised regarding the meaning of human existence, no discipline should isolate itself (or be isolated) from the conversation. Truth in all disciplines has nothing to fear from broadening the knowledge base in each discipline. Narrative theology should be in conversation with philosophy and science. It should also be in conversation with the humanities and the arts. Literature, drama, poetry, and film, along with other art forms, explore the same questions theology deals with—the world in all of life's complexity, banality, inhumanity, compassion, longing, cowardice, and heroism. Wisdom is ennobled when facts are seasoned with discernment. Discernment is enhanced by the humanities and the arts. Faith must be willing to engage in vigorous thinking about thinking within the full panoply of other narratives of human existence and meaning-making. It is the *narrative of faith* within the *faithful community* that makes possible conversation between all fields of human endeavor.

25

A Coherent Christian Faith

"To discover how to be truthful now, is the reason I follow the star.
To discover how to be living now, is the reason I follow the star.
To discover how to be loving now, is the reason I follow the star.
This journey is long, we want our dinners,
And miss our wives, our books, our dogs,
But have only the vaguest idea why we are what we are.
To discover how to be human now is the reason we follow the star."
—W. H. AUDEN, *The Christmas Oratorio*
   Poet

"Why do I follow him? Well, well . . . I like him."
—SANCHO PANZA, regarding Don Quixote
   Miguel de Cervantes
   Novelist, Poet, Playwright

DESIRE PROVIDES THE SPARK, *narrative* conveys the story, and *faith* supplies the trust to live life as an affirming flame.

Desire is at the heart of the divine/human love story. Passion fires an erotic faith in an erotic God. It is the dynamic that leads to passionate commitment, authentic connection, and confessional living—yearning heart to yearning heart. Lift the Jewish toast, "*L'chaim!*" To Life!

Narrative's function is to provide identity and coherence. Identity addresses the who, where, and why of our personhood. Coherence combines logic and consistency. This demands critical thought—Axial thinking. In the search for coherence, experience reveals there is always some measure of incoherence. Coherence does not remove complexity, ambiguity, and paradox. Perhaps that is what we learn from Sigmund Freud's probing of the subconscious, Heisenberg's Indeterminacy Principle, and quantum physics. Primal narratives must be thoughtful, but still leave room for things unresolved and things mysterious. The only theological question that interests us after nearly a century and a half of combined human experience is, "What is the word that gives life?" Authentic life. Abundant life. Redeemed life. Life-alive! This question is central in the life, work, and death of a historical figure by the name of Jesus who stated his mission clearly: "I have come that you might have life and have it abundantly." His story is divulged in narrative form in the New Testament Gospels. The story is neither nebulous nor unfocused. It does challenge conventional thinking. It also challenges belief. The question must be raised: "Is faith in this story outside the realm of rationality?"

Faith is composed of two elements: question and affirmation. *Question* has to do with the nature of faith. The nature of faith is trust. Trust, for the Christian, is in a person—Jesus—and the One to whom Jesus points. Jesus lived his life in trust—or to put it another way—Jesus' faith was trust in God. His life was a living parable of this trust. *Affirmation* deals with the vocation of faith. The affirmation of faith is confession in word and deed. Quite simply, we cannot tell our stories without reference to the story and invitation of Jesus.

The very idea of a life of faith—any faith in anyone or anything—has been challenged from the earliest cultures. Perhaps it was easier to believe religious explanations of life's realities in primitive cultures when primitive science had little to offer. Perhaps, but we doubt it. But when evidence-based science produced a dazzling display of proofs, the laboratory became the cathedral and the database became the pantheon of truth. Scientific realities became first among equals in truth-making. Faith-based thought lost authority and power. There are areas of the world today where religion continues to flourish, but in Western technocultures religion—particularly mainstream Christianity—is in decline. Increasing numbers of people believe religion is an anachronism left over from unenlightened eras. But after everything, faith-based explanations and faith-based living have endured. The point must be made that the irreligious, the agnostic and atheistic, nevertheless live faith-based lives. Faith in a narrative establishes an identity through which every individual engages life. Confession is an expression of the way we are and the way life is. Confession is not a series of sterile propositions, no matter how passionately believed, but living faithfully toward a bedrock purpose (science, religion, politics, business, law, the arts, the warrior tradition, *la familia*, money, power).

Confession is used in three ways in the Christian tradition. First, it is used as taking an oath of Jesus' lordship. "You are the Christ (Annointed One), the son of the living God" (Matt 16). Or, "Jesus is Lord" (Rom 10). It is an affirmation of a relationship with Jesus and the One whom Jesus revealed, not, we repeat, an affirmation of propositions about Jesus. Second, confession is made through a life lived in "the Way." Christians love God, neighbor, and self with the totality of their being (heart, soul, mind, and strength—unfragmented). We embrace with awe the mystery of a life marked by the good, the bad, and the ugly, and yet retain the capacity to hope and be surprised. Third, confession is the admission of sin (our harmful, evil thoughts and ways, our brokenness, perfidy, and alienation). Confession is the difficult-to-do, actual expression of sin that is personal (to the one wronged) and corporate (communally in public worship). Naming the sin makes tangible its intent and result. But the Judaeo-Christian story makes clear that sin is the fallen nature of humanity.

The Jesus story stands against everything that doesn't make room for life-alive with love, hope, peace, and justice—open to all "others," not just some "others." This is discipleship toward and for the "least of these," and rejects the dull, dreary, deadly, noninclusive conformity and uniformity of a closed community. The narrative of Jesus crosses racial, gender, political, economic, national, and religious boundaries. Jesus in his passion, death, and resurrection points to the Way of life-alive in the present and in the beyond—across even the final boundary of death.

Important theological distinctions must be made on the nature of the Christian faith we strive to confess and the classic Christian creeds. They are not the same thing. Creeds are historical documents that arose when the church grew in numbers and broadened its geographic and cultural reach. All creeds were formulated to clarify standards of orthodoxy in light of particular issues in a particular time. The historic creeds (Nicene [fourth century], Chalcedonian [fifth century], Athanasian [sixth century], and Apostles [eighth century]) are important to "thinking about thinking" on the story of Jesus, but they are not the story. Take, for example, the Apostles Creed:

> Jesus was conceived by the Holy Ghost, born of the Virgin Mary, suffered under Pontius Pilate, was crucified and buried, descended into hell, and the third day he rose again from the dead.

Absent from the Apostles Creed is the story of the life, ministry, and teachings of Jesus—all essential to the unfolding, sustaining narrative of Jesus. The creeds attempted to do the impossible—express a living relationship in propositional formulas and to capture the mystery of the faith in rational language—as we often do in our own time and place. In their restricted content and purpose, creeds became stamped by the authority of institutional, historical churches in their struggles to express the nature of Jesus.

The creeds are a part of the tradition that points to the one whose narrative the church proclaims. As part of the tradition they can both explain and distort. It is a mistake to deify historical documents, doctrines, and creeds, including the Bible. Paul's admonition to the Christian community in Corinth was to "make love your aim." Not spiritual gifts, an infallible Bible (the only Bible in Christian experience at that time was the Jewish Bible—the Old Testament), an institutional authority, or a wide variety of traditions. Do not even make "faith in faith" your aim. Not even a preposition gets in the way of Paul's expression of faith: "I know *whom* I have believed." Faith as relationship! The most important thing about creeds is "who" is their content, not "what" is their content.

Faith is not reason, but neither is faith irrational. Faith can be confessed while admitting the inability to fathom the depths of a mystery. We are to love God with the mind and faith can be, and must be, critically pondered. But the intellect will not prove God, rationalize God, domesticate God, or bind God within fixed, manageable attributes. Dogmatism reduces faith's relational life in Jesus to concurrence with a set of codified propositions. Faith is never simply contemplation. Faith is an act of the will, a motivating force making possible our on-the-road journey of experience, encounter, engagement, and involvement. Faith is neither anti-emotional nor unemotional. Faith laughs, weeps, and loves. Faith is infused with desire, including anger. (Remember Jesus cleansing the temple.) Faith can blow your mind; it has guts and grit; sometimes it makes you want to puke. Faith is filled with mystery that is fundamental to the Christian experience.

The opposite of faith is not doubt. The opposite of faith is certitude. Evil is often the result of thinking and acting with thoroughgoing certitude. Life's most rewarding moments are launched by faith. Who ever danced the tango with certitude? Who ever played Beethoven's *Violin Concerto Number Two* with certitude? Who ever stepped on stage to play Cordelia in King Lear with certitude? Who ever lofted the winning buzzer shot basketball with certitude? Has anyone ever married with certitude? Or faced martyrdom with certitude? We recall Jesus' cry of despair on the cross: "My God, my God, why have you forsaken me?" Christian faith is risk. Faith doesn't "know everything." Faith is able to ask questions. Faith is the ability to live with questions that are experienced as having no answer. Faith is the practice of seeking. Faith is different from solidifying power in order to enforce institutional goals. Faith is not propaganda or programs. It is the dynamic that enables us to step out on an unknown road, to walk in the holy mystery of the ongoing, unending, and inexhaustible gospel story. The words of Jesus from Mark's gospel provide the constant reminder: "Go on ahead!"

Just so, faith opens up horizons, prompts questions, and piques the imagination. In fact, it has long been said that we *believe in order to understand*. Faith makes good thinking possible. Zen Buddhism calls this *satori*—seeing with the third eye. The third eye allows a truer seeing: enlightenment. It may come in an "ah ha!" moment, or after years of study, or at the end of a lifetime of reflection, or through a lover's quarrel with the church of your origin, or after seventy years of arguing with your brother. Jesus constantly challenged mute consent to the way things are and the way things are said to be. He was frustrated by those who had eyes that didn't see and ears that didn't hear. This references the danger of our religion being one in which we gain information without insight, knowledge without enlightenment, and strategize without imagination. Jesus' life and language shocked the received wisdom, the habits, the culture, the religious, the irreligious, the civil authorities, and above all, the imagination of his culture. The failure of imagination in the life of faith refuses the reality of a horizon that beckons. The failure of imagination not only erodes faith's capacity, but also love's and hope's capacity. Love, compassion, sympathy, and empathy require imagination. Complex ethical decisions demand imagination. Failure of imagination drains life of its full potential and leads to the death of hope.

Faith is not ethereal. It is incarnated—in the flesh. It infuses the beating heart, the hank of hair, the hunk of bone, the walking, talking honeycomb of marrow and mind. Faith's doubt contains the leaven of courage that inspires a Jesus believer (relationship, not propositions) to risk placing one foot in front of the other on the the Way. Faith is not destination; it is journey. Faith has a past, but is future-oriented with a vision of hopeful expectation. Faith may be accompanied by tears, but should never take the form of a whine. Nor should faith be shouted in strident, Christian imperialism. Faith is not boasted; it is modest. Faith is not imperious; it is sacrificially lived. Faith is not proven; it is prayed. Faith is not knowledge; it is commitment. Faith is not emptied of mystery; it gratefully embraces mystery. Christian faith is deeply personal but it is never private. Faith is belonging in community. Faith is not achieved, it is a gift of God. Gratitude opens the gift and plays with it.

26

Giving an Account

"The formation of Christian community has become increasingly difficult. The increasing coldness of human life, the increasing inability to feel with others and thus to form communal relationships, is the most ominous threat to the human future in Western society. Without the formation of communities there can be no solutions to the dehumanization which is taking place in the political, economic, cultural and natural dimensions of life."
—Jim Wallis
 Sojourners

STORIES OF DESIRE AND narratives of faith were written by the authors' search for coherent meaning-making in this pluralistic world. Our experience of life and the desire to live it fully, our encounter with many stories, the company of others on our journey, and the grace of the Christian confession of faith compels a sense of wonder in this two thousand and nineteenth year of the Common Era.

Knowledge is discovered when the right questions are asked of the right sources. It took a long time—still ongoing—for humankind to even ask the array of questions it confronted, let alone devise answers. Over time, facts and figures accumulated. Thinking about thinking sifted through this huge pile of information and called it data. Progress established (within a range of certainty) what was true, false, or contained a smidgen of truth. This was saved in a file we labeled, "What?" But, truth is elusive. Absolute truth is humanly unattainable, and any such claim closes off paths to learning. Claims of absolute truth are not just wrongheaded, but dangerous, and lead to violence against someone or something. Humankind operates within the realm of approximate truth. Stretched end-to-end, proximate truth leads to accumulated knowledge. What good is it? It's very practical: it works!

Comprehension can be achieved when attention is given to the myriad of stories experienced over time and filtered through discriminating thought. Everyone, acknowledging the exceptions that prove the rule, reaches that moment when knowledge expands into comprehension and is put in their "So What?" file. It is their gyroscope for life. It must work on the practical day-to-day level. The jaw-dropping surprises that occur along the way are discernment. Absent that, which we believe is a spiritual insight, one is lost.

The authors accept and respect the "givens" of natural science as outlined in Part One ("What?"). We reject, however, a worldview that restricts itself to understanding cosmos and creature through a methodology of sheer molecular, animal physicality. We believe there is a spiritual dimension to the cosmosphere that we have experienced as baptized believers in the Jesus story striving to walk the Way in company with other Follow-Me ones. An account of our faith requires that we speak not only of the meaning of believing, but also the nature of belonging.

Jesus began his public ministry by inviting people to join him in a communal journey. He taught and lived a communal narrative rooted in the divine nature of the God that grew out of Jewish monotheism, expressed with an expansive understanding of a God of love who was manifest as a Trinity in which he was the incarnate Son. At his post-resurrection glorification, Jesus gave his disciples marching orders: "Go into all the world and preach the gospel." This great commission urges no more—and no less—than to tell his story in its fullness. Living out of this specific faith narrative should not be domineering. Jesus' story compels respect for other people, other stories, and other faiths. In giving an account of our faith, we are not proselytizing, but confessing. Nor is it a claim to have all the answers.

The stories of the nine great, text-based, meaning-making narratives of world civilizations previously summarized sprang from many cultures, spoke in many voices, and employed many images. They had sundry differences, which shouldn't be overlooked. *Vive la difference!* Yet the questions posed were similar and the answers, at the very least, shared some common themes, motifs, and ideals. The fact is, all world religions have been, and still are, variously engaged in wars against each other, and each of these religions have engaged in fratricidal conflicts within their own ranks. Denominationalism and sectarianism diminish witness and result in venom and violence. The Christian religion certainly labors under this schismatic burden.

The two major divisions of Christianity (Catholic and Protestant)—despite much common ground—have been at each other's throats (literally and figuratively) for some 500 years. The authors' own Christian heritage, whose central plea to a fragmented Protestant world was unity, separated itself from the broad Protestant heritage. Our tradition generally took refuge in absolutism—only to subsequently divide into several sects. Denominations and sects have several things in common. They have muddled illusions about their roots, delusions expressed as distinctive doctrines believed to be uniquely correct, a blind eye for internal distortions and inconsistencies, and a shared denigration of sister denominations.

One common motif of most world religions was the use of light as a common symbol of religious/philosophical enlightenment. The authors wish to expand the metaphor of light and religion by noting that natural light projected through a prism is refracted into component wavelengths represented by the spectrum of colors. The varied, sacred, meaning-making stories of civilizations may be likened to a beam of ultimate sacredness passed through a cosmic prism and separated into single, distinct wavelengths. Each story of the sacred is unique, but monochromatic. We are persuaded that it takes all of the world's sacred stories to cast the full kaleidoscopic, meaning-making light of religion. The beam of ultimate sacredness passed through the Protestant prism separated into monochromatic wavelengths of denominationalism. It takes the whole church to tell the whole Christian story. The goal is not to homogenize religions, including Christianity, but to inspire faithful, meaning-making discipleship while preserving the unique insights offered by each.

The post-resurrection beginning of the Christian churches' story found devoted disciples of Jesus gathered in an upper room in Jerusalem. The Holy Spirit moved them to begin their mission of gospel proclamation on the Jewish Festival of *Shavuoth* (a festival held on the fiftieth day after the second day of Passover). Peter proclaimed the narrative of Jesus to a responsive number of Jews who had assembled for *Shavuoth*. Christians came to call that day Pentecost (Greek: *pentēkostē*, fiftieth day) and celebrated it in the church calendar. The confessing community was referred to variously as "the way" (*hodos*), disciples (the "follow-me" ones), fellowship (*koinonia*), Christians, and the church (Greek: *ekklesia*, "assembly," translated "church" more than 100 times in the New Testament). There is no definition of "church" in the New Testament—only images. Perhaps the most profound image, theologically, is the "body of Christ." Those in the body are "in Christ." From Pentecost until the present time, there has always been the human church in the presence of Christ. And from apostolic times, and in every age and on every continent since, the questions for Christians have always been the same. "Who and where is Jesus?" "What and where is church?"

WHO AND WHERE IS JESUS?

This question has answers rooted in *history* and *theology*, both of which had their origin when Jesus Christ was proclaimed (*history*) and explained (*theology*). In succeeding years, the message and its meaning were written in documentary, epistolary, monographic, and apocalyptic genres, some of which were preserved, collected, and canonized as the New Testament. Just as Old Testament writings include history that was theologized, the New Testament texts record history that, at one and the same time, were history theologized and theology historicized. This underscores the power and purpose of narrative theology, whereby *historical* answers to Jesus' identity were preserved: to wit, Jesus was a semitic male of the lineage of Judah birthed by Mary in a stable in Bethlehem of Judaea during a specific historical period. A Nazarene carpenter by trade, with a prophetic mission beginning in Galilee, he was crucified in Jerusalem by Roman authorities at the instigation of certain Jewish religious leaders. He was bodily resurrected three days after his death, rallying his disciples for a preaching ministry of the Good News he both enunciated and lived.

The same texts provide *theological* answers to the question, "Who and where is Jesus *since his historical life ended*?" Jesus once told his disciples that where "two or three" gathered in his name, he would be in their midst. Again, Jesus taught that he would be encountered in actual people who were hungry, thirsty, alienated, naked, sick, and imprisoned (the "least of these"). The shocked exclamation of his detractors says it all: "This man eats and drinks with sinners!" As an example, we share an incident told us by a first-line responder—a paramedic in a prominent city of wealth and power. A pastor one day discovered an old man stretched out in a velvet pew at the rear of his church sanctuary. He called emergency services. Our paramedic friend and his co-workers responded to the pastor's call in an ambulance. The paramedic examined the old man and discovered he had simply been sleeping. He was neither drugged, drunk, nor ill. They packed up and prepared to leave. The pastor inquired if they intended to take the bum with them. "No," said the paramedic. "He's just old, tired, homeless, and lonely. He needs a church, not a hospital or a jail." A secular arm of society needed to remind a pastor of the church of the encounter with Jesus in history.

The final *theological* expression of an encounter with Jesus is the *historical* Passover meal. On the night Jesus was betrayed, he took bread ("this is my body") and wine ("this is my blood"), invoked a blessing, and explained the covenantal significance as he shared it among his apostles. Paul made it clear to the Corinthian Christians that covenantal eating of the bread and the wine was an encounter with Jesus.

Narrative theology—the *historical* record leavened with *theological* reflection—establishes that Jesus is found where two or three are gathered in his name, where the disenfranchised are welcomed and sustained, and in the Eucharist.

WHAT AND WHERE IS CHURCH?

Church has always been believed to be a living organism of people more than an institution—a "way" more than a "place." Looking back, it seems inevitable that the living Christian organism would become institutionalized. "We've got to get organized!" is the great rallying cry of humanity. The church, as it came out of history and culture, conversed with history and culture, shaped and was shaped by history and culture, and lived in the ambiguity of history and culture, has exhibited many forms. From upper rooms to homes, from catacombs to cathedrals, from tents to store fronts, from fugitive pariahs to citizens of empire, from desert fathers and mothers to Vatican Councils and World Councils, and from local congregations to national and ecumenical organizations, the institutional church has operated under many names and flown many flags. Through both devotion and distortion, the church has left behind a regrettably mixed record.

The church is marked by faithfulness and unfaithfulness to the primal gospel narrative. It wavers between acceptance and denial of its calling. Development and growth is undermined by digression and stagnation. The church perpetrates and suffers apostasies and schisms, resistance to empire and collusion with empire, internecine wars and political infighting, as well as hypocrisy, venality, pretentiousness, bigotry, arrogance, and abuses of all kinds. Bloody crusades, book burnings, heretic burnings, inquisitions, and witch hunts can be contrasted with banality beyond belief. The world points to the harm done and the hypocrisy displayed by church and Christians throughout history as a major obstacle to faith. Church and Christians can only confess in tears and repent in grief. There is no excuse and should be no rationalization. Religion has played a role in perpetrating the terror of history that religion set out to address.

And yet, church and Christians have also performed deeds of transforming love. Social, racial, and gender barriers have been broken down. Charities have been established, hospitals have been built, mercy and forgiveness practiced, truth spoken to power, and justice promoted. The church has worked for peace, enabled education, and protected the helpless and hopeless. It has proclaimed a redeeming gospel and kept alive sacred spaces and places of intellectual, moral, and ethical reflection.

Church and Christians are simply knee-deep in the "wheat and weeds" of Jesus' parable. Life is lived in the ambiguity of good and evil. While there is no pure church or pure community, being part of a confessing, practicing faith community is nevertheless central to being Christian. And it is a given that association with *any* Christian community will at some point disenchant and disappoint. This should not surprise us. It is Christ's human body. But authentic Christian community strives to work through disappointments because we are made *one* through being in Christ, not by negotiating some ultimate human construct.

The questions, "Who and where is Jesus?" and "What and where is church?" are indivisibly linked by three realities informed by narrative *history* and *theology*. The church of Jesus Christ is a *sacramental community*, a *wisdom community*, and an *open community*.

THE CHURCH AS SACRAMENTAL COMMUNITY

The word *sacrament* is taken from the Latin *sacramentum*, a translation for the Greek word *musterion* (a mystery; that which is difficult to, or cannot be, explained). In a Christian context, sacrament refers to an act of mysterious and sacred significance that is a visible sign of a spiritual reality. Catholics and Protestants together identify several religious sacraments: baptism, confirmation, communion, ordination, marriage, penance, anointing the sick, and last rites. We comment here on baptism and communion, both crucial sacraments of divine/human encounter and central in the practice of both Catholic and Protestant traditions.

Immersion baptism is a *musterion* freighted with symbolism—washing and cleansing, burial and resurrection, a death died and a life made alive. Jesus, identifying with our humanity, began his ministry with baptism. In baptism, the confessing believer dies with Christ and is raised with Christ to a new life inspired, like Jesus, for the life-alive, cross-shaped journey.

The Lord's Supper is also a *sacramentum* of Christ's presence where Jesus is both host and guest. This encounter is a mysterious realm of covenantal eating, central to the life of the church, where bread is body and body is church. This sacrament has been referred to over the centuries as the Lord's Supper, the Table of the Lord, the Communion, the Eucharist, and the Mass. Implicit in observing the Mass is that celebrants return to the Mess and expend themselves in a life of suffering service in a broken world. If Christians can't see Jesus in the disenfranchised, we won't see him in the Communion (and *vice versa*).

THE CHURCH AS WISDOM COMMUNITY

The spirit-filled community of Jesus is a reality of alternative wisdom made known in the proclamation of narrative gospel grasped only by those who have eyes that can see and ears that can hear. The Apostle Paul wrote, in a lyrical passage to the church of God in Corinth, that it was God's good pleasure through the foolishness of preaching to save those who believed; designating as sanctified all those in every place that call upon the name of the Lord Jesus Christ. Christ crucified, which was Paul's proclamation, was a stumbling block to Jews and foolishness to Greeks. The Jews were scandalized by the Jesus narrative because they envisioned a Messiah of power who would establish God's kingdom on

Earth by conquering Empire. A servant Messiah who lived in a spirit of love, justice, and mercy only to be executed by Empire on a criminal's cross was simply impossible. The Greeks lived in a culture of acquisition and power. Anything less was foolish. God chose the foolishness of the world to shame the wise. God chose the weak things of the world to shame the powerful. The spirit-filled community of Jesus lives an *alternative wisdom* of transforming love, reconciliation, mercy, and justice.

THE CHURCH AS OPEN COMMUNITY

God's inclusive love shatters any sense of Christian exclusiveness. The church is *oikomene* (Greek: "God's big house"). The church is a place of hospitality (Greek: *philoxenia*, "love of the stranger"). Jesus welcomes all people, moving beyond social strictures and limiting worldviews. The church is a community of radical diversity—Jew and Greek, male and female, slave and free, tax collector for the Roman Empire, Zealot plotting the overthrow of Roman Empire, Roman centurion and the eunuch of foreign bureaucracy. All are invited. All share the blessing of a radical unity in their radical diversity.

* * * * * *

But we must be practical. Right? How does a disciple of Jesus decide, in today's parlance, which church to join? Should one align oneself with one of the Catholic orthodoxies, one of the many Protestant denominations, or simply freelance one's Christianity?

We first note, that just as Jesus began his ministry with baptism, so do we, and God does not place confessants in the wrong church. We may be confused, but God is not. Following baptism we take up our yoke and follow Jesus living in the Way of grace through faith. It's impossible to make a purely *theological* decision on which *institutional expression* of church to be a part. That is to say, we cannot simply tote up the earmarks of the church and create a checklist for the truest, the bluest, or the best. Neither should church preference be just all style and scruples. The parameters of *sacrament*, *wisdom*, and *openness*, just discussed, assist us in finding a tradition within our fractured church where we may gather in the name of Jesus.

The sacramental community *itself* is a visible sign of the mystery of human experience with divine love. *So we must ask*, is our community's basic principle too limited to contain our human experience? Is it too constricted to allow freedom? Too narrow to be faithful? Too broad to have specificity? Too warped to encourage wholeness? Too judgmental to enable love? Too mean-spirited to make us compassionate? Too pious to sanction passion? Too rationalistic to open the eyes of the heart? Too deaf to hear questions? Too bleak to feel empathy? Too stubborn to free the imagination? Too close-minded to learn? Too uncompromising to admit mistakes? Too rigid to free the imagination? Too materialistic to make room for divinity? Too mechanistic to make us human? Too saintly to dirty our hands in service? Too "good" and irreproachable to involve ourselves with the "others"?

The core Jesus story is an overarching narrative that joins desire with faith to hold together the paradoxical mysteries and unresolved truths of human and divine natures, of transcendence and immanence. The core Jesus story is also compelling in its simplicity. Jesus is the parable of God and begs the question, "*What happens if you live in the narrative of Jesus?*" Jesus crossed all cultural, social, religious, philosophical, and political boundaries of his day. In his domain of borderlands—physical, metaphysical, and metaphorical—he crossed back and forth with passion and compassion. He lived at boundaries both hospitable and inhospitable, defined and imprecise, known and unknown. He called his disciples to the boundaries, often entreating them, "Go to the other side."

Boundary lines are places of invitation, of mutual conversation (listening as well as speaking), of generosity, of establishing trust and exchanging gifts, and where both danger and comfort are shared, along with food, stories, questions, and concerns. It is inevitable that in our Christian journey, following Jesus in the Way, we will sometimes be called to cross a boundary or be pushed across a boundary. Crossing boundaries is necessary to connect church and world; to connect the church pew with the city's mean streets; to connect communion table with dinner table; to connect the gourmet banquet with destitution's barren board. Jesus took people and places as they came and gave himself in service. Christians have found Jesus and church everywhere—in the exotic and the unremarkable, among the alien and the kindred spirit, through tedium and peril. What if the choice really is where Jesus put it—between God and mammon (greed, wealth, and power)?

Jesus, as recorded in the Gospels, used the phrase "the *power* and the *glory*" when he taught his disciples to pray. The synoptics, speaking of the power of Jesus' miracles, use the Greek word *dunamis*, from which our word *dynamite* is derived. John's gospel speaks of miracles using the word *sameion*, Greek for "sign." In surveying the "What?" of life, we have looked at the power, the dynamite, embedded in the cosmosphere. In pondering the "So what?" of life, we have looked at signs that point toward meaning-making and transcendence. Humankind's struggle has been to find an overarching, coherent story in processing both the "What?" and "So What" of their world. The tragedy in the long history of Christianity's sacred story is seeing the event and missing the meaning—of observing what happened and missing the point. Paying attention to the fundamental questions that accompany all of our living ("What?" and "So What?") through the lenses of desire, narrative, and faith, enables us to weave past, present, and future into life-alive. The mystery is made known and signifiers recognized as the experience of life-alive bring us into the embrace of faith and grace—the lived experience of the *power* and the *glory*.

27

A Coherent Christian Hope

"The devout Christian of the future will either be a mystic,
one who has experienced something,
or he/she will cease to be anything at all."
—Karl Rahner
   Jesuit Priest and Theologian

"Anyway, I don't know why mystic should be such a bad word. It doesn't mean much more than the word religion which some people still speak of with respect. What does religion say? It says that there is something in human beings beyond the body and the brain and that we have ways of knowing that go beyond the organism and its senses. I've always believed that. My misery comes, maybe, from ignoring my own metaphysical hunches. I've been to college so I know the educated answers. Test me on the scientific worldview and I'd score high.

But it's just head stuff."
—Saul Bellow, Novelist
   From *Humboldt's Gift*

NATURAL SCIENCE, BUT CERTAINLY not all natural scientists, claims there is no reality in the cosmos that cannot be perceived by temporal weights and measures. If that view of the cosmos is correct, there is nothing more to discuss. But if there is a cosmic reality that is non-material, as understood by temporal metrics, then science labors under a misapprehension when it thinks it can explain the non-material by its methodology.

Theology, too often, has mixed temporal weights and measurements with mystery. Such thinking takes different forms. The theology of our personal, early religious narrative mixed the stuff of natural science with the stuff of biblical texts. Passages of the Bible were claimed to be *in sync* with the latest scientific findings as a way to infer proofs of God and proofs of Bible. It was a sly inference: "You see—nudge, nudge; wink, wink—God knew . . . He told the writers of the Bible that the world was round, or knew the proper dimensions of sailing vessels for Noah's instruction, or understood ocean currents as 'paths in the sea,' or that the Earth would end in a fiery flame-out. Or . . ."

The theology of our youth cast Christian faith as extracting facts from an inerrant Bible and restoring an ancient order. Looking back, it was an Enlightenment-inspired, rational, scientific/theological investigation of the God of the *ancients*. Science and sophistication had produced a faith that was adverse to experientially *knowing* a *present God* journeying with us into our unknown future. Proving dogma was preferable to confronting mystery. Faith that was mystical, or believed empowered by the Holy Spirit, was too loosey-goosey and just got out of hand. Controlling the content of a belief system was practical (a posture of defense), whereas engaging the dynamic of a faith narrative was an enchantment (as much heart as head). The theology of our youth offered more answers than questions, propositions than confessions, and positions held than journeys taken. There were quasi-spiritual dreams patterned on the successful American business model: get organized, raise money, build an impressive building, or finance a religious television program, or rally the resources to plant a "new church" or evangelize a foreign land. And sometimes, to establish an orphan's home or do medical missions. But in such efforts, the "brethren" often fell out over scriptural arguments regarding church cooperation and proper financing. Still, heaven was out there as the big pay-off, but faith as transformed living was eclipsed by correct theological codification rather than narrative experience. Our summons was to walk the straight-and-narrow while quoting book, chapter, and verse, instead of ranging across boundaries necessary to a life of faith.

We return again to our thesis. *Desire* erupts full-blown from our biological nature, and includes longing for coherent meaning to our lives. The Judaeo/Christian *narrative* is a proclamation of comprehension, ending with good news rooted in the *history* and *theology* of the Jesus story. The story calls for a decision—to act or not to act. *Faith* is an act of trust in the summons to step into a future, anticipating the mysterious reality coming toward us.

Confessional faith works with a God story and a human story. There is ideological tension among theologians and philosophers as to which story came first—the God story or the human story. "Start with the God story," is an echo of Karl Barth. "Start with the human question," resonates from Paul Tillich. Both men stand in the ranks of the twentieth century's greatest theologians. Theology continues to be the universe of discourse that operates at the interface of the God story and the human story. Examining where and in what way the God story and the human story intersect is a concern of Christian scholarship, but *is not the primal narrative of the Bible that establishes the Christian community.*

Faith's work is to divulge—make known—an encounter with God. Faith knows presence and absence. It holds us even as we hold it. It is trust. It is meaning-making. It thrives on the tension between the "already" and the "not yet." It holds the mystery of life and God in awe and reverence. Belief in God assumes mystery and the people of God are mystics by definition (Webster: a person who seeks by contemplation and self-surrender to obtain unity with or absorption into deity or the Absolute by apprehending truths that are beyond pure intellect). Faith is the link between security and risk, between believing and doubting, between life and death. Faith shapes us into beings who reject despair and nihilism, while at the same time rejecting triumphalism and certitude. It experiences openness rather than exclusion. It's the way we live toward all that we face and experience, and the way we interpret all that happens to us. Faith does not make us stupid before the complexity of the world in which we live, nor should it require us to deny the obvious in science and its methodology. Faith engages world cultures and civilizations in all of their strengths and weaknesses, possibilities and threats. Faith affirms that every person counts and that humankind is included in a meaningful universe. It confronts the body, mind, and spirit—the wholeness of our human personhood and creaturely existence—with disciplines and decisions, mercies and joys, rebukes and consolations, mystery and knowing, the power and the glory. It brings forgiveness and forgiving, worship and work, patience in waiting, meaning-making in action, life-alive—and yes, finally—resurrection and life beyond with God's forever-welcome-in-grace. Thus, faith's work is interpretation toward life's meaning, life's action, and life's hope. It is encounter. It is trust. It is announced with the words, "Be not afraid." It ends with the words, "I will be with you always."

Epilogue

"To play a wrong note is insignificant;
To play without passion is inexcusable."
—Ludwig van Beethoven

The authors have lived in various narratives—complex and simple, scientific and religious, naive and labyrinthine, violent and pacifist, ecstatic and mundane, historical and mystical. We have been passionate and apathetic; engaged and withdrawn. We're the product of the long development of cultures and civilizations, as well as particular geographic locales, definitive historical and religious customs, and heritages and habits. We've looked through telescopes and microscopes. We have listened to the heart through stethoscopes and in stories. We have accepted and rejected creeds (written and oral), we've pondered theology and theologies, we've worshiped and railed before the divine/human mystery. We have been battered, lifted, healed, disappointed, loved, rejected. We've been believers, would-be believers, disbelievers, doubters, and doubters of our doubt. We've loved and lusted, celebrated and grieved, been to the far country and come home. We have wounded others and have been wounded. We've helped and we've hurt. We've wept tears of both deep joy and unutterable sorrow. "We been doin' some hard travelin', Lord."

The central narrative of our lives has been the encounter with the gospel story and the faithing life to which that story summons. It has not been the only narrative of our lives, but it is the one that has absorbed all others. We have tried to live the story and we have failed in its living.

We have been true believers, honest doubters, willful sinners. We have been convicted and convinced, wayward and timid. We have affirmed and denied. We have studied long hours and we have given up. We have worshiped, knowing that without awe and a dumbfoundedness before the mystery of it all, we would simply shrivel. We have prayed, knowing that without kneeling at the altar we could not stand in the world. We have been engaged and walked away discouraged, preached and endured long silences in both prayer and proclamation. We have studied the faith, prayed the faith, raged at the faith, whispered the faith, wept the faith, laughed the faith, and occasionally danced the faith. We have been baptized and we have baptized—in ornate or simple church baptisteries, in mountain streams, foreign lakes, seas and oceans, in city ponds, backyard swimming pools and hot tubs, household bathtubs, and prison cafeteria mashed-potato pots. We have communed and received communion among most all expressions of the Christian faith. From fundamentalists and conservatives to liberals and progressives. With Roman Catholic priests and the Eastern Orthodox. With Anglicans and in Mennonite households. With Anabaptists and Pentecostals. With nondenominationalists to ecumenists and emerging church enthusiasts. We have done it in a number of different nations and different cultures, with different races using different languages and dialects, and among the highly educated and the barely literate.

We have shared the story in magnificent sanctuaries and unadorned, darkened undercrofts of ancient churches. Among young drug addicts and aging alcoholics. We have shared the story with the very rich and the very poor, the well-housed and the homeless. We have shared the story on battlefields and in war zones. We have shared the story on peace marches, in civil rights meetings, and social justice convocations. We have shared it in scientific labs, hospital rooms, and prison cells. We have shared it in coffee houses and bars and pubs. We have shared it in university lecture halls and primary school classrooms, at grass roots neighborhood meetings and international civic organizations. We have shared it in embassies and chambers of commerce. We have shared it in ecumenical conferences and interfaith meetings, as well as denominational assemblies and sectarian gatherings. We have shared it in large city churches, ghetto store front churches, small country chapels, in rented halls, hootches in Vietnam's central highlands, and in house churches. We have shared it in disciples' houses, liberty houses, safe houses, and retreat centers. We have shared it at Communion tables and common tables. We have shared it in maternity wards, emergency rooms, mental hospitals, hospices, funeral homes, cancer clinics, crematoria, and in grave yards, military cemeteries, unmarked pauper's graves, and gleaming mausoleums. It is the story recounted in the inscripturated Word and encountered in the Word incarnate. It's about making belief, making love, making hope, and it instills life-alive. It is about being mystics: confronting mystery, enduring mystery, believing mystery, and being held by mystery.

This inventory is not to say anything about us but something about the story itself. It is the story that has been large enough, deep enough, broad enough, universal enough, local enough, challenging enough, inviting enough, critical enough, inclusive enough, and personal enough to speak to, give meaning to, bring judgment upon, contain, save, and redeem the "all" of our blessed, sinful, and wounded lives. It's the story that has shaped us, occupied us, haunted us, inspired us, commanded us, enraged us, and comforted us. We are part of it and it is part of us. We don't know where one stops and the other begins.

Bibliography

Stories of Desire and Narratives of Faith: From Neanderthals To The Postmodern Era

"We are what we are by virtue of the 'relevant others' with whom we speak. First and foremost, theology has to do with the 'relevant others' whom we include in our dialogue concerning the problem of our day-to-day life."

—Rubem Alves
   Theologian, Philosopher, Poet
   From *Frontiers of Theology in Latin America*

Allen, Diogenes. *Love: Christian Romance, Marriage, Friendship.* Cambridge, MA: Cowley, 1987.
Alves, Rubem. *I Believe in the Resurrection of the Body.* Minneapolis: Fortress, 1986.
———. *The Poet, The Warrior, The Prophet.* London: SCM, 1990.
———. *Theology of Human Hope.* New York: Corpus, 1969.
———. *Tomorrow's Child.* New York: Harper and Row, 1972.
———. *Transparencies of Eternity.* Miami, FL: Convivium, 2010.
———. *What is Religion?* Maryknoll, NY: Orbis, 1984.
Assmann, Jan. *The Mind of Egypt.* New York: Metropolitan, 2002.
Barzun, Jacques. *From Dawn to Decadence: 1500 To The Present (500 Years of Western Cultural Life).* New York: Harper Collins, 2000.
Bauckham, Richard. *Bible and Mission: Christian Witness in a Postmodern World.* Grand Rapids: Baker Academic, 2003.
Beker, J. Christiaan. *Suffering and Hope: The Biblical Vision and the Human Predicament.* Grand Rapids: Eerdmans, 1994.

BIBLIOGRAPHY

Bellah, Robert. *Religion in Human Evolution: From the Paleolithic to the Axial Age.* Cambridge, MA: Belknap Press of Harvard, 2011.
Berger, Peter. *The Sacred Canopy.* New York: Anchor, 1967.
Berger, Peter, and Thomas Luckmann. *The Social Construction of Reality: A Treatise in the Sociology of Knowledge.* New York: Anchor, 1967.
Bettelheim, Bruno. *The Uses of Enchantment.* New York: Random House/Vintage, 1975.
Borg, Marcus. *Christian Speaking: Why Christian Words Have Lost Their Meaning and Power—And How They Can Be Restored.* New York: Harper Collins, 2011.
———. *Meeting Jesus Again for the First Time.* New York: Harper Collins, 1994.
Born, Max. *The Born/Einstein Letters: 1916–1955.* New York: MacMillan, 2005.
Broadbent, R. J. *A History of Pantomime.* New York: The Citadel, 1965.
Bronowski, Jacob. *The Ascent of Man.* Boston: Little, Brown and Company. 1973.
Brueggemann, Walter. *The Bible Makes Sense.* Atlanta: John Knox, 1983.
Brueggemann, Walter, ed. *Hope for the World.* Louisville: Westminster John Knox, 2001.
Buechner, Frederick. *The Eyes of the Heart.* New York: Harper Collins, 1999.
Campbell, Joseph (with Bill Moyers). *The Power of Myth.* Edited by Betty Sue Flowers. New York: Doubleday, 1988.
Coffin, William Sloane. *Creedo.* Louisville: Westminster John Knox, 2004.
———. *Letters to a Young Doubter.* Louisville: Westminster John Knox, 2005.
Cox, Harvey. *The Future of Faith.* New York: Harper Collins, 2009.
Diamond, Jared. *Guns, Germs, and Steel.* New York: W. W. Norton, 1997.
Dukas, Helen, and Banish Hoffman. *Albert Einstein: The Human Side.* Princeton, NJ: Princeton University Press, 1981.
Eliade, Mircea. *Cosmos and History: The Myth of the Eternal Return.* New York: Harper and Row, 1959.
———. *Myths, Dreams, and Mysteries.* New York: Harper and Row, 1975.
———. *The Sacred and the Profane: The Nature of Religion.* New York: Harcourt, 1959.
Farley, Wendy. *Eros Toward the Other: Retaining Truth in a Pluralistic World.* University Park, PA: Pennsylvania State University Press, 1996.
———. *Gathering Those Driven Away: A Theology of Incarnation.* Louisville: Westminster John Knox, 2011.
———. *The Wounding and Healing of Desire: Weaving Heaven and Earth.* Louisville: Westminster John Knox, 2005.
Fiero, Gloria K. *The Humanistic Tradition: Book 3—The European Renaissance, the Reformation, and Global Encounter.* New York: McGraw Hill, 2002.
———. *The Humanistic Tradition: Book 4—Faith, Reason, and Power in the Early Modern World.* New York: McGraw-Hill, 2002.
Gibellini, Rosino, ed. *Frontiers of Theology in Latin America.* Maryknoll, NY: Orbis, 1983.
Hall, Douglas John. *Confessing the Faith.* Minneapolis: Fortress, 1998.
———. *Professing the Faith.* Minneapolis: Fortress, 1993.
———. *Thinking the Faith.* Minneapolis: Fortress, 1989.
Harari, Yuval Noah. *Sapiens.* New York: Harper Collins, 2015.
Hauerwas, Stanley, and L. Gregory Jones, eds. *Why Narrative: Readings in Narrative Theology.* Eugene, OR: Wipf and Stock, 1997.
Hause, Steven, and William Maltby. *Western Civilization: A History of European Society.* Belmont, WA: Wadsworth, 1999.
Hawking, Stephen. *A Brief History of Time.* New York: Bantam, 1998.

Heltzel, Peter Goodwin, ed. *Chalice Introduction to Disciples Theology*. St. Louis: Chalice, 2008.
Holloway, Richard. *Leaving Alexandria*. London: Cannongate, 2012.
Irwin, Alexander C. *Eros Toward the World: Paul Tillich and the Theology of the Erotic*. Minneapolis: Fortress, 1991.
Jaspers, Karl. *The Origin and Goal of History*. Translated from German, 1949. London: Routledge and Kegan Paul, 1953.
Johnson, Elizabaeth A. *Quest for the Living God: Mapping Frontiers in the Theology of God*. New York: Continuum, 2007.
Kelsey, David H. *Eccentric Existence: A Theological Anthropology*. Vol. 1. Louisville: Westminster John Knox, 2009.
———. *Eccentric Existence: A Theological Anthropology*. Vol. 2. Louisville: Westminster John Knox, 2009.
King, Margaret L. *Western Civilization: A Social and Cultural History, Vol. I, Prehistory–1754*. Upper Saddle River, NJ: Prentice Hall, 2000.
———. *Western Civilization: A Social and Cultural History, Vol. II, 1500–The Present*. Upper Saddle River, NJ: Prentice Hall, 2000.
Küng, Hans. *On Being a Christian*. Glasgow: Collins/Fount, 1978.
Lee, Charlotte I. *Oral Interpretation*. Boston: Houghton Mifflin, 1952.
Lewis, C. S. *The Four Loves*. New York: Harcourt Brace and Company, 1960.
Loy, John, ed. *The Paradoxes of Play*. West Point, NY: Leisure, 1982.
MacGregor, Neil. *A History of the World in 100 Objects*. New York: Viking, 2011.
Marney, Carlyle. *The Coming Faith*. Nashville: Abingdon, 1970.
———. *The Crucible of Redemption*. Nashville: Abingdon, 1968.
———. *Faith in Conflict*. Nashville: Abingdon, 1957.
McClendon, James Wm., Jr. *Biography as Theology: How Life Stories Can Remake Today's Theology*. Eugene, OR: Wipf and Stock, 2002.
McNamara, William. *Mystical Passion: The Art of Christian Loving*. Rockport, IL: Element, 1977.
Montgomery, Scott L., and Daniel Chirot. *The Shape of the New: Four Big Ideas and How They Made the Modern World*. Princeton, NJ: Princeton University Press, 2015.
Nelson, James B. *Embodiment: An Approach to Sexuality and Christian Theology*. Minneapolis: Augsburg, 1978.
Niebuhr, H. Richard. *The Meaning of Revelation*. New York: MacMillan, 1941.
Nygren, Anders. *Agape and Eros*. Chicago: University of Chicago Press, 1982.
Oatman, Johnson. "When Upon Life's Billows." In *Great Songs of the Church* 2, compiled by E. L. Jorgenson, 304. Hammond, IN: Great Songs, 1979.
Pelikan, Jaroslav. *The Vindication of Tradition*. The Jefferson Lecture in the Humanities 1983. New Haven, CT: Yale University Press, 1984.
Perry, Marvin, et al. *Sources of the Western Tradition: From the Scientific Revolution to the Present*. Vol. II. Boston: Houghton Mifflin, 1987.
Polhemus, Robert M. *Lot's Daughters: Sex, Redemption, and Women's Quest for Authority*. Stanford, CA: Stanford University Press, 2005.
Rahner, Karl. *Theological Investigations*. London: Darton, Longman and Todd, 1966.
Reilly, Kevin. *The West and the World: A History of Civilization*. Vol. I. 2d ed. New York: Harper and Row, 1989.
Robinson, Marilynne. *The Givenness of Things*. New York: Farrar, Straus and Giroux, 2015.

Smith, James K. A. *Desiring the Kingdom*. Grand Rapids: Baker Academic, 2009.
Stengel, Richard, ed. "The 100 Most Influential People Of All Time." Special ed. *Time*, 2012.
Stroup, George W. *Before God*. Grand Rapids: Eerdmans, 2004.
———. *The Promise of Narrative Theology: Recovering the Gospel in the Church*. Eugene, OR: Wipf and Stock, 1997.
Tickle, Phyllis. *Emergence Christianity*. Grand Rapids: Baker, 2012.
Tillich, Paul. *Christianity and the Encounter of World Religions*. Minneapolis: Fortress, 1994.
———. *Love, Power, and Justice*. London: Oxford University, 1954.
———. *Systematic Theology*. 3 vols. Chicago: University of Chicago Press, 1951–63.
Wakefield, Dan, ed. *Kurt Vonnegut: Letters*. New York: Delacorte, 2012.
Webb, Glenn Taylor. "The Art of Living in the World with Awareness, Respect and Trust-Responding to Buddhism." Palm Desert: St. Margaret's Forum, January 17, 2014.
———. "Zen Funerals, Rinzai Style." Monograph. Palm Desert, 2017.
Wilson, Edward O. *The Social Conquest of Earth*. New York: Liveright, 2012.
Wolpe, David J. *The Healer of Shattered Hearts: A Jewish View of God*. New York: Penguin, 1990.
Wright, N. T. *Simply Jesus: A New Vision of Who He Was, What He Did, and Why He Matters*. New York: Harper Collins, 2011.

The Authors

The authors are brothers. Victor Hunter is a pastoral theologian who has spent more than fifty years in the pastor's study and parish pulpit, while working with pastors, seminary students, renewing congregations and judicatories in a variety of settings. Lanny Hunter is a physician whose background is in the sciences. He has spent more than fifty years in the consultation room and the operating theater, while serving as a lay leader in Christian congregations. They have celebrated their 50th wedding anniversaries and are surrounded by children and grandchildren.

With over 150 years of lived experience between them, they have engaged in a lifelong conversation between their disciplines of science and theology. They are the authors, separately and together, of six books and many articles. They have been actively engaged in the church, both in its more traditional forms and in new and developing ways of being church and community in the postmodern world.

Lanny Hunter　　　　　　**Victor Hunter**

www.ingramcontent.com/pod-product-compliance
Lightning Source LLC
Chambersburg PA
CBHW020410230426
43664CB00009B/1243